ENVIRONMENTAL LITIGATION IN CHINA

A STUDY IN POLITICAL AMBIVALENCE

This is a book about the improbable: seeking legal relief for pollution in contemporary China. In a country known for tight political control and ineffectual courts, *Environmental Litigation in China* unravels how everyday justice works: how judges make decisions, why lawyers take cases, and how international influence matters. It is a compelling account of how the leadership's mixed signals and political ambivalence play out on the ground, propelling some – such as the village doctor who fought a chemical plant for more than a decade – even as others back away from risk. Yet this remarkable book shows that even in a country where expectations are that law would not much matter, environmental litigation provides a sliver of space for legal professionals to explore new roles and, in so doing, probe the boundary of what is politically possible.

Rachel E. Stern is an assistant professor of law and political science at the University of California, Berkeley. Her earlier articles on law, social activism, and environmental issues in China and Hong Kong have appeared in *Comparative Political Studies*, *Law and Policy*, *China Quarterly*, and other journals. She is also a former junior Fellow at the Harvard University Society of Fellows.

D1193479

CAMBRIDGE STUDIES IN LAW AND SOCIETY

Cambridge Studies in Law and Society aims to publish the best scholarly work on legal discourse and practice in its social and institutional contexts, combining theoretical insights and empirical research.

The fields that it covers are: studies of law in action; the sociology of law; the anthropology of law; cultural studies of law, including the role of legal discourses in social formations; law and economics; law and politics; and studies of governance. The books consider all forms of legal discourse across societies, rather than being limited to lawyers' discourses alone.

The series editors come from a range of disciplines: academic law; socio-legal studies; sociology; and anthropology. All have been actively involved in teaching and writing about law in context.

Series Editors

Chris Arup
Monash University, Victoria
Martin Chanock
La Trobe University, Melbourne
Sally Engle Merry
New York University
Susan Silbey
Massachusetts Institute of Technology

Books in the Series

Diseases of the Will
Mariana Valverde

The Politics of Truth and Reconciliation in South Africa: Legitimizing the Post-Apartheid State
Richard A. Wilson

Modernism and the Grounds of Law
Peter Fitzpatrick

Unemployment and Government: Genealogies of the Social
William Walters

Autonomy and Ethnicity: Negotiating Competing Claims in Multi-Ethnic States
Yash Ghai

Series list continues following the Index.

Environmental Litigation in China

A STUDY IN POLITICAL AMBIVALENCE

Rachel E. Stern

University of California, Berkeley

CAMBRIDGE
UNIVERSITY PRESS

CAMBRIDGE
UNIVERSITY PRESS

32 Avenue of the Americas, New York NY 10013-2473, USA

Cambridge University Press is part of the University of Cambridge.

It furthers the University's mission by disseminating knowledge in the pursuit of education, learning and research at the highest international levels of excellence.

www.cambridge.org
Information on this title: www.cambridge.org/9781107460027

First published 2013
First paperback edition 2014

A catalogue record for this publication is available from the British Library

Library of Congress Cataloguing in Publication data

Stern, Rachel E.
Environmental litigation in China : a study in political ambivalence / Rachel E. Stern.
   p.   cm. – (Cambridge studies in law and society)
Includes bibliographical references and index.
ISBN 978-1-107-02002-3 (hardback)
1. Environmental law – China.   2. Environmental law – Political aspects – China.
3. Pollution – Law and legislation – China.   4. Liability for environmental damages –
China.   I. Title.
KNQ3127.S74   2013
344.5104'6–dc23   2012037771

ISBN 978-1-107-02002-3 Hardback
ISBN 978-1-107-46002-7 Paperback

Contents

List of Abbreviations

ACEF: All-China Environment Federation
ACLA: All China Lawyers Association
ALL: Administrative Litigation Law
BLA: Beijing Law Association
BPCs: Basic People's Courts
CASS: Chinese Academy of Social Sciences
CCP: Chinese Communist Party
CLAPV: Center for Legal Assistance to Pollution Victims
CPPCC: Chinese People's Political Consultative Conference
EIA: Environmental Impact Assessment
EPB: Environmental Protection Bureau
HPC: High People's Court
INGO: International Non-Governmental Organization
IPC: Intermediate People's Court
MEP: Ministry of Environmental Protection
MoJ: Ministry of Justice
NAEC: Non-Litigation Administrative Execution Case
NGO: Non-Governmental Organization
NPC: National People's Congress
SEPA: State Environmental Protection Agency
SPC: Supreme People's Court

Introduction

THIS IS A BOOK ABOUT THE IMPROBABLE: SEEKING LEGAL relief for environmental pollution in contemporary China. It is an account that involves judges, lawyers, and international non-governmental organizations (NGOs), as well as the individuals who file civil environmental lawsuits. This last group includes such people as the herdsmen from Inner Mongolia who sued a paper factory over poisoned groundwater and the Shandong villager who demanded compensation for noise that allegedly killed 26 foxes on his farm.[1] Empirically, this book is a close-to-the-ground account of everyday justice and the factors that shape it. In a country known for tight political control and ineffectual courts, the pages that follow unravel how litigation works: how judges make decisions, why lawyers take cases, and how international influence matters. Conceptually, civil environmental lawsuits illustrate how litigation can contribute to social change in China and, by implication, other authoritarian states.[2] Even pursuing

---

1 While I occasionally make reference to key administrative cases, my focus is on civil litigation. Overall, civil cases comprise the vast majority of cases in Chinese courts – 87 percent in 2010 – and touch fewer political nerves than cases that entail direct confrontation with state agencies (China Law Yearbook 2011, 1051). For more on administrative environmental litigation, see Zhang (2008).
2 I borrow political scientist Lisa Wedeen's definition of authoritarian states as places "where leaders are intolerant of people or groups perceived as threatening to the regime's monopoly over the institutions of the state" (1999, 26). Throughout this book, the terms "authoritarian" and "illiberal" are used interchangeably.

legal remedies with slim hopes of success, in a country where expectations would be that law wouldn't much matter, litigation can provide a limited opportunity for judges, lawyers, academics, and NGOs to explore new roles and, in so doing, gently expand the universe of political possibilities.

My focus is on environmental litigation for two reasons. First, the environment is an area with high, real-world stakes. By 2005, when I started this research, the severity of China's environmental degradation was splashed across headlines around the world. More than 300 million Chinese citizens lack access to safe drinking water, as a start, and China is home to some of the most polluted cities in the world (Wang 2013). But with few exceptions, there was also little up-to-date research on either the political story behind such dramatic environmental problems or proposed solutions.[3] Part of the appeal of this project lay in its policy implications. Could litigation play a role in either stopping pollution or spurring environmentalism?

As a student of politics, I found environmental lawsuits interesting for a second reason as well. One of the first insights of my fieldwork was that civil environmental lawsuits occupy a "safety belt" (*anquan dai*), as one Chinese lawyer put it, between cases that are unequivocally forbidden by the state (like defending the banned spiritual group Falun Gong) and cases that are relatively uncontroversial (like defending children's rights). Falling in the middle of this spectrum, pollution cases enjoy a sliver of political opening that renders them less risky to complainants than other rights-related cases while remaining "a little bit sensitive" (*you yidian mingan*) – somewhat politically touchy, but not taboo. Sometimes environmental lawsuits proceed quietly, with no more impediments than any other private dispute. But at other times, cases spark interest from political power holders who pressure litigants, lawyers, and judges to meet their wishes, or drop litigation altogether.

3 When I started the project in 2005, exceptions included Jahiel (1998), Jing (2000), and Economy (2004). Much more on Chinese environmental issues was published in the mid- and late-2000s, a reflection of the growing importance of the topic.

Variously undermined, ignored, or encouraged, environmental cases sit near the boundary of the politically permissible. This places them on the outskirts of allowable legal action in an authoritarian state, an excellent vantage point to assess the potential and limits of law.

My starting point is the observation that courts pose a dilemma to authoritarian states. Although law can resolve disputes and boost legitimacy, all but the most orchestrated show trials can also threaten government interests or authority. One strand of the growing literature on law in authoritarian states explores this tension, particularly the reasons regimes devolve power to courts and the ways in which they control them.[4] But how does the authoritarian dilemma concerning courts – a high-level desire to control and capitalize on the law – affect daily routines among those whose jobs entail regular interaction with courts, litigants, or legal concepts? Or, to ratchet up one level of abstraction, how do official attitudes toward law tamp down or inspire social change?

Political Ambivalence

Environmental Litigation in China: A Study in Political Ambivalence investigates these questions. Until now, most accounts of litigation and social change have focused on democracies, especially the United States.[5] This is not surprising insofar as democracies tend to house the type of feisty, activist courts that deliberately dip into social and political issues. Yet it hardly seems likely that there is no relationship between law and social change outside the democratic world. Building on a resurgence of social science interest in Chinese law, the chapters that follow

---

4 For a partial selection, see Markovits (1996, 2010), Moustafa (2003, 2007, 2007a), Solomon (2007, 2008, 2010), Moustafa and Ginsburg (2008), Ghias (2010), Cheeseman (2011), Hendley (2011), Rajah (2011, 2012), and Massoud (forthcoming). Earlier work on courts in authoritarian states includes Toharia (1975), Tate (1993), Hendley (1996), and Epstein, Knight, and Shvetsova (2001).

5 For example, see Hazard (1969), Muir (1973), Upham (1987), Rosenberg (1991), McCann (1992), and Roach Anleau and Mack (2007).

track the interaction between state signals over environmental litigation and legal professionals' response.

Here, environmental litigation offers a window onto what I call political ambivalence: conflicting official (or quasi-official) signals, defined as observable indications of official preferences, regarding the desirability of certain types of citizen action. Ambivalence, meaning the simultaneous existence of opposing preferences, sums up the official attitude toward environmental litigation. It is not that individual bureaucrats or political leaders are conflicted, although this is certainly possible, but that citizens are confronted with opposing information about state preferences. Simultaneous impulses to promote law but control courts, to protect the environment and yet pursue economic growth, generate a medley of conflicting statements, cases, and regulations. In contemporary China, this often translates into ground-level uncertainty. When information is conflicting, and also often incomplete or unreliable, it is difficult to gauge the government's "tolerance interval," let alone figure out how to act accordingly (Epstein, Knight, and Shvetsova 2001).

Let me emphasize that writing about political ambivalence does not mean the Chinese state is a single-minded organism, any more than a reference to the body politic describes a being that might sit up and start walking. On the contrary, the Chinese state is "a heap of loosely connected parts" with divergent perspectives on the wisdom of suing polluters (Migdal 2001, 22).[6] Rather than delving into bureaucratic politics, however, this book looks at the state as reflected in society, or how individuals experience the state. Here, variation about which parts of the state support and oppose environmental litigation pale beside the larger truth that both low-level bureaucrats and normal citizens often encounter a state that behaves *as if* it is ambivalent. Political ambivalence, in other words, describes the state as seen from below, from the perspective of people trying to suss out political attitudes without perfect

---

6 For other work that advocates disaggregating the state, see Perry (1994), O'Brien (2003), and O'Brien and Li (2006).

information. The phrase is shorthand for a common experience of everyday Chinese politics – that of interpreting signals sent by different parts of a state that can't seem to make up its mind.

Some reasons for political ambivalence are universal. Whenever multiple bureaucracies or levels of government take part in policymaking, mixed signals are likely. Including more officials from more agencies inevitably introduces different interests, agendas, and voices. Hierarchy, especially many layers of hierarchy, also decreases the likelihood of a single, clear message as policies make their way from higher to lower levels with opportunities for distortion (both deliberate and inadvertent) each step of the way (Wedeman 2001).

But even if political ambivalence is difficult to avoid in all but the most tightly controlled regimes, it seems amplified in China. One reason for this is the country's physical size – just slightly smaller than the United States - and unusually high degree of decentralization.[7] For some time now, decision-making has been fragmented, with a range of bureaucracies and officials enjoying latitude to adjust and make policies (Lieberthal and Oksenberg 1990). Bargaining, increasingly with pressure groups as well as bureaucrats, is an enduring presence in Chinese policymaking, and behind-the-scenes jockeying often produces conflicting cues (Kennedy 2005; O'Brien and Li 2006; Mertha 2008).

Political ambivalence also reflects a "guerrilla policy style" that dates back to the revolutionary mobilization of the 1930s and 1940s. Guerrilla policymaking, as political scientists Sebastian Heilmann and Elizabeth Perry explain, is a process of "continual improvisation and adjustment" that prioritizes flexibility and accepts "pervasive uncertainty" (Heilmann and Perry 2011, 12 and 22). Local officials are given leeway to try new approaches and good ideas are sometimes rolled out nationwide

---

7 Even after recentralizing revenues in the mid-1990s, spending by local governments still accounted for nearly 70 percent of government spending, a level of fiscal decentralization surpassing that of nearly every other authoritarian state. China's level of fiscal decentralization has been exceeded only by Yugoslavia in the years immediately preceding its breakup (Landry 2008, 3–6).

(Heilmann 2008). Mixed signals are a feature of today's political land-scape, in part owing to this tradition of experimentation and comfort with variation. Demonstration areas for economic and political innovation dot the nation and, at times, what economist Albert Hirschman once called a "disparity of attention" while leaders are occupied with "more vital *other* interests" can serve as a green light (Hirschman 1978, 47).

All these sources of mixed signals precede the obvious fact that the Chinese state is more divided over some subjects than others. Certain topics, like Taiwanese or Tibetan independence or the right to practice Falun Gong, are uniformly off limits. There is no such clarity over environmental litigation. Pollution cases touch on two debates in Chinese politics: the pros and cons of encouraging court cases and disagreement about how to weigh environmental considerations against economic growth. The tent of the Chinese Communist Party is big enough to encompass differing opinions, and, so far, the leadership has not stepped in with a definitive policy statement.

By diving into one area in which political ambivalence is particularly pronounced, this book highlights two responses to uncertainty. Often, mixed signals about the desirability of legal solutions lead to self-censorship. Judges protect polluters when higher-ups demand it (Chapter 5), lawyers screen out politically sensitive cases (Chapter 6), and international NGOs gravitate toward less controversial programs (Chapter 7). At the same time, mixed signals also leave creative leeway for bottom-up experimentation. In an inhospitable environment for both law and activism, conflicting signals crack open enough political space to allow the formation of new institutions (Chapter 4), give breathing room to limited judicial innovation (Chapter 5), permit legal activism (Chapter 6), sustain international encouragement (Chapter 7), and promote environmental policy ideas (Chapter 8).

These are significant changes, especially given the tightening tenor of the times. Under President Hu Jintao and Premier Wen Jiabao, both of whom came to power in 2003, there was a widespread sense that space for legal advocacy was shrinking. Certainly, the lawyers pushing for government accountability, civil rights, and social justice had a difficult time in the 2000s, a decade replete with high-profile roundups, warnings, and arrests. Nor did political change appear to be anywhere on the agenda, despite Premier Wen's occasional calls for political reform. Instead, the Chinese leadership was preoccupied with "maintaining stability" (*weiwen*) and preventing protest. In 2009, the Chinese budget for internal policing reached the equivalent of US$95 billion, surpassing the People's Liberation Army budget for the first time (Lam 2011). For the most part, this worked. In a decade full of mass mobilization, from the Color Revolutions in the former USSR and Balkan states to the Arab Spring, China appeared so stable that many social scientists turned their analytic attention to the roots of authoritarian resilience.

Yet no political system is static. Even in the absence of opposition politics (no one in these pages is much interested in regime change), there is room to bend the rules of who gets what, when, and how. This is especially true in areas such as law that are changing rapidly. All of the changes described here happened in the first ten years of the twenty-first century. Keep in mind that as recently as 1995, the vast majority of lawyers were state employees, and the Ford Foundation was one of very few international non-governmental organizations with an office in Beijing. By the mid-2000s, nearly all lawyers had joined the private bar, and it was impossible to overlook the presence of international groups looking to influence and improve environmental law. These kinds of small-scale social shifts help track how the Chinese Communist Party's well-documented turn toward law is also changing China itself. After all, as legal scholar Martha Minow reminds us, "Legal language, like a song, can be hummed by someone who did not write it and changed by those for whom it was not intended" (quoted in McCann 1992, 733).

The Cases

Outside China, the most common reaction to this project is surprise that China has environmental lawsuits. This reaction, I think, is two-fold. First, people are surprised that cases are interesting enough to be worth studying in a place widely known for weak, closely monitored courts.[8] Indeed, Chinese courts rely on local government for yearly budgets even as Party representatives vet key appointments and occasionally intervene in individual decisions (Peerenboom 2002, 302–309; Zhu 2007, 179). Yet despite this, Chinese judicial politics are increasingly vibrant. As in other authoritarian states, courts are not simply extensions of state power, but sites of "vigorous and meaningful legal struggles" that make visible daily conflicts over class, citizenship, and power (Moustafa 2007a, 3).[9] At times, especially when broad-based mobilization proves difficult, lawsuits can also be a tool of social activism.[10] Even when cases fail (as they frequently do), litigation can bring attention to an issue and serve as "an effective tool of political theater" (Moustafa 2007a, 40).

The second surprise is that ordinary Chinese citizens are willing to stand up to polluters. But grassroots action does not necessarily indicate nascent environmental consciousness. Rather, most environmental cases are filed out of desperation and compelled by an immediate threat. So-called "typical cases" (*dianxing anli*), a prominent phrase in the Chinese legal lexicon, nearly always involve compensation for economic losses. In rural areas, lawsuits often arise when local residents blame pollution for the death of fish, livestock, or crops. Chinese villagers, as anthropologist Jun Jing observes, "can become instant political activists when their livelihood is threatened" (2000, 219). In urban areas, claims of economic loss are more frequently joined by complaints about pollution that is affecting quality of life, such as noise or restaurant smoke. And in both places, lawsuits are often inspired by crisis events like an oil or chemical spill. Disruptions to quotidian routines concentrate outrage far better than ongoing problems (Snow, Cress, Downey, and Jones 1998; Stern 2003, 797; van Rooij 2010, 59). Certainly, the number of

---

8 See Lubman (1999), Peerenboom (2002), Cai (2004), Cai and Yang (2005), and Liebman (2007).

9 For more on how courts make conflicts visible see Lee (2007, 33) and Gu (2008, 260).

10 For more on legal activism in China, see Zhao (2003), China Labour Bulletin (2007), Lee (2007), Kellogg (2007), Pils (2007), Fu and Cullen (2008), and Lü (2008).

pollution-related complaints and protests are rising. There were 696,134 environmental complaints nationwide in 2009, an increase of 53 percent from the year 2000 (China Environment Yearbook 2001 and 2010, 687 and 604). Pollution was also responsible for 13 percent of rural disputes in a 2010 survey, ranking just below disagreements with neighbors as the second most common type of countryside grievance.[11]

What about the number of environmental lawsuits? In 2010, the Supreme People's Court (SPC) counted 12,018 pollution compensation cases (SPC 2011). Although official data should be treated with skepticism, this number is a valuable reference point because government statistics on civil environmental litigation are rarely released.[12] Although twelve thousand cases is a tiny fraction of the more than six million civil cases heard annually, it marks a significant increase over the volume of civil environmental litigation earlier in the decade. A 2008 article from Xinhua, the official government news agency, reported 4,453 pollution-compensation cases in 2004, followed by 1,545 cases in 2005, and 2,146 in 2006.[13]

11 Data from the survey has not yet been published. The numbers cited here come from personal communication in May 2010 with Ethan Michelson, associate professor at Indiana University. The survey covered sites in six provinces. In a 2012 lecture organized by the Standing Committee of the National's People's Congress, the vice-chairman of the Chinese Society for Environmental Science, Yang Chaofei, also reported that the number of environmental protests grew an average of 29 percent annually between 1996 and 2011 (Caijing 2012).

12 In general, official numbers warrant caution. To take one example, data from the annual China Environment Yearbook shows the number of environmental complaints plummeting in 2007 to 123,357 from 616,122 the year before. The next year, the number of environmental complaints popped back into the 600,000 range. Without a reasonable explanation for the drop – surely China's environment did not markedly improve for a single year – it is hard to avoid the conclusion that official statistics are sometimes either accidently inaccurate or manipulated for political reasons. In any case, the China Environment Yearbook contains annual data on the number of administrative environmental lawsuits, but not the number of civil environmental lawsuits.

13 Alongside these numbers, which are nowhere near as complete as would be ideal, observers agree that environmental litigation is slowly becoming more popular (Interviews 45, 103, 106). An official at the SPC, the highest court in China, told me in 2007 that pollution cases were rising 25 percent per year (Interview 103). That same year, the Vice Minister of Justice publicly agreed that "conflicts over … environmental policies are growing by the day" (quoted in Human Rights Watch 2008, 28–29).

The largest collection of environmental cases currently available, more than 700 civil decisions collected by a team at Zhongnan University of Economics and Law, highlights two key aspects of environmental cases.[14] First, there is a class dimension to lawsuits. Two-thirds of civil cases in the Zhongnan sample were brought by workers or peasants, two groups largely left behind by China's economic boom (Lü, Zhang, and Xiong 2011, 85). Likely, workers and peasants suffer more exposure to pollution. They may also be forced to turn to courts when their money or connections prove insufficient to engineer a backdoor solution instead. The Zhongnan project also found that plaintiffs won at least some financial compensation in 43 percent of first-instance cases (Lü et al. 2011, 89). This win rate suggests that once a case is accepted by the court – no small obstacle – plaintiffs' prospects improve markedly. Going to court can sometimes pay off, even against long odds.

Of course, there are many ways to pursue disputes without recourse to courts. In focusing on litigation, my point is not that lawsuits are the most common way, or even the best way, to address environmental problems. The vast majority of environmental disputes are handled through government-brokered deals, private concessions, or simply when plaintiffs give up and go away. Still, low-frequency events can illuminate social dynamics as well as high-frequency ones. In microcosm, the origins, dynamics, and outcomes of environmental lawsuits offer one way to take stock of the shifting balance between political control and citizens' rights.

Sources

Like many interesting topics in China, environmental lawsuits are hard to study. The biggest problem is that there is no comprehensive

---

14 In 2007 and 2009, researchers from Zhongnan fanned out across the country to visit courts and request copies of environmental decisions. Although the decisions they amassed are not a complete record, as it proved impossible to visit every court, and local enthusiasm for unearthing cases varied, they created the largest collection of environmental cases currently available: 782 civil decisions, 61 criminal decisions, and 111 administrative decisions in total.

central repository of court decisions. Court decisions are not public documents, and, unless court officials decide differently, they are usually only released to the parties in the case.[15] This makes basic information, like the number of civil environmental cases or patterns of regional variation, difficult to know with certainty. In addition, courts are typically off limits to foreign researchers. While Chinese nationals can show an ID card to gain admittance (although they are sometimes denied access too), foreigners need both luck and connections to get inside. Finally, environmental lawsuits are rare enough that my research often felt like a hunt for anyone who had dealt with such an offbeat type of case. It was so hard to find environmental lawyers, in fact, that I started cold calling those whose name and law firm appeared in news reports or publicly available court decisions.[16]

As a result, this book draws on a wide array of sources. Above all, my perspective was shaped by months of conversations with lawyers, plaintiffs, judges, Environmental Protection Bureau (EPB) officials, journalists, legal experts, and representatives of international NGOs in the United States, Hong Kong, and twelve Chinese provinces.[17] This added up to more than 170 open-ended interviews conducted either during my longest stay in China, the fourteen months between November 2006 and January 2008, or shorter research trips in 2009, 2011, and 2012. Twenty-nine of these conversations were repeat interviews, when I sat down a second or a third time with someone to get updated on a case, hear the latest gossip, or see how their thoughts had changed. Conversations typically took place in Mandarin Chinese unless I was talking to a native English speaker. Although a Chinese research assistant accompanied

---

15 Sometimes, courts will put decisions online or make them available to Web sites that aggregate legal decisions.

16 This strategy worked because lawyers often list their phone number online to attract clients. Most lawyers I called were willing to speak to me in person after I explained the project.

17 Inside mainland China, I conducted interviews in Beijing, Chongqing, Guangdong, Guangxi, Hebei, Heilongjiang, Hubei, Jilin, Shanghai, Jiangsu, Zhejiang, and Yunnan. The coastal bias reflects the fact that most lawyers live and work along China's more developed east coast.

me on several occasions, I conducted most interviews alone. I typically received permission to take notes, although this was sometimes impractical in informal venues like restaurants. In all cases, I tried to type up my handwritten notes directly afterward.

In addition to these interviews, which ranged in length from 30 minutes to a full day, I compiled more detailed information, including court decisions, media reports, legal briefs, e-mail exchanges, and blog archives, for the four disputes discussed in Chapter 3. These four cases, evenly divided between northern and southern China and between disputes resolved inside and outside of courts, helped illustrate the ways in which local politics and individual personalities shape strategy and results. The following chapters, however, are not an explanation of success and failure in environmental lawsuits based on case studies. Rather, details from my four cases are woven into a larger account of the everyday practice of law and the relationship between law and social change. In a place like China, where research is difficult and every piece of information is hard-won, one advantage of organizing the book around themes rather than cases is the creative flexibility to build the arc of an argument on disparate fragments of insight. In addition to interviews and case studies, I opportunistically draw on other sources, including forty-two decisions in pollution lawsuits, a review of over sixty Chinese-language articles on environmental law, an original small-scale survey, and analysis of survey data collected by Chinese researchers. On occasion, I also cite unpublished documents provided to me by the author.[18]

Finally, a significant part of what follows is based on personal observation and involvement. Day to day, I spent a significant amount of time in China attending workshops on public interest law, environmental law, and environmental activism. These gatherings, which ranged in length from a morning to five days, attracted a group I came to think of as the usual suspects: the lawyers, NGO representatives, and academics

---

18 To protect anonymity, unpublished documents are marked in the text with the footnote "unpublished document on file with the author."

most interested in environmentalism and legal activism. Through the conference circuit, I also learned a great deal about how people talk in unguarded moments, over coffee or in whispers in the back of the room. Inevitably, as I became more tightly integrated into this world, I started doing things such as forwarding court decisions to lawyers working on similar cases, translating Web site updates into English, and alerting friends to American fellowships, grants, and opportunities.[19] The ties that eased my work also made me part of the research on international exchange that appears in Chapter 7. Any quotation in this book that does not cite an interview number comes from my field notes, a record of my everyday interactions and observations.

Roadmap

Environmental Litigation in China: A Study in Political Ambivalence is divided into two parts. The first three chapters offer an empirical look at how environmental litigation works, including an introduction to law and environmental issues in post-Mao China (Chapter 1), a step-by-step account of how a court case unfolds (Chapter 2), and four sketches of environmental disputes (Chapter 3). What stands out in this section is the human dimension of these cases. In the end, environmental lawsuits are brought and fought by individuals with the grit to overcome what sometimes seems like an endless stream of obstacles. These three chapters unquestionably speak to the difficulties and limits of environmental litigation, even as they also illustrate possibilities occasionally made real by gutsy choices and sheer stubbornness.

The second section of the book examines environmental litigation from multiple angles. Each of the next four chapters introduce a new actor's perspective on environmental lawsuits and, by extension, political

---

19 Although this core group of attendees typically lived in Beijing, many conference organizers worked hard to reach out to people outside the capital. During conferences in Guizhou, Heilongjiang, Hubei, Shanghai, and Zhejiang, I benefited greatly from talking to locals that were not part of the usual crew.

ambivalence. Roughly speaking, each successive chapter also increases distance from the central government, moving from discussion of political ambivalence and the state (Chapter 4), to judges on the frontlines (Chapter 5), to lawyers (Chapter 6), to international NGOs (Chapter 7). In addition to providing an organizing logic, working from inside to outside the state also offers a way to track the interaction between top-down signals and bottom-up experimentation. The final chapter makes this connection explicit, weaving different actors' perspectives into a broader account of the relationship between mixed signals, environmental litigation, and change to internal legal culture.

For me as a writer, one challenging (and occasionally rewarding) aspect of this approach was writing with multiple audiences in mind. From a public law perspective, the pages that follow fit comfortably into two long-standing threads of socio-legal research: how legal institutions work and the relationship between law and social change. For those coming out of a comparative politics tradition, however, this book is also an account of how individuals navigate political uncertainty and, at times, seize mixed signals as an opportunity for innovation. Others interested in comparative authoritarianism may want to explore where else political ambivalence aptly describes the experience of everyday politics, or perhaps pick up on the idea that there is much to be learned by viewing the state from below. Students of international relations will gravitate toward the view of transnational exchange found in Chapter 7, while China watchers will want to carefully consider the possibility that political ambivalence is central to the experience of contemporary Chinese politics. And anyone worried about China's tremendous environmental problems will want to head to Chapters 2, 3, and 8 to find out how lawsuits work and how much impact they have.

Despite forays into recent history, *Environmental Litigation in China: A Study in Political Ambivalence* largely starts in the year 2000. That year not only marked the turn of the century, but also the start of a major campaign to convert all remaining state-owned law firms into private partnerships. It is a good place to begin because pushing lawyers off the state payroll significantly changed the landscape of environmental litigation. Suddenly responsible for making an independent living, lawyers had new incentives to pick cases, keep clients happy, and even find new strategies to win in court. A year later, in 2001, the SPC also shifted the burden of proof to defendants, effectively requiring polluters to disprove any link between their behavior and plaintiffs' losses. Like the privatization of the bar, this seemingly small change had significant implications. At least on paper, it became far easier for pollution victims to win in court, and, although still extraordinarily hard, an improbable type of legal action became a bit more possible.

1 Post-Mao

Economic Growth, Environmental Protection, and the Law

ANY ACCOUNT OF ENVIRONMENTAL LAW quickly intersects with the well-known story of China's rapid economic growth. When Deng Xiaoping rose to power in 1978, he faced a challenging economic situation. The amount of grain produced per person had fallen below 1957 levels and the per capita income of Chinese peasants, then 80 percent of the population, was just $40 per year (Vogel 2011, 1). Deng pledged to quadruple the GDP by the year 2000 and, for the next thirty years, China posted annual growth rates near 10 percent. Economic growth became an unwavering byword of post-Mao politics, and China's economic success helped drive, a renewed interest in law. Deng and, later, President Jiang Zemin saw law as necessary to enforce contracts, break up monopolies, and attract investment to a "socialist market economy."

At the same time, economic growth helped create widespread pollution. China is now the world's largest emitter of greenhouse gases and produces more mercury than the United States, India, and Europe combined (Kirby 2011). Ninety percent of urban river water is polluted, and environmental groups estimate that a quarter of the population lacks access to safe drinking water (Freeman and Lu 2008, 6; Xinhua 2009). And the list goes on. In addition to air and water pollution, two of the most high-profile issues, China faces an array of other pollution-related problems, from ongoing struggles to curb noise to soil contamination left by polluting factories. It is no wonder that Minister of Environmental

Protection Zhou Shengxian calls reducing pollution an "increasingly heavy task" (Xinhua 2011).

This chapter looks at two legacies of China's emphasis on economic growth: the re-building of legal institutions after Mao Zedong's death in 1976 and the leadership's increasing concern about pollution. The turn towards law and, later, environmental protection gave rise to law that makes it possible to sue polluters and, equally important, to an atmosphere in which it is imaginable to do so. Still, it is far from clear where these trends will culminate. How law fits into the delicate balance between economic and environmental protection is part of an ongoing debate about where China should be headed and the best way to get there. After all, the Chinese state is visibly committed to three core contradictions. In economics, China is a communist country pursuing capitalism, an irony rife with ideological tension. In politics, China is a one-party state running long-term experiments in village elections, intra-party democracy, and other types of public participation. And in law, China has spent thirty years of legal reforms working toward an efficient, predictable legal system despite certain knowledge that law can subvert as well as support those in power.

China's Turn Toward Law

At Mao's death, formal law in China was close to non-existent. The near lawlessness of the 1960s and 1970s was the result of a politicized struggle in which champions of flexibility and revolutionary values edged out proponents of rules and legal expertise (O'Brien 1990, 158). When the People's Republic of China was founded in 1949, however, it was less clear which side would win. The 1950s pitted "new cadres" bent on making justice accessible to the masses against legal specialists who saw a detailed legal code and bureaucracy as a critical step in setting up a new nation capable of running a planned economy (Li 1978, 22–26). A group of educated, well-traveled legal specialists was behind the 1954 Constitution, a document that borrowed heavily from the Soviets to draw up a blueprint for legal institutions and principles that is still recognizable today. This first constitution, urged on the leadership by Stalin as a way to cement Chinese Communist Party (CCP) legitimacy, marked the high point of what historian Glenn Tiffert calls "a brief surge of legal construction" that would remain "unmatched until the reforms of the 1980s" (Tiffert 2009, 70). As part of the surge, law schools expanded, Chinese delegations traveled abroad to learn about Soviet experiences, and famous law journals were founded (Tiffert 2009, 71).

This experiment with socialist legality ended with the Hundred Flowers Campaign of 1957.[1] Mao's idea of letting "a hundred flowers bloom" and "a hundred schools of thought contend" was widely interpreted as official encouragement to vent constructive complaints. There was an outpouring of criticism surrounding the new legal system, including concerns about judicial independence, restraints on Party power, and lack of due process (Baum 1986, 78; Tiffert 2009, 71–72). Seemingly surprised by the vehemence and quantity of dissatisfaction, the Party responded with the Anti-Rightist Movement. The Anti-Rightist Movement hit the legal community especially hard. Many legal scholars and professionals were criticized, purged from the Party, transferred to other jobs, arrested, and imprisoned. The Ministry of Justice shut down in 1959, and the dwindling number of law schools that remained shifted focus from professional to political training (Li 1978, 31). Chairman Mao, who had long been wary of excessive bureaucracy, did not seem displeased by the change. As he commented, "the Civil Law, the Criminal Law, who remembers those texts? I participated in the drafting of the Constitution, but even I don't remember it" (quoted in Tiffert 2009, 72).

Following a flare of interest in new legal codes in the early 1960s,[2] political distrust of law reached its apogee during the violent political

1 An earlier campaign to re-examine the work of the bureaucracy in 1951 and 1952 had already led to the transfer of a large number of judges. In an early victory for the new cadres, remaining judges were warned to avoid elitism and adhere to the mass line (Li 1978, 29).

2 See Baum (1986, 80).

turmoil of the Cultural Revolution. Widespread attacks on the "four old" elements within Chinese society – old customs, old habits, old culture, and old ideas – included law. A typical article from a Guangzhou Red Guard journal published in 1968 laid out the critique that law was a tool of "bourgeois powerholders" used by counter-revolutionaries to "take advantage of their right to defense, their right to appeal and legal restrictions on the instruments of dictatorship to pursue their legal struggle." True revolutionaries should "rely on people, not on the law, for government" (quoted in Baum 1986, 81–82). In practice, government by the people meant that courts, the procuracy, and law schools ceased operation. Local residents' committees and work groups typically resolved day-to-day disputes, such as tensions over a shared bathroom or even a divorce, while revolutionary committees often meted out justice in more serious cases. At all levels, political instructions were not conveyed through law, but via Central Party documents, speeches by leaders, and the media (Yang, Chen, and Zhang 2010a, 19).[3] In 1975, revisions to the constitution formalized some of these changes. The procuracy was abolished, and the courts were placed under the jurisdiction of revolutionary committees (Baum 1986, 83). By Mao's death in 1976, years of striving toward the ideal of revolutionary justice had left the courts, codes, and legal education in shambles.

Re-Establishing the Law

Deng Xiaoping's rise to power in 1978 marked a turning point in the PRC's legal development. After the chaos of the Cultural Revolution, many were ready to trade in Mao's vision of "continuous revolution" for a newfound commitment to stability and law. Adherence to law symbolized a rejection of class struggle as well as a more explicit assurance that abuses of power during the Cultural Revolution would not be repeated

---

3 Three of the most important news outlets were People's Daily (*Renmin Ribao*), People's Liberation Army Daily (*Jiefangjun Bao*) and Red Flag Magazine (*Hongqi Zazhi*) (Yang et al. 2010a, 19).

(O'Brien 1990, 158; Lubman 1999, 124). In 1978, the CCP Central Committee called for strengthening the legal system:

> There must be laws for people to follow, these laws must be observed, their enforcement must be strict, and lawbreakers must be dealt with…Procuratorial and judicial organizations must…guarantee the equality of all people before the people's laws, and deny anyone the privilege of being above the law (quoted in Baum 1986, 85).

Over the next several years, law schools started to re-open, the Ministry of Justice and the People's Procuratorate were re-established, and new regulations on lawyers restored the legal profession (Peerenboom 2002, 6–7; Chen 2008, 158, 162, and 167). Legal drafting resumed after the hiatus of the Cultural Revolution, and the number of court cases started to pick up. Unlike the 1950s flirtation with socialist legality, post-Mao efforts to write new laws, professionalize the judiciary, and strengthen the courts proved considerably longer lived. The Chinese leadership turned toward law for many reasons, discussed in Chapter 4, and this historic project of legal construction was accompanied by a dramatic rise in the numbers of judges, procuratorate employees, lawyers, law firms, and law schools (Table 1.1).

Table 1.1. *The Growth of Legal Institutions*

	Start of reforms	2000s
Number of judges	60,439 (1981)	189,531 (2009)
Number of lawyers	8,571 (1981)	195,170 (2010)
Number of procuratorate staff	97,330 (1986)	223,334 (2010)[4]
Number of law firms	79 (1979)	17,230 (2010)
Number of law schools & departments	less than 15 (1978)	634 (2008)

Sources: Zou (2006, 14); Zhu (2007, 273); Chen (2008, 167 and 169); Xinhua (2009a); Ji (2010, 299); China Law Yearbook (2011, 1054 and 1067).

In the 1990s, growing high-level support for law paralleled efforts to recentralize political power. The idea of "rule by law" (*yifa zhiguo*),

---

4 This includes administrative assistants and the judicial police (*sifa jingcha*).

endorsed by President Jiang Zemin in several key speeches in the mid-1990s, complemented initiatives designed to uphold central authority and unify standards across the country (Chen 2012, 501–504). In 1999, the first SPC five-year plan for court reform listed fifty specific goals, many aimed at improving the competence of judges and the quality of their decisions (Liebman 2007, 624–625). The plan marked a step toward professionalism, visible in the degree to which judges' educational levels improved in response to new policies. The 1995 Judges Law introduced age and experience requirements for judges, followed by a 2001 amendment requiring that new appointees pass the national judicial exam along with lawyers and procurators (Standing Committee 2001). Although complaints about uneducated judges persist, especially in rural areas, judges today are much better educated than their 1980s counterparts.[5] Including vocational training, only 17 percent of Chinese judges had post-secondary education in 1987. By 2000, nearly all did (Chen 2008, 152).

Alongside the growth of legal institutions, the Standing Committee of the National People's Congress (NPC) approved the first campaign designed to disseminate national law (*pufa yundong*) in 1985.[6] The goal was to "place the law in the hands of the masses...so that [they] will learn to use the law as a weapon against all acts committed in violation of the Constitution and the law" (quoted in Gallagher 2006, 793). Media coverage of legal information increased, accompanied by law classes, educational materials, and slogans. The *Beijing Evening News*, for example, ran a legal advice column from 1989 to 1998 called "Dear Lawyer Bao." As the paper's editor wrote in a preface to the first column, "as society advances toward a system of law, every citizen needs to...raise

---

5 There is a shortage of judges outside coastal areas, particularly in the countryside. Low salaries make it especially difficult to retain young, well-trained judges in these areas (Zhu 2007, 193; Balme 2010, 172).

6 The 1985 campaign built on efforts dating back to at least 1979. In 1979, the Central Committee of the CCP called for legal education and the introduction of law classes into curricula (Central Committee 1979).

his or her legal awareness, and know the law, understand the law, adhere to the law, and use the law" (quoted in Michelson 2008, 44). By 1990, the end of the first five-year legal dissemination plan, official statistics claimed that 70 percent of the population had participated in some form of legal study (Zhu 2007, 580).

Four more legal dissemination campaigns followed, each five years long. Officials uncovered ever more creative ways to raise legal awareness, from legal hotlines (once telephones became common) to TV shows produced by the state-owned stations. In environmental disputes, legal outreach efforts quickly became visible in complaints that invoked the law alongside the traditional language used to petition aloof officials. For example, one letter written to a municipal Environmental Protection Bureau (EPB) head in Anhui province in the 1990s asks: "From ancient times, 'heaven is high and the emperor is far away,' but why is the Environmental Protection Law never properly enforced in my home town?" (quoted in Weller 2006, 118). Beyond environment, too, twenty-five years of popularizing legal knowledge anchored the idea of rights protection in the popular consciousness.[7]

Law and the Party

The overall trend toward increased reliance on law should not mask ongoing, hard-fought arguments about the role the legal system should play in Chinese society. How should the law prioritize goals such as maintaining social order, resolving disputes, implementing policy, protecting citizens, and aiding the CCP? China's legal community debated the raison d'être of law throughout the post-Mao period, and new initiatives often reflected shifts in emphasis. There was a notable change in 2007,

---

7 There is a great deal of variation across China in legal awareness and knowledge. Among other issues, the budget for legal outreach efforts is higher in rich provinces than in poor ones. During the third five-year plan to popularize law, for example, Shanghai spent 700,000 RMB (US$111,111) compared to just 20,000 (US$3,174) RMB in all of Xinjiang Province (Zhu 2007, 590).

for example, when President Hu Jintao stated that judges and procurators should "regard as supreme the Party's cause, the people's interest and the constitution and laws" (quoted in Cohen 2008). Because it placed the Party's interest on par with the law, Hu's formulation of the "Three Supremes" (*san ge zhishang*) – the Party, the people, and the law – was widely seen as a retreat from policies emphasizing judicial independence. Around the same time, judges also found themselves under rising pressure to mediate cases rather than try them. In 2009, 62 percent of civil cases were resolved through mediation, compared to just 31 percent in 2004 (Minzner 2011, 944). Together, the stress placed on mediation and the Three Supremes convinced some scholars that a "turn against law" was under way, or at least a retreat from earlier reforms centered on litigation and professionalism (Minzner 2011; see also Jiang 2010). Reformers hoping to nudge forward government accountability, civil rights, and social justice through law agreed that what felt like a tailwind in the 1990s became a headwind by the mid-2000s (Interview 150).[8]

What was dubbed a "turn against law" can also be seen as a waning of interest in a particular vision of autonomous law.[9] In contrast to the 1990s, when judges were celebrated for "rationality" and "adherence to neutrality," judges in the 2000s were supposed to be Solomon-like mediators (Minzner 2011, 954). In other words, the job of the judge was to defuse tension and craft compromises rather than faithfully apply rules. That change in role conception marked a shift away from the ideal of law as a "model of rules" toward the belief that mediation could achieve fair, efficient, and cost-effective dispute resolution equally well (Nonet and Selznick 2008, 54). So far, it is unclear how well mediation is succeeding. The generic advantages of mediation – decreased costs, shorter decision times, and creative solutions – are accompanied by a real danger that backroom negotiations will favor the powerful.

Meanwhile, the concept of Three Supremes fits comfortably within the long-standing mainstream view of law among top leaders: that it

8 See interviews 148, 152, 154, 156, and 167 as well as Minzner (2011, 964).
9 For more on autonomous law, see Nonet and Selznick (2008, 53–72).

should serve the CCP. After all, the growth of legal institutions occurred under the aegis of the Party, and channels of Party influence are a long-standing part of the legal system. Article 126 of the Constitution shields courts from interference by agencies, organizations, and individuals, but not the Party itself (Li 2012, 854). Inside courts, presidents and vice-presidents are elected by the local people's congress only after being vetted by the Party committee (Zhu 2007, 179). Each court also assigns "significant, difficult or complex" cases to an adjudication committee of senior judges, most of whom are usually also Party members.[10] Overall, the CCP has proved remarkably reluctant to diverge "from a principle it has followed since the PRC was established; policy, as defined and implemented by the CCP, must be supreme over law" (Lubman 1999, 130). Post-Mao leaders have always looked to law to help the Party meet its goals.

Pollution and Political Will

As the Chinese leadership built legal institutions and debated the purpose of law, environmental problems such as smog, water shortages, acid rain, river pollution, and oil spills started to intensify.[11] Particularly under Deng Xiaoping, China's environmental track record resembled that of nineteenth-century industrial England. The 1980s and 1990s was the era of "pollute first, control later" (*xian wuran, hou zhili*) and, especially in rural areas, industrialization was key to economic expansion. With the end of collective farming in the early 1980s, local

10 The court president and vice-president always serve on the adjudication committee. The other committee members are nominated by the president and approved by the local people's congress at the corresponding level. For more on the adjudication committee, see Chen (2012, 510–512) and He (forthcoming).

11 For a more complete account of the origins of China's environmental problems, see Shapiro (2001) and Elvin (2004). China's ongoing reliance on coal to supply roughly 70 percent of its energy needs also deserves mention as a significant source of air pollution. Coal combustion remains responsible for 70 percent of China's soot, 75 percent of sulfur-dioxide, 85 percent of nitrogen dioxide, and 80 percent of carbon dioxide as well as the release of toxic heavy metals like mercury and lead (Economy 2010, 740).

governments found themselves under pressure to find other, non-agricultural sources of income for unemployed villagers (Oi 1999, 77). Many began investing in township and village enterprises (TVEs), which were relatively low-tech, labor-intensive factories that could offer jobs, boost incomes, and supply taxes. Compared to state-owned factories responsible for set quotas, TVEs were flexible and could adjust output in response to demand. They could also keep salaries and benefits relatively low by selectively hiring young workers (Vogel 2011, 447). As Deng later recalled, TVEs were "a new force that just came into being spontaneously;" a great, unexpected success (quoted in Vogel 2011, 445). TVE output grew by 35 percent per year throughout most of the 1980s (Meisner 1999, 465) and, by the 1990s, approximately one-third of China's 500 million rural labor force was working in metal smelters, brick furnaces, cement plants, and the like (Tilt 2010, 36–37).

By the 2000s, rural factories (many now privatized) accounted for one-third of national GDP and were widely blamed for severe air and water pollution (Economy 2010, 63; Tilt 2010, 3).[12] Rural pollution was so severe that nearly 70 percent of letters sent to the Ministry of Environmental Protection (MEP) in the late 2000s related to issues in the countryside (Zhang 2012). Pan Yue, deputy director at what was then the State Environmental Protection Agency (SEPA), summed up the prevailing view in 2006:

> China's environmental crisis has arisen, basically, because our mode of economic modernization has been copied from Western, developed nations. In twenty years, China has achieved economic results that took a century to obtain in the West. But we have also concentrated a century's worth of environmental issues into those twenty years. While becoming the world leader in GDP growth

12 Estimates from the early 2000s hold TVEs responsible for somewhere between half (Economy 2004, 63) and two-thirds of China's total air and water pollution (Tilt 2010, 3). China's first pollution census, released in 2010, indicates that pesticide runoff from agriculture has now eclipsed factory effluent as a source of water pollution (Watts 2010).

and foreign investment, we have also become the world's number one consumer of coal, oil and steel – and the largest producer of carbon dioxide (quoted in Tilt 2010, 64).

As incomes rose, at least in some parts of the country, increasing affluence also became a source of pollution itself. In July 2011, the World Bank Group reclassified China as an upper-middle-income economy, a change that highlights a growing group of people who understandably want hot water, refrigerators, and computers.[13] In cities, many are exchanging new disposable income for private cars, which are accompanied by traffic and air pollution. China surpassed the United States in passenger car sales in 2009, and counted more than 100 million automobiles on its roads in 2011 (Economy 2010, 77; Xinhua 2011a). Car sales have room to grow, too, as only 10.9 percent of urban households owned a car in 2009 (China Statistical Yearbook 2010). Even eating habits are changing with affluence. China's per-capita consumption of meat and milk increased four-fold, and its consumption of eggs increased eight-fold between 1978 and 2002 (Liu and Diamond 2005). This means more agricultural waste, more fish food and fertilizer for aquaculture, and likely more pollution.

Rewarding Economic Growth

Since Mao's time, the connection between economic growth and pollution has been tightened by a political system that has yet to effectively prioritize environmental protection. The nub of the problem is an evaluation system that ties officials' career prospects to goals that prioritize economic growth and tamping down protest (van Rooij 2006a,

13 According to the 2011 World Bank definition, upper middle-income economies have an average per capita income of $3,976 to $12,275. Although the half of the Chinese population that lives in cites largely already own most durable household goods, few in the countryside do. In 2009, 37 percent of rural households owned a refrigerator, 53 percent a washing machine, and 12 percent an air conditioner (China Statistical Yearbook 2010).

271; Weller 2006, 144; Cary 2011).[14] To set the tone for the province, provincial governors usually pick an EPB head whose background suggests he will be sympathetic to plans for economic development.[15] As of 2010, only eight provincial EPB heads had been promoted from within the EPB itself. The remaining three-quarters came from elsewhere in government, not infrequently with experience working for an economic bureau or state-owned enterprise (Kostka forthcoming). The emphasis on economic growth means that local governments often protect economic interests at the expense of existing environmental laws, regulations, and policies. Even periodic national environmental campaigns, such as the one to close down small polluting enterprises in 1996 or clean up the Huai River in 1998, rarely sustain improvement after political pressure ends.[16] Here is Vice Minster Pan again:

> The main reason behind the continued deterioration of the environment is a mistaken view of what counts as a political achievement...The crazy expansion of high-polluting, high-energy industries has spawned special interests. Protected by local governments, some businesses treat the natural resources that belong to all the people as their own private property (quoted in Kahn and Yardley 2007).

Lower down in the bureaucracy, there are many examples of local officials, like a county head or Party secretary, intervening in EPB work to protect polluters that provide revenue from taxes or jobs (Ma and Ortolano 2000; Zhang 2008; Ma 2010).[17] EPBs must send a notice before formally issuing a pollution-related fine, a warning that often serves as

---

14 According to one account, local officials opposed plans to introduce Green GDP (an adjusted measure of GDP that accounts for the costs of environmental degradation) because of the potential impact on promotions (Cary 2011).

15 As of 2010, none of the thirty-one provincial EPB heads were women (Kostka forthcoming).

16 On the ineffectiveness of the Huai River campaign, see Economy (2010, 1–11). For more on pollution campaigns in general, see van Rooij (2006a, 332–351).

17 Local leaders will also sometimes ask EPBs for a favor on behalf of close friends or relatives (Zhang 2008, 55–56).

an opportunity for the enterprise to petition county officials to reduce or waive the fee (Zhang 2008, 53). "We'll stand in the complainant's corner if it's a small company, but not if it's a big one," one provincial EPB official explained (Interview 99).

In situations where the local government is competing for outside investment (packages offering new entrants tax breaks, low land-use fees, or subsidized electricity are common), compromising on environmental protection is even more likely. A willingness to overlook pollution can be a perk used to lure investors, especially in places without other enticements to offer (Zhang 2008, 53; Luo 2010, 91; Stalley 2010, 105; Tilt 2010, 151). Many outside investors in a county in Hubei province, for example, have agreements with local leaders stipulating the maximum amount of environment-related fees they will pay (Zhang 2008, 53). In 2010, Guzhen county in Anhui province went as far as to suspend six EPB officials, including the bureau chief, for damaging efforts to attract investment by visiting a tire manufacturer three times in a month (Ma 2010).

China's industrial parks (*gongye qu*) are sites of some of the fiercest competition to attract investment and can easily turn into pollution hotspots if political support for environmental monitoring falters.[18] In the early 2000s, in the midst of what the Chinese media dubbed a "chemical park fever," it was widely reported that many new parks were sidestepping Environmental Impact Assessment (EIA) requirements and allowing chemical plants to start production before wastewater treatment plants were completed (Stalley 2010, 98–104). This "simultaneous construct and pollute" (*yibian jianshe, yibian wuran*) approach was possible, in part, because most permits are approved by the park administrative committee (*guanli weiyuanhui*) without oversight from city or provincial authorities. Even after a park is complete, pollution can be strategically ignored by environmental authorities who report to park

---

18 A Shanghai EPB official suggested that newer industrial parts with more modern equipment and parks run by the city government (as opposed to the district government) do a better job with environmental protection (Interview 105).

management and have little contact with the local EPB (Stalley 2010, 103–104). When a reporter called Funing County Chemical Park in 2006 and asked about investment opportunities, he was openly told: "The more you invest, the more preferential treatment you get. As long as your investment is at least 10 million RMB (US\$1.6 million), 45,000 RMB per *mu*,[19] all emissions issues will be easy to solve" (quoted in Ye 2006).

Building Local Revenue

The attitude that "investors are gods," as a road sign in Jiangsu province proclaimed, stems not only from pressure to meet quotas, but also from the need to keep local government solvent (Ye 2006). Building a tax base is critical, especially because many township governments are deep in debt. Areas with industry tend to be in better fiscal health than those reliant on agriculture alone (Oi and Zhao 2007) and, in good times, taxes from industry provide public goods like roads, schools, running water, and electricity that benefit the whole community. Especially in poorer parts of China, township cadres are frustrated by pressure to step up environmental enforcement while simultaneously maintaining a tax base and keeping up employment (Tilt 2010, 128–131). Officials in one Sichuan township saw industrial tax receipts fall to zero after a decision by higher-ups to close all factories exceeding emissions standards.[20] As one vice mayor put it, "the upper level of government invites you to dinner, but the local government pays the bill" (quoted in Tilt 2007, 927).

Given the importance of economic growth for the careers of local political leaders, it is not surprising that EPBs frequently lack the resources and incentive to enforce environmental regulations (Jahiel

---

19 A mu is one-sixth of an acre.
20 The decision was made at the district level after Sichuan Television Station aired an exposé on pollution from a zinc smelter in the township. The closed factories were a vital source of revenue for the township, but not for the overall district (Tilt 2010, 115–118).

1998; Ma and Ortolano 2000; van Rooij 2006; Tilt 2007). Despite a significant rise in the amount spent on environmental protection (0.6 percent of
the GDP in 1989 compared to 2.5 percent in 2009), the sources of funding
undermine the bureau's independence (Stalley 2010, 35; China Statistical Yearbook 2010). Most money comes from local government, and the
power of the purse makes officials' requests to go easy on polluters hard
to ignore. Especially in poorer areas, some EPBs also rely on pollution-
discharge fees for basic funding. Dependence on fines, ironically, leaves
EPBs reluctant to eradicate pollution entirely (van Rooij 2006, 64; Zhang
2008, 37).[21] Often, EPBs aim for enforcement strict enough to avoid criticism without upsetting powerful polluters or officials (van Rooij 2006a,
297). After all, EPBs have no coercive power to force compliance. A former EPB head in Hubei province explained, "If we issue a fine, but the
violator does not hand it over, we cannot do anything, literally" (quoted
in Zhang 2008, 36).[22]

EPBs also remain underfunded and understaffed, especially in
poorer parts of the country. Lack of resources means less oversight
and an overall shortage of environmental information. A 2011 Natural Resource Defense Council report on industrial lead pollution in
Yunnan province, for example, found that county EPB staff neither
routinely monitored lead levels nor enjoyed regular access to a car for
inspections (15–18). Even in a city as rich as Shanghai, the government collects environmental information from less than 30 percent of
small-scale enterprises (Warwick and Ortolano 2007, 244). And without
routine monitoring, pollution continues. Coal plants install state-of-the-
art sulfur-dioxide scrubbers and fail to turn them on (Steineld, Lester,
and Cunningham 2008)[23] or chemical factories discharge at night when

---

21 Officially, all pollution fees and fines are supposed to go directly to the local finance
   bureau, and the EPB is not guaranteed a portion of revenues. However, there is local
   variation in how well this system has been implemented (Lo and Tam 2007, 48).
22 In contrast, the Industrial and Commercial Bureau can confiscate goods or materials
   until violators pay fines (Zhang 2008, 37).
23 An alternative explanation for the high reported levels of sulfur-dioxide emissions is
   that plants are burning sub-standard coal that overwhelm scrubbers even when they
   are turned on (Steinfeld et al. 2008).

the roads are dangerous and inspections are practically impossible (van Rooij 2006, 65).

Often, the EPB finds itself in a reactive role, scrambling to demonstrate progress on political priorities or responding to public complaints. As the number of environmental complaints soared from 369,712 in 2000 to 696,134 in 2009, partly thanks to the proliferation of phone hotlines and online forms, complaint handlers have found themselves coping with a nearly unfinishable pile of work (China Environment Yearbooks 2001 and 2010; Cheng 2011). An ethnographic study of one EPB in southeast China shows complaints get priority when they are easy to solve, enjoy backing from powerful people, have been reported in the media or involve a group. "Anonymous complaints never get prioritized," an agent explained. "I ignore most of them" (quoted in Cheng 2011).

The Turn Toward Environmental Protection

Everyday headaches at the EPB reflect the lack of priority placed on the bureau's mandate. For the last quarter of the twentieth century, businessmen, government officials, and most of the public agreed on the importance of economic growth and saw deterioration in the quality of water and air as a price they were willing to pay. In the 2000s, however, political will to tackle pollution started to build alongside rising environmental consciousness. Of those surveyed in a 1997 study in Anhui province, 63 percent had never heard the term "environmental protection" (*huanjing baohu*) (Alford et al. 2002, 497). Ten years later, more than eighty percent of respondents in a national survey knew about environmental protection, even if their proffered definitions were not always on target (China Awareness Program 2008, 2).[24]

At the same time, the central leadership began displaying increasing concern over environmental issues, a change which some observers

---

24 Although these surveys are not directly comparable, these two data points suggest rising public awareness of environmental issues in the 2000s.

termed "the greening of the Chinese state" (Ho and Vermeer 2006).[25] As early as 2002, then-president Jiang Zemin talked about sustainable development and "better[ing] the natural environment" as a key part of reaching a "well-off society" (*xiaokang shehui*) (Tilt 2010, 11). And in recent years, the Hu Jintao-Wen Jiabao government has routinely mentioned environmental protection alongside economic growth. A 2006 speech by Premier Wen Jiabao, to take one example, stressed the importance of moving "from a mindset of cleaning up after economic development to a simultaneous emphasis on environmental protection *and* economic growth" (quoted in Tilt 2010, 139).

Alongside rhetoric, there are concrete signs that environmental protection is a rising policy priority. The number of EPB staff increased from 70,000 to more than 170,000 between 1991 and 2007, during which time government spending on environmental protection jumped from 10 billion RMB (US$1.6 million) to 340 billion RMB (US$54 million) (Mol 2009, 96). As part of a government reshuffle in 2008, the NPC also elevated the former State Environmental Protection Administration to the Ministry of Environmental Protection. MEP became one of just five "super ministries" with a seat on the State Council, a highly visible upgrade in status.[26] Penalties for environmental violations are increasing too, as shown by the 208 percent jump in the average fine per case between 2001 and 2006 (van Rooij and Lo 2010, 18).

Accountability

Most important, higher-ups started holding local governments accountable for plans to reduce energy intensity by 20 percent and key

---

25 Many interviewees talked about the greening of the state (especially see interviews 7, 30, 36, 72, 78, 82, 87, 94, 105, 122, 127, 135, 137, 167).

26 The other four "super ministries" are the Ministry of Industry and Information, the Ministry of Human Resources and Social Security, the Ministry of Housing and Urban-Rural Construction, and the Ministry of Transport (Xinhua 2008).

pollutants by 10 percent during the eleventh Five-Year Plan (2006–2010).[27] In 2007, after China fell behind its goals for two years running, Premier Wen Jiabao announced that energy efficiency and emissions targets "cannot be changed, and must be unswervingly achieved" (Wen 2007; see also People's Daily 2008). The same year, the State Council announced that monitoring results would be used to help determine promotions and bonuses for provincial officials and 1,000 key firms. Some provinces went even further.[28] Regulations in Hebei province, for instance, specified that county leaders who failed to meet targets would be fired. And in Shanxi, environmental enforcement officials prioritized closing small cement, iron and steel plants as the easiest way to meet sulfur-dioxide reduction goals (Kostka and Hobbs 2012). In the last six months of 2010, officials were under so much pressure to make their numbers by the end of the five-year period that some provinces started forcing blackouts. Anping, a town of 600,000 in Hebei province, shut off traffic lights for a week to save energy (Hook 2010). Ratcheting up incentives to meet energy-efficiency and pollution reduction targets was effective: national energy intensity dropped by 14.3 percent between 2006 and 2009 (Xu 2010).

Under the twelfth Five-Year Plan (2011–2015), it appears officials and leaders of state-owned enterprise will remain accountable for environmental targets, including a 16 percent nationwide reduction in energy intensity. In addition to further reductions to the key targets listed in the last Five-Year Plan, sulfur-dioxide emissions, and chemical oxygen demand (a measure of water pollution), the new plan also calls for a 10 percent decrease in levels of nitrogen oxide and ammonia nitrogen as well as a 15 percent drop in heavy metals in five key control

27 Key pollutants include chemical oxygen demand (COD), a measure of water pollution, and sulfur-dioxide. For an early call to incorporate environmental criteria into annual evaluations, see State Council (2005).
28 In order to meet national targets, lower levels of government often inflate goals. In one Shanxi county, for example, cadres were responsible for a 27 to 30 percent targeted reduction in energy intensity (Kostka and Hobbs 2012).

areas (Natural Resources Defense Council 2011, 20). Provincial goals, shown below and assigned by the State Council, generally make wealthier provinces responsible for deeper cuts than poorer areas (Table 1.2).

Table 1.2. *Sulfur-Dioxide Reduction Targets in China's Twelfth Five-Year Plan (2011–2015)*[29]

less than 1% reduction	1–4% reduction	4–9% reduction	more than 9% reduction
Gansu	Inner Mongolia	Anhui	Beijing
Hainan	Jilin	Fujian	Tianjin
Qinghai	Heilongjiang	Jiangxi	Hebei
Tibet	Yunnan	Hubei	Shanxi
Xinjiang	Ningxia	Hunan	Liaoning
		Guangxi	Shanghai
		Chongqing	Jiangsu
		Sichuan	Zhejiang
		Guizhou	Shandong
		Shaanxi	Henan
			Guangdong

Source: State Council (2011).

Ambitious targets, of course, are no guarantee of environmental improvement. Localities may just cook the numbers to look as if they are in compliance. One county in Shanxi, for example, decided to meet environmental targets during the eleventh Five-Year Plan by closing factories in rotation. This "sleeping management" (*xiumian guanli*) approach was effective – shutting factories is surely a fast way to cut emissions – but suggests a panicked, last-minute effort rather than a long-term commitment to reducing pollution (Kostka and Hobbs 2012). Polluters, too, still by and large believe that pollution can be solved with money. The average fine for exceeding emissions standards was just 10,000 RMB (US$1,587) in 2006, an amount easily absorbed into the cost of business (van Rooij and Lo 2010, 18). As a leader of a paper factory located in a township with a high cancer rate explained, "As long as we compensate, there is no problem" (quoted in van Rooij 2010, 74).

29 This is the percent reduction over 2010 levels.

Top-Down Environmentalism

In contrast to polluters' resistance, the central leadership is starting to see the strategic sense of environmental protection. Newfound interest in the environment reflects hardheaded considerations at least as much as values-driven environmentalism. Especially following the 2008 Olympics, China is firmly connected to the outside world and the CCP derives substantial legitimacy from international recognition. The need to project an image of up-to-date, internationally engaged leaders requires not only hosting foreign dignitaries, but also taking international pressure to address environmental issues seriously. Domestically, state environmentalism reflects a considered assessment of the potential for pollution to disrupt long-term growth and stability. Environmental crises, in particular, have played a key role in forging this understanding by showcasing the destabilizing effects of pollution. An early crisis, in which a number of Beijing residents fell ill after eating fish from a polluted reservoir in 1972, was followed by rumors that class enemies poisoned the water in an attempt to kill Mao and other CCP leaders (McElwee 2011, 22). Just over two decades later, in the mid-1990s, severe pollution along the Huai River turned the water black and left hundreds of thousands without drinking water. In response to local anger (at one point, officials were pelted with eggs when they tried to keep journalists from filming the river), central leaders stepped in and closed hundreds of polluting factories (Hertsgaard 1997).

The 2000s have been punctuated by environmental disasters as well. After major chemical spills along the Tuo River and the Songhua River in 2004 and 2005, over thirty NPC delegates wrote a joint brief pushing for public interest environmental litigation to stop the deleterious influence of industrial accidents on "the construction of a harmonious society" (Bie 2007, 449). Sometimes, high-profile accidents directly channel new resources to cash-strapped EPBs. In Jilin province, after the Songhua spill, the provincial EPB received new equipment for on-the-spot water analysis to avoid the delay caused by sending samples back to the lab for testing. "It's ironic," one EPB official commented, that "we suddenly had status" after a major crisis (Interview 87).

How much has environmentalism trickled down from the pinnacle of the state? New resources allocated to EPBs have surely helped, and there are occasional echoes of pro-environment rhetoric throughout the bureaucracy. Officials in Guizhou province, for example, made a cliché of the phrase "protecting green mountains and blue water is a political achievement" (*bao zhu qing shan lü shui ye shi zhengji*) in the late 2000s. But on the other hand, it is also clear that the majority both inside and outside of government see pollution as acceptable. Even EPB employees often limit their ambition to finding a balancing point between economic growth and environmental protection. It remains hard for most to imagine seriously sacrificing economic development goals.

Environmental Law and Litigation

Environmental law lies at the intersection of these two fitful currents in post-Mao politics: re-building the legal system and finding a balance between economic growth and environmental protection. Against this backdrop, it seems reasonable to ask how environmental litigation fits into efforts to limit pollution. In a country with serious pollution and weak regulatory agencies, could citizen-initiated lawsuits serve as a backstop to the usual mélange of fines, mediation, and social suasion?

Although it will take most of this book to explore this question, it is worth beginning by recognizing how much China's environmental laws have changed since Mao's departure. The 1979 trial enactment of the Environmental Protection Law marked the first major environmental law of the post-Mao era and, in fact, Article 41 lays out the legal basis for civil environmental litigation.[30] It holds polluters responsible for

---

30 There are also references to environmental protection in the 2004 Constitution. Notably, Articles 9 and 26 hold the state responsible for the "the rational use of natural

damages and grants complainants the right to sue if a government-negotiated settlement is unsatisfactory. Over the next decade, this omnibus legislation was followed by a set of topic-specific laws, including the 1982 Marine Pollution Law, the 1984 Water Pollution Law, and the 1987 Air Pollution Law.[31] As state control over the economy waned in the 1990s, and pollution worsened, all three laws were revised and new laws like the 1995 Solid Waste Law and the 1996 Noise Pollution Law introduced.[32] Still, thanks to low fines, feeble enforcement, and vague provisions, the prevailing view at the turn of the twenty-first century was that environmental law was weak and ineffective.

Around 2000, the broader turn toward environmental protection became visible in the stepped-up pace of efforts to write and revise environmental laws. "Laws are being drafted at all times, on all subjects," a Beijing-based environmental official commented in 2002 (quoted in Ferris and Zhang 2002, 587), a burst of busyness also captured in MEP documents indicating plans to revise nearly every major environmental law during the eleventh Five-Year Plan (2006–2010).[33] Much of this ambitious agenda was realized and, throughout the 2000s, national environmental laws and regulations delved into new areas, strengthened environmental standards, and increased penalties for violations. Highlights included the 2002 Environmental Impact Assessment Law, the 2002 Clean Production Law, the 2007 Measures on Open Environmental Information, and the 2008 Circular Economy Law. By the end of the first decade of the 2000s, there were over 29 national environmental laws and 1,300 environmental standards (Wang 2010a; State Council 2011a). China had also ratified many international environmental agreements, including the 2002 Kyoto Protocol and the 2004 Stockholm

resources" and pollution control. Chinese courts, however, do not have the power to strike down laws that contravene the Constitution.

31 These dates refer to when the law was adopted rather than enacted. For an overview of these pieces of legislation, see McElwee (2011, 60–65).

32 For more on the revisions to the Air Pollution Law, see Alford and Liebman (2002). For more on the national law-making process in general, see McElwee (2011, 34–50).

33 State Environmental Protection Agency, *11th Five-Year Law Plan on National Environmental Protection Laws and Regulations*. Document on file with the author.

Convention. Despite obvious gaps, such as the lack of a law requiring polluters to restore the environment, law on the books had improved such that some observers could plausibly credit China with "an admirable set of environmental laws" (Stalley 2010, 22).

This set of environmental laws allows three types of environmental lawsuits, outlined in Table 1.3. The high-level overview is that civil cases concern private controversies between polluters and individuals, criminal cases deal with violations of laws defining criminal conduct, and administrative cases involve claims by or against government agencies.[34] In China, administrative litigation also includes "non-litigation" administrative execution cases (NAECs, or *feisu xingzheng zhixing anzi* in Chinese). Through NAECs, government agencies can enlist judicial help in enforcing decisions.[35] For EPBs, the courts' coercive capacity to detain individuals for up to 15 days or confiscate property has sometimes been a huge aid in collecting fines that were approaching hopeless write-offs (Zhang et al. 2010, 314–315). Even if polluters rarely paid fines in full, one restaurant owner explained, "You know you need to pay once judges come" (quoted in Zhang et al. 2010, 318).

Criminal lawsuits punish responsible individuals for extreme pollution incidents, as well as illegal mining, fishing, or logging.[36] These kinds of cases punish individuals and assign blame, which can be an expedient

34 Agency decisions can also be challenged through administrative review (*xingzheng fuyi*). Administrative review is a bureaucratic process that does not involve the courts. For more on administrative review, see the Administrative Review Law (National People's Congress 1999).

35 Courts have benefited from NAECs too. In the 1990s, shortly after the passage of the Administrative Litigation Law (ALL), courts found themselves under pressure to maintain a robust administrative litigation caseload in order to justify the existence of the administrative division and meet annual targets. NAECs helped courts make their numbers while also generating revenue through court fees (Zhang et al. 2010, 315–317).

36 Nearly three-quarters of defendants in a sample of 61 decisions were involved in agricultural work, a proportion that suggests environmental crimes are tied to limited economic opportunities in rural areas (Lü et al. 2011, 86). In 2010, the Standing Committee of the NPC widened the definition of criminal liability to enable prosecution for pollution even in the absence of major financial losses, injuries, or deaths (Gao 2010).

Table 1.3. *Types of Environmental Litigation*

	Types of litigation			
	Administrative		Criminal litigation	Civil litigation
	Administrative lawsuits	Non-litigation administrative execution cases		
Who sues?	A citizen, a legal person, or other organization	Government agencies	The procuratorate, on behalf of the state	Individuals and organizations that have suffered direct harm due to pollution
Who gets sued?	Administrative agencies	Parties in non-compliance with agency decisions	Individuals and organizations	Polluters
Common causes of action	Agency inaction or contested decision	Failure to comply with administrative decisions	Major pollution incidents, illegal mining, logging and fishing[a]	Monetary losses, emotional distress, health-related claims
Selected outcomes	Revocation or upholding of decision	Court enforcement	Fines, prison sentences	Compensation for losses, elimination of danger, restoration to original status, apology[b]

[a] For a complete list of environmental crimes, see Articles 338–346 of the Criminal Law. For a more complete explanation of the kinds of situations that lead to a criminal case, see "The Interpretation of the Supreme People's Court on Some Issues Concerning the Specific Application of Law in the Trial of Criminal Cases Involving Environmental Pollution" (Supreme People's Court 2006).

[b] For a full list of potential remedies, see Article 15 of the Tort Law (Standing Committee of the National People's Congress 2009).

way to find a scapegoat for well-publicized pollution accidents. In 2011, for example, the chairman of Biaoxin Chemical Company was sentenced to eleven years in prison for the crime of "spreading poison." It was a notable exception to the usual seven-year maximum sentence for an environmental crime and the first conviction under Article 115 of the Criminal Law.[37] In that same year, the procuratorate reported 17,725 criminal cases, a fair number considering the agency's reputation for disinterest in environmental cases (Supreme People's Procuratorate 2012).

Finally, citizens can sue polluters for damages through civil litigation. Although there will be much more to say about this kind of lawsuit over the next seven chapters, first a few words on how the basics work. To start, would-be plaintiffs have three years from when they became aware of losses to file a claim. Most prospective plaintiffs are people who have directly suffered harm. Until the late 2000s, only direct victims of pollution, not environmental activists or sympathetic lawyers, had the right to sue (a legal concept known as standing).[38] Starting in the late 2000s, the exception became the specialized environmental courts discussed in Chapter 4. Under local regulations in the cities of Guiyang, Wuxi, and Kunming, concerned bystanders like the EPB, the procuratorate, and social organizations can bring forth public interest environmental litigation.[39] More recent revisions to the Civil Procedure Law also allow lawful authorities (*falü guiding de jiguan*) and relevant organizations (*you guan zuzhi*) to initiate environmental public interest

---

37 Article 115 of the Criminal Law allows sentences as harsh as a ten-year prison term, life imprisonment, or death (McElwee 2011, 252).

38 Standing is also limited in American environmental law. In the landmark case *Sierra Club v. Morton* (1972), the Supreme Court held that NGOs must show a tangible link to an area before to be granted standing. Environmental NGOs usually do this by showing that their members have an economic, aesthetic, or recreational interest in the area.

39 In Guiyang, all three of these groups plus concerned citizens are permitted to bring environmental public interest litigation. In Kunming, standing is limited to the EPB, the procuratorate and NGOs. And in Wuxi, only the procuratorate and NGOs can initiate environmental public interest litigation (All-China Environment Federation and the Natural Resources Defense Council 2011, 22).

lawsuits (Standing Committee of the National People's Congress 2012). Although it not yet clear how "lawful authorities" or "relevant organizations" will be defined in practice, the change indicates growing support for the idea that China should "give law greater clout in [the] battle against pollution" (Jiang 2006). Following these local experiments, the Civil Procedure Law was revised in 2012 to allow lawful authorities (*falü guiding de jiguan*) and relevant organizations (*you guan zuzhi*) to initiate environmental public interest lawsuits (Standing Committee of the National People's Congress 2012). Although it not yet clear how "lawful authorities" or "relevant organizations" will be defined in practice, the change indicates growing support for the idea that China should "give law greater clout in [the] battle against pollution" (Jiang 2006).

Taking stock of law on the books makes clear just how much China's environmental laws have improved since the 1980s. In environmental law, as in so many other areas, Chinese law drafters are working hard to perfect the legal system. Their efforts are visible in an ever-expanding host of regulations, from laws improving access to environmental information to experiments with public interest litigation in environmental courts. Yet there is still an extraordinary gap between written law and how the law works in practice. As the next chapter explores, plaintiffs who try to use courts to stop pollution or win compensation encounter a host of challenges.

2 From Dispute to Decision

TO START, CONSIDER THIS SKETCH OF WHAT *LEGAL DAILY* and the All China Lawyers' Association (ACLA) would later name one of 2005's ten most influential lawsuits: Pingnan village is located in what was, in 1992, one of Fujian province's poorest counties. It was a place where local sayings like "Pingnan, Pingnan is poor and hard" verged on lamentations and villagers were initially willing to welcome Rongping Chemical Plant as a source of more than 300 new jobs. Over the next ten years, however, enthusiasm gave way to discontent as crops started dying and health problems spread. When complaint letters and media reports failed to solve the problem, 1,721 villagers filed a class action lawsuit against the factory in 2002. Three years and one appeal later, the Fujian Provincial High People's Court ordered Rongping to clean up industrial waste and pay 684,178 RMB (US$108,600) in compensation. This translates to roughly 397 RMB (US$63) per plaintiff, an ambiguous victory for what many observers saw as a landmark environmental case.[1]

One hard lesson learned from the Pingnan case is that civil environmental litigation in contemporary China is difficult. As lawyers and

---

1 All exchange rates are calculated at 6.3 RMB to 1 US dollar throughout. Much has been written about the Pingnan case. In English, see Oster and Fong (2006), Wang (2007, 212–218), and China Dialogue (2011). In Chinese, He (2004), Lai (2006), and Zhang (2006a) are a good starting place.

plaintiffs often recount, new challenges accompany each phase of litigation. Wringing concessions out of polluters requires remarkable persistence. As one of China's most prominent environmental lawyers explains, "It's incredibly hard to win environmental lawsuits. Even if you win, it's no use because the victims, most of whom are from the lowest levels of society, [hardly] get any of the compensation. Litigation is hard [and] post-litigation enforcement is also hard" (quoted in Sha 2003). There is near consensus that, as one plaintiff put it, lawsuits should be "the last road" (*zuihou yitiao lu*) or final resort when government bureaus prove unresponsive or mediation fails (Interviews 51, 68, 75, 106).

At the same time, the fact that many see litigation as a last resort suggests that environmental lawsuits, however imperfect, still tell us much about how China's most aggrieved and stubborn citizens experience the legal system. Before turning to individual actors' perspectives on environmental litigation in Chapters 4 to 7, this chapter traces an environmental lawsuit from dispute to decision as a way of understanding both how law works (e.g., process and institutions) and how lawyers and litigants try to work the law (e.g., obstacles and strategies). The examples recounted below are not representative, but illustrative of problems encountered and solutions attempted. Above all, environmental cases show how the courts work when power is unequal. Cases with powerful plaintiffs or weak polluters are rare. What, then, are the best strategies when the odds are stacked against you?

Chinese Courts

For anyone coming to Chinese law with knowledge of judicial politics elsewhere, one good place to begin is by thinking of Chinese courts as dispute resolution mechanisms rather than as courts.[2] Cutting across cultures, courts resolve disputes in keeping with what political scientist

2 I'm indebted to Benjamin Liebman for this idea.

Martin Shapiro calls the logic of the triad: two parties turn to a third to adjudicate a conflict with the implicit understanding that they will obey the resulting decision (1981). Yet the process of judging – how the decision is made and who makes it – can vary a great deal. Here, the noun "courts" is loaded with cultural assumptions about how authorities can and should behave. Avoiding the word, even just as a brief thought exercise, opens up space to stop expecting Chinese courts to behave like courts elsewhere and to take them on their own terms instead.

To start, contemporary Chinese law is rooted in a statute-oriented, civil law tradition, which places judges closer to rule-interpreting bureaucrats than values-driven lawmakers. In contrast with the adversarial, lawyer-driven American legal system, Chinese judges have historically been responsible for demanding relevant documents, identifying relevant laws, and summarizing the evidence.[3] The Chinese legal system also reflects a strong Soviet influence because the Chinese leadership consciously modeled its legal institutions after those of the former Soviet Union in the 1950s. The Chinese procuratorate, for example, is directly analogous to the Soviet public procurator – a national bureaucracy responsible for criminal investigation and prosecution. As in the former Soviet Union, the Chinese Communist Party (CCP) remains largely outside the law. Cases involving Party members are often not heard by the courts but dealt with as internal disciplinary matters (Lubman 1999, 10). Although the constitution stipulates that the leadership of the Communist Party should guide all legal work, the role of the Party in judicial proceedings is not clearly defined. Instead, Party influence is typically ad hoc, felt when a major case comes to the attention of the political-legal committee, the procuratorate, or another government agency.[4]

---

3 For more on adversarial legalism in the United States, see Kagan (2001). On the role played by judges in civil law systems, see Shapiro (1981, 150–154) and Kagan (2001, 105).

4 The political-legal committee includes representatives from courts, the procuratorate, the Public Security Bureau (PSB) and the Justice Bureau. The committee routinely discusses major cases, especially criminal cases, and is typically chaired by the head of the PSB.

Ordinary courts in China are divided into four levels. As of 2012, there were 3,117 Basic People's Courts, 404 Intermediate People's Courts, 32 High People's Courts, and one Supreme People's Court (SPC) (Supreme People's Court 2012). Under the Basic People's Courts, there are more than 10,000 subdivisions known as people's tribunals (*renmin fating*) located in towns and villages (Chen 2008, 150). Intermediate People's Courts are located in municipalities and prefectures, whereas High People's Courts are generally in provincial capitals. The SPC, in addition to its work as a court of final appeal, also helps interpret laws, administer the judiciary, and draft new legislation. With the exception of death penalty cases, which have additional appeal procedures, and SPC decisions, which are always final, cases are allowed a single appeal to a court one level higher than where the case was initially heard (Zhu 2007, 174).

Internally, courts are organized into divisions responsible for different tasks. A civil environmental lawsuit will be handled by at least three divisions. In the 1990s, Chinese courts started establishing case-filing divisions (*li'an ting*), and, by October 2003, these divisions had become the first stop for litigants in 95 percent of courts (Zhu 2007, 188). The idea was to divide responsibility such that the act of bribing judges would become more difficult, more expensive and, it was hoped, less common.[5] After judges in the acceptance division accept a case, they assign it to a presiding judge in the civil division. One option at this point is court-brokered mediation. In 2011, 67 percent of first-instance civil cases were either withdrawn or mediated (Supreme People's Court 2012).[6]

If mediation either breaks down or doesn't take place, civil environmental cases are typically heard by a panel of three judges and decided by majority vote.[7] In contrast to other countries where police enforce

---

5 It is not clear if this worked. Some litigants complain that reform only increased the number of people they need to bribe (Li 2012, 860).

6 For more on mediation in administrative environmental cases, see Zhang (2008, 97–100).

7 The exception is that relatively straightforward cases are sometimes heard under simplified procedures by only one judge.

court judgments, Chinese courts are responsible for enforcing their own decisions. Post-decision, civil environmental cases are reassigned to the enforcement division where judges attempt to ensure compliance with court orders. The main tools at their disposal are the ability to impose fines, detain individuals for up to fifteen days, and seize, freeze, or auction assets (Zhu 2007, 247; Zhang 2008, 83). Still, enforcement of civil judgments is notoriously difficult, especially because seizing assets requires coordination with banks, bureaus, and other institutions that sometimes prove less than cooperative.

Getting a Case into Court

In environmental disputes, even getting a day in court is a hard-won privilege. Under the Environmental Protection Law, would-be plaintiffs have three years from when they became aware of pollution-related losses to file a claim. Sometimes, as in the Pingnan case, the court counts time spent seeking administrative solutions against the statute of limitations – a real problem when bureaucracies move slowly or fail to act altogether (Wang 2007, 210). The right to sue, a legal concept known as standing, is also limited to those who have directly suffered harm. Only victims of pollution (*wuran shouhaizhe*) can bring a case.

Not even law-abiding pollution victims are necessarily guaranteed a court hearing. Judges at the case-filing division of the court routinely refuse cases, and, although case refusal is supposed to be accompanied by a written rationale, judges often leave plaintiffs without the record of refusal necessary to formally appeal the decision. Judges say that they turn away cases for a variety of reasons, perhaps due to lack of evidence, or because an administrative bureau is handling the dispute, or because law is not an appropriate way to solve the problem (Interviews 57, 74, 164).[8] In practice, subjective decisions about the appropriateness of law give judges latitude to avoid volatile disagreements that

---

8 An SPC training manual suggests that judges consider: 1) legal criteria and whether the case "falls within the scope of laws and regulations," and 2) political criteria because

might affect social stability and, equally important, annual court evaluations. Day to day, this means that judges at the case-filing division often
have the unenviable task of convincing angry people to seek redress
elsewhere. In so doing, judges sometimes exercise individual discretion
and sometimes follow orders. Confidential regulations (*neibu guiding*)
from higher courts or other government agencies occasionally instruct
courts to refuse certain types of cases or to handle them in a certain way.
A recurrent rumor during my fieldwork, for example, was that lower
courts received instructions from the Supreme People's Court to turn
away major environmental cases (Interviews 12, 13, 19).[9] Although I
was unable to confirm the existence of a written document, politically
inspired directions are certainly not uncommon.

The difficulty of maneuvering cases past the case-filing division is no
secret.[10] Even consultants to the government-backed All-China Environment Federation (ACEF) publicly admit that "the overwhelming
majority of cases [are] stopped at the doors to the courts due to difficulties getting them accepted and obtaining sufficient evidence" (Li 2008).
For many would-be plaintiffs, the primary emotion associated with law is
frustration. In Hunan province, one man spent five months in 2004 trying
to get a pollution dispute into court. He kept a journal of his unsuccessful
struggle, which included ten trips to the basic-level court, three trips to
the intermediate court, and two trips to the high court. Here is a typical
entry:

> [October 18, 2004] Three days later, I went to the intermediate court
> to tell them about the situation and hand over my written docu-
> ments... throwing the materials I had written aside, assistant division

"questions that involve national defense, foreign relations, state interest, and other
matters that go beyond the scope of the power of the judiciary and are not suitable to
be adjudicated by the courts" (quoted in Fu and Peerenboom 2010, 99).

9 This rumor also came up outside formal interview settings.

10 In practice, basic-level courts also frequently turn away disputes that have previously
been through administrative mediation (*xingzheng tiaojie*) although there is no legal
basis for this (Liu 2009, 75).

head Ding said: 'Go to the basic level court! Don't come back looking for us!' Swallowing my anger, I picked up the documents from the
floor and put them back on the counter. I wanted to go to the central
court offices to find the court leaders, but the gatekeeper wouldn't let
me in.[11]

The commonness of exclusion leaves some environmental lawyers ready
to declare success as soon as a case is accepted (Interviews 110, 147, 157).
Getting a case turned down is a "huge blow" (Interview 147), lawyers
say, because "there's no place to even talk" without a hearing (Interview 33).

The case-filing division also has the discretion to break up collective
lawsuits into individual cases. Like the United States, China allows lawsuits on behalf of a large group of people with the same grievance. Under
the Civil Procedure Law, citizens can bring collective lawsuits led by
two to five representatives – a logical course of action when widespread
pollution affects an entire neighborhood or village.[12] Often, however,
judges in the case-filing division divide up class actions in order to maximize per-case court fees, boost the number of cases handled, or dis-
arm collective action (Wang 2007, 217–218; Interview 106).[13] But filing paperwork for dozens of identical cases is a burden (Interviews 106,
115, 117). Photocopying documents and hauling boxes is enough of a
deterrent that lawyers say even convincing a court to treat each family
as a unit instead of as individuals constitutes a minor accomplishment
(Interview 117).

11 Unpublished document on file with the author.
12 These representatives make most decisions for the group although the Civil Procedure
   Law includes a clause requiring group approval to drop requests or initiate mediation.
   For more on the details of different kinds of group litigation, see Palmer and Xi (2009)
   and Liebman (1997–1998).
13 A 2005 notice from the Supreme People's Court allows courts to split up class-action
   lawsuits if "it is not easy" to handle the case as a class action (van Rooij 2010, 69). In
   an interesting parallel, judges did the same thing in 1950s Czechoslovakia. Otto Ulc, a
   former Czech judge, writes about how a quota system created incentives to break up
   cases as much as possible (1972, 43).

Many local observers interpret trouble getting on the docket as an outgrowth of local economic protectionism (*difang baohu zhuyi*). Local protectionism, far and away the most frequently cited explanation for most litigant difficulties, refers to the widespread perception that the local government shelters large polluters who prop up the local economy through either tax revenues or job provision.[14] The Pingnan case is a particularly good example of how focusing on economic growth can create a situation where, as one Environmental Protection Bureau (EPB) employee put it, "If there weren't a factory, there wouldn't be a government" (Interview 87). By 2003, tax revenues from Rongping Chemical accounted for more than a quarter of the county's 20 million RMB (US$3.2 million) annual budget (News Probe 2003). While local protectionism is not always a factor, powerful political protectors can certainly sway courts dependent on local government to provide funding for salaries, benefits, housing, and facilities. Judges tend to listen when local officials make their preferences known if only because, as one judge put it, for "everything the judge does, he must ask for help" (quoted in Lubman 1999, 265).

Finding (and Keeping) a Lawyer

Lawyers' fluency in the language of the law makes them a natural asset in beating back local protectionism by drawing up legal briefs, submitting preliminary evidence, and talking a case into acceptance by courts.[15] The trouble for many complainants lies in finding a lawyer willing to

14 For more on local protectionism in environmental enforcement, see van Rooij (2006a, 191–209) and Zhang (2008, 51–53).

15 Plaintiffs are allowed to represent themselves in a civil lawsuit, and how often lawsuits move forward without legal representation is an open question. In the sample of 782 decisions collected by researchers at Zhongnan University of Economics and Law and discussed in the introduction, either a lawyer or legal worker represented 53.3 percent of those requesting compensation. Another 29.6 percent of lawsuits moved forward with a citizen representative speaking on behalf of the plaintiff, and 17.1 percent of plaintiffs represented themselves (Lü et al. 2011, 85). This sample, in combination with information gleaned from interviews and the cases discussed in Chapter 5, suggests that legal representation is fairly widespread but not universal.

take their case. Mainstream Chinese lawyers, like attorneys in many countries, typically screen out unprofitable cases, particularly those that involve challenging local power holders (Cai and Yang 2005; Michelson 2006). However, contrary to the common view of poverty-stricken pollution victims, some would-be plaintiffs can raise money for a competitive attorney fee. *Nongmin*, the Chinese term for those involved in agricultural work, covers workers with a range of incomes. In 2007, I observed a ninety-minute contract negotiation between a group of *nongmin* and two environmental lawyers which centered on the relative wealth of the villagers (as one lawyer said during the discussion, "I've seen people much poorer than you!"). The two sides settled on a 60,000 RMB (US$9,523) fee paid in installments, a lot of money considering that successful mid-career Beijing lawyers net about 20,000 RMB per month[16] and that per-capita rural income was 4,140 RMB per year in 2007 (Wen 2008). Although the group may have had hidden sources of income (possibly remittances or past profits from a bumper harvest), it is also possible that they simply decided was worth saving up to pay for a legal team.

Still, even when clients scrape together a market-rate fee, many lawyers remain wary of environmental cases because of the potential political sensitivity and the amount of legwork involved. Collective lawsuits are particularly hassle-filled because plaintiffs must individually *opt in*, which means that the legal team must submit a copy of each litigant's identity card to the court.[17] And even those willing to track down dozens

16 This is an estimate based on the salaries of lawyers I spoke to during my fieldwork. By way of comparison, a 2007 survey of more than 1,300 lawyers in eight provinces found a median income of 100,000 RMB (US$15,870) per year (Liu 2008). Salaries vary a great deal, however, and education and years of experience generally translate into more money. A 2009 survey of 1,019 full-time lawyers found that the median income for lawyers with B.A. degrees, M.A. degrees and Ph.D. degrees was 88,000 RMB (US$13,992), 138,000 RMB (US$21,904) and 231,000 RMB (US$36,666) respectively (Michelson and Liu 2010, 316).

17 In China, litigants must individually opt in to a lawsuit. Providing a copy of an identity card (or for litigants less than eighteen years old the household registration card) is one way to indicate that the lawsuit has their support. In the United States, in contrast, civil actions cover an entire class of people (say, those who bought a certain brand of

(or hundreds) of identity cards sometimes balk at situations in which the polluter enjoys strong local government support. These lawyers delicately inquire about the extent of local protectionism during preliminary interviews or simply refuse cases where the polluter is a major taxpayer (Interview 16). Physical danger is also a concern (Interview 37, 131). One Beijing lawyer, for example, was afraid that the mafia investors behind polluting enterprises would beat him up on investigatory trips to isolated factories (Interview 37).[18]

Coaxing a lawyer into taking a case is often easier with law firms registered outside the immediate area.[19] Neither polluters nor their local government supporters usually have the high-level connections necessary to cause trouble for non-local lawyers (Interviews 10, 108, 115, 125). Lawyers' daily conduct and, more importantly, annual license renewal are overseen by their local justice bureau, and it is not easy to orchestrate bureaucratic pressure from far away. As a criminal lawyer in Zhejiang explains, "Local lawyers won't accept the case [so they] go to lawyers in other places, maybe more famous, so they will not offend local leaders. I often go to other counties to handle cases" (quoted in Halliday and Liu 2008, 29). Sometimes, local and non-local lawyers also team up to combine outsiders' prestige and relative freedom with insiders' local connections and on-the-ground ability to collect evidence and file paperwork (Interview 115).

However, signing up plaintiffs and assembling a legal team is no guarantee that either side will see a case through. When harassment picks up,

laptop during a defined period of time). While individuals in the class must be notified of pending litigation and can opt out, they do not need to opt in individually. If there is a monetary settlement, however, class members usually need to do something (like file a claim form) to get compensation.

18 While these lawyers reported fears of violence on trips to rural areas, violence can also occur in cities. In April 2009, Shanghai lawyer Yan Yiming was beaten up in the conference room of his office by thugs posing as potential clients (Lim 2009).

19 See Fürst (2008, 90–91) for an example of a case that was turned down by local lawyers before plaintiffs found legal representation in Beijing. Of course, non-local lawyers can also face local suspicion. As one Chengdu lawyer asked, "How could a Guizhou law firm do business in Beijing? ... [and] in Guangdong or Shanghai, nobody would hire a Sichuan law firm" (quoted in Liu 2009, 119).

even committed lawyers reconsider their priorities. One Hebei lawyer, for example, dropped an environmental case after the suddenly overzealous local water bureau intensified inspections at his law firm (Interview 139). Disappearing plaintiffs are also common. Several lawyers I interviewed spent significant time investigating cases and collecting evidence only to find complainants unwilling to sue (Interviews 53, 90, 125). The fact that collective lawsuits require appointing representatives (*daibiao ren*) to act for the group makes it particularly easy to identify, cajole, and discourage leaders. In a 2002 case in Beijing, a construction company offered two representatives, Mr. Wan and Mr. Sheng, 50,000 RMB (US$7,936) to relocate and drop a lawsuit they were involved in. Even though Mr. Sheng was making only 400 RMB per month, he refused, saying "Fine, if you give everyone else 50,000 to move first, I'll be the last to move" (quoted in Liang 2006, 27).[20] Plaintiffs in other cases report widespread use of intimidation tactics, such as local officials entering homes, eating food, and using the bathroom without invitation (Liang 2006, 46). In addition to bribes and threats, inertia also drains energy during a long lawsuit. Maintaining hope, especially in collective lawsuits, requires both persistence and leadership. The Pingnan case was successful, in large part, because the village unified around the head representative, a middle-aged man named Zhang Changjian who ran the local medical clinic. Zhang, a natural leader by virtue of age, occupation, and gender, was aware of the importance of his role. Dubbed the lawsuit's "spiritual leader" (*jingshen lingxiu*) by the press, Zhang told a reporter in 2004 "I can't move. Right now, everyone is watching me. If I retreat, everyone will disband" (quoted in He 2004).

Case Acceptance Fees

Front-loaded court case acceptance fees (*anjian shouli fei*) also force even the angriest plaintiffs to calculate the monetary value of court-brokered justice. Although the State Council lowered litigation

---

20 Interviews 53, 125, and 158 also discussed attempts to buy off plaintiff leaders.

Table 2.1. *Acceptance Fees for Civil Cases Under 2007 State Council Regulations*

Amount of requested compensation		
In RMB	In US Dollars	Case acceptance fee
Less than 10,000	>1,587	50 RMB
10,000–100,000	>15,873	2.5% of requested compensation
100,00–200,000	>31,746	2.0% of requested compensation
200,00–500,000	>79,365	1.5% of requested compensation
500,000–1 million	>158,730	1.0% of requested compensation
1 million–2 million	>317,460	0.9% of requested compensation
2 million–5 million	>793,650	0.8% of requested compensation
5 million–10 million	>1.58 million	0.7% of requested compensation
10 million–20 million	>3.17 million	0.6% of requested compensation
More than 20 million	<3.17 million	0.5% of requested compensation

Source: State Council (2007).

fees in 2007 to make it easier for average citizens to bring civil claims to court, acceptance fees are high enough to warrant reconsideration (see Table 2.1).[21] Many Chinese scholars believe complainants need more financial help. Some authors suggest fee-shifting provisions that would force losing defendants to pay litigation and attorneys' fees (Shi 2003; Xing 2004).

Under the current system, poor plaintiffs' best recourse is to obtain proof of poverty and petition the court to waive litigation fees or delay payment.[22] In poorer areas of China, fee waivers can be hard to get because the courts are reliant on litigation fees (Interview 74). Some courts depend so heavily on fees that judges scout out potential cases in the surrounding area (He 2011, 257). In better-financed courts, where a fee waiver is a realistic possibility, decisions rely on a judge's assessment

---

21 Before the 2007 regulations took effect, the case acceptance fee ranged from one-half to 4 percent of requested compensation (Wang 2007, 211). There are reports that some courts have delayed implementation of the new regulations because of concerns about lost revenue (Peerenboom and He 2008, 22).

22 Proof of poverty can come from the local party committee, the neighborhood committee, the civil affairs department of the local government, or the local labor bureau and is accepted at the court's discretion.

as to whether applicants are troublemakers (*diaomin*) or the deserving poor.

Venue Shopping

At this point, litigants and lawyers still undeterred by the risk, expense, and nuisance of litigation face a strategic decision: where to sue. Important cases (*zhongda anjian*), defined in the Civil Procedure Law as cases "with a significant impact within their jurisdiction," bypass the basic court and go straight to the intermediate court or high court. In practice, the definition of an important environmental law-suit varies by province, but often involves a baseline level of requested compensation.

As scholars note – and lawyers on the ground agree – higher-level courts are better insulated from local pressure, staffed by better-educated judges, and more likely to return favorable decisions (O'Brien and Li 2004, 85–6; Interviews 3, 15). Starting with the intermediate court and appealing to a higher court if necessary is commonly seen as one way to lessen the obligation that accompanies basic-level courts' budgetary reliance on local government and, by extension, major taxpayers. Some-times this works. In a 2002 water pollution case in Tangshan, for instance, the high court admonished the intermediate court for a grave legal error (*yanzhong falü cuowu*). The case was sent back on remand, and the intermediate court re-decided in favor of the plaintiffs.[23] Yet skipping levels is increasingly difficult, at least in the mass cases that inspire the most official unease. A 2005 SPC notice effectively limited most environmental cases to the lower rungs of the court hierarchy by man-dating that all collective lawsuits go through basic-level courts (Wang 2007, 215). And on the rare occasions when non-mass cases involve

---

23 The intermediate court re-decided in favor of the plaintiffs. Hebei High Court (2004), *Liu Honggui et al. v. Tangshan Jiaohuachang Youxian Zeren Gongsi.* All court deci-sions cited are on file with the author.

sufficient losses to qualify as an "important" case, individual plaintiffs may have to lowball requested compensation to afford case-acceptance fees.

Another choice is to work horizontally to find a court outside the polluter's immediate bailiwick. When pollution crosses borders, several different courts are likely to have jurisdiction, and filing a case as far away from the polluter as possible usually makes sense (Fürst 2008, 97; Interview 118). In particular, some lawyers claim that China's fourteen maritime courts are good places to bring water pollution lawsuits (Interviews 28, 85, 147). Like China's specialized intellectual property tribunals, maritime courts handle a high number of cases involving foreign companies. Judges, who are appointed by the central government, have a reputation for being professional and well educated, both advantages for environmental litigants.[24]

Evidence

Once inside the court, litigants struggle to even demonstrate that pollution exists. Here, government reports are the gold standard, seen as "very authoritative" (*feichang quanwei*) (Interviews 39, 100, 172) and "comprehensive" (*quanmian*) (Interview 110). Some lawyers even find major cases easier to litigate because of the increased likelihood of government reports documenting pollution (Interview 40). The most obvious source of information is the local EPB, an agency whose helpfulness varies. In some places, lawyers find that the EPB efficiently conducts tests on request without demanding fees (Interview 76). Elsewhere, however, the EPB is less responsive. When Zhang Changjian started lodging complaints in Pingnan, for example, the local EPB didn't even have pollution-monitoring equipment. The closest EPB capable of

---

24 For more on the maritime courts in English, see Hamilton (2002) and Dimitrov (2006). In 2012, an experienced Chinese environmental lawyer reported that maritime courts were becoming less willing to take on lawsuits in which jurisdiction is unclear, particularly cases in which water pollution is caused by land-based sources (Xia 2012).

inspections was three hours away, making impromptu inspections nearly impossible (News Probe 2003). In places with uncooperative EPBs, lawyers and plaintiffs can sometimes work around the bureau. One repeat plaintiff in Hebei province, described by his Beijing-based lawyer as a "graduate of the system who knows more than many lawyers," now requests help from the relatively sympathetic agricultural bureau (*nongye bu*) instead (Interview 147).

When it exists, there is also no guarantee that pollution data will be accurate or accessible. In some places, long stretches of county-mandated "enterprise quiet days" (*qiye anjing ri*) prohibit environmental monitoring from interrupting production and leave EPBs very little time to collect fines, deliver documents, and conduct inspections (Zhang 2008, 51).[25] Factories are also adept at hiding pollution from even assiduous inspectors. Tricks include polluting only at night, building secret underground discharge pipes, and storing wastewater in pools that flood during rainstorms (McMullin 2008–2009). And when government agencies do manage to document pollution, the resulting reports are often tightly guarded. In the Pingnan case, the plaintiffs' lawyers could pry documents out of the EPB only when they knew enough to request them by name (Interview 34). Yet despite the difficulty of tracking down government data, independent scientific analysis is relatively rare. Outside expertise is expensive and, litigants fear, too easily dismissed as biased (Interview 15). In politically sensitive cases, it can also be hard to find labs willing to run tests. In Shanxi, lawyer Yan Yiming was unable to get water samples analyzed because environmental monitoring stations uniformly claimed that they lacked the necessary equipment (Xu 2009).

Although courts can track the history of pollution through routine government reports, day-to-day environmental monitoring does not typically touch on the two trickiest legal questions surrounding civil

25 Enterprise quiet days are a national problem according to a 2007 interview with the head of the Ministry of Environmental Protection's Environment Supervision Bureau (Zhang 2008, 51). In two of the counties Zhang studied in Hubei province, enterprise quiet days lasted twenty-five days of the month.

environmental litigation: causation and damages. Across legal systems, pollution-related compensation claims hinge on causation – the tricky business of linking pollution to losses. This is hard because damages, like a fish kill, could be caused by factors other than pollution, such as over-feeding or overcrowding. Although the burden of proof in China rests with the defendant to prove that pollution did *not* cause damages, local courts routinely rule against plaintiffs because of doubts about causation. Cases involving multiple small enterprises are especially challenging because individual responsibility is difficult to untangle (Interview 106). Small companies are also more likely to be unregistered, so tracking down an owner to sue can also be a challenge (Interview 118). To bypass the morass of causation, lawyers occasionally turn to zoning law or contract law. In Beijing, for example, an owner in an upscale housing complex sued the developers for a contract violation because the marketing materials promised 41 percent green space and delivered only 16.3 percent. The owner saw green space as an environmental rights issue, but she structured the case as a contract dispute in the hopes the court would be more likely to accept it (Chen 2006a). Another strategy is to rely on a clear-cut standard. A case in Tangshan City, for example, hinged on whether the factory violated a 1986 regulation requiring a 1,000-meter buffer zone between industry and a residential neighborhood (Interview 40).

Appraisals

In the absence of clear-cut standards, judges typically rely heavily on outside appraisals conducted by either a government bureau or a private appraisal agency.[26] Judges often lack the time or skills to investigate environmental cases and, in theory, a scientifically informed assessment helps improve the quality and efficiency of decisions. In fact, cases often hinge on appraisals, as judicial decisions rarely deviate far from a report

---

26 Appraisals are especially common in water pollution cases that involve fish kills (Lü et al. 2011, 87). For a critique that judges are overly reliant on appraisals, see Lü et al. (2011, 86).

the court regards as unbiased. Especially in politically sensitive cases, pointing to a third-party evaluation can shield judges from criticism. Two of the most critical legal issues, causation and damages, are often outsourced to appraisers. Three-quarters of the civil decisions collected by the team at Zhongnan University of Economics and Law show judges turning to an appraisal or a clear-cut legal standard to determine causation. Appraisals are "the king of evidence" and it is a significant setback if the court turns down a request to conduct one (Lü et al. 2011, 87).[27]

Appraisals are both critical to the success of a case and of greatly uneven quality (Interviews 15, 104, 110, 157; see also Lü et al. 2011; Natural Resources Defense Council 2011, 25). The local justice bureau is responsible for licensing both appraisal organizations (*jianding jigou*) and individual appraisers, and the qualifications for the job are relatively flexible. Appraisers can get a license with just five years of relevant work experience and a related undergraduate major.[28] Clued-in judges know that a license does not necessarily indicate competence, and that deeper evaluation is necessary. After several phone calls, one judge passed up a prestigious Tsinghua University-affiliated organization because employees lacked the necessary skills (Interview 93). Scrupulous appraisal organizations will also turn down a commission if they don't have the requisite expertise (Interview 158).

Too often, however, cases move ahead with a less-than-capable appraiser responsible for the key piece of evidence. In an environmental hearing I observed in Hebei province in 2008, the appraisal team did not include a single plant expert even though its primary task was evaluating damage to a fruit orchard. Or, in the Pingnan case, plaintiffs complained that the court-appointed appraiser spent less than a day in the village and only eyeballed a small piece of forest located relatively far from

---

27 For an example of a case that suffered because the court turned down the plaintiffs request for an appraisal, see Luo (2010).
28 Appraisers must have five years of relevant work experience and one of the following: 1) a high-level technical title, 2) equivalent professional qualifications, or 3) a related undergraduate or graduate major. See State Council (2005a).

the factory (Caijing 2006). Sometimes, plaintiffs also suspect that experts are pressured or bought off rather than incompetent. In a case in Inner Mongolia, an appraisal was written and stamped the same day inspections took place and *before* test results were available (Fürst 2008, 53). Political influence is a distinct possibility too, especially if the appraisal organization is an offshoot of a government bureau.[29]

Sometimes, litigants commission their own appraisal, picking an organization based on personal ties, efficiency, technical competence, and location (Interviews 110, 130, 157). Some lawyers say that picking a northern appraiser for a case in the south and vice versa enhances objectivity (Interview 110). Others select a government agency to lend the appraisal an official and trustworthy imprimatur (Interview 157). In a legal system with a history of judge-led investigations, the problem is that hired experts are often seen as biased. More immediately, they are also expensive. As well-known environmental lawyer Wang Canfa put it, "After the pollution, the economic situation just gets worse and worse. Who has the money to hire an organization to do an appraisal?" (quoted in Lin and Ding 2009). Although the cost of an appraisal depends on the amount of work involved and who is hired to do it, all appraisals are expensive for plaintiffs who are typically already suffering economic losses. Nor is documentation necessarily a first impulse after pollution. Dead fish or rotting crops are often cleared away before would-be plaintiffs ever consider litigation (Interview 46). The combination of inexperience and bureaucratic foot-dragging can also significantly extend the lag time between pollution incidents and evaluation. The fruit-orchard appraisal in Hebei took place three years after the alleged pollution, making it even more difficult to demonstrate causation.

Closing Statements

After collecting appraisals and other evidence, one of the best remaining opportunities for lawyers to sway the bench is the closing statement,

---

29 This is a particular issue in administrative cases when the government agency itself might be the defendant in the lawsuit (Yang 2010, 307).

known in civil cases as the *dailici*. Lawyers see this as an opportunity to lay out an argument that flawlessly demonstrates their legal logic and education (Interviews 110, 116). The clearest sign of success is when court decisions echo lawyers' legal arguments, as they occasionally do (Interview 110). For the more theatrically inclined, closing statements also provide a platform to dramatize the case and appeal to judges' empathy, ego, and patriotism. Playing on the government's historical sympathy for claims related to economic distress, lawyers often cast their clients as members of a weak and disadvantaged group (*ruoshi qunti*). Consider how this Beijing lawyer opened a 2003 closing statement:

> My client is a middle-aged laid-off worker who is the backbone of a family with two children in middle school and a grandmother over 80 years old....He borrowed 30,000 RMB [US$4,411] from the bank, friends, and relatives and signed a contract to raise fish in Lake X....He took this much risk and bore the hopes of his entire family! Imagine, a person of this age without a high school education or specialized skills. As soon as fish farming fails, he not only has no opportunity to get back the money but may drag three generations into his difficulties....[30]

When it arises, environmentalism is primarily couched as what political scientists Kevin O'Brien and Lianjiang Li call "rightful resistance" and framed "in reference to protections implied by ideologies or conferred by policymakers" (2006, 3). One lawyer sees environmental slogans as "supporting points" (*zhichengdian*) to buttress rhetorical questions like "How can a harmonious society exist when everything is polluted?" (Interview 125). Others neatly interweave environmentalism and patriotism, as in this excerpt from the closing statement in the Pingnan case:

> I am a Beijing lawyer and university professor. The reason I'm paying attention to an environmental case thousands of kilometers away is not because I'm going to get any benefit from the case. Rather, it is because I see piece after piece of my country's green mountains

---

30 All closing statements cited are unpublished documents on file with the author.

turned desolate and bare by corrupt profiteers and section after section of clear river turned into a dirty gutter devoid of fish and shrimp. As a Chinese person who has not lost his reason, I cannot help using the law to help protect environmental rights and to protect our weak and disadvantaged groups who rely on the homeland to live.[31]

After reminding the judges of his status ("I am a Beijing lawyer and university professor"), the lawyer evokes Chinese pride in support of environmental rights. Reasonable Chinese people, he implies, should protect the homeland from destruction.

In these final remarks, lawyers often urge judges to uphold justice and even make history. One lawyer defending an environmental protester told the court that "those who should be judged are neither the defendants whose human rights and property rights were violated nor those weak and disadvantaged groups living at the bottom rungs of society, but those at the chemical companies responsible for the major pollution accident!... They will stand accused by history."[32] Strategically overlooking the possibility of political pressure or flat-out corruption, this aspirational view of the court calls on judges to live up to the best traditions of Chinese justice.

Elite Allies

Many plaintiffs understand that judicial decisions can depend as much on what happens outside the court as within it. In the search for sympathetic allies willing to enter the "bargaining arena" on their behalf, they typically both exhaust their net of personal connections and petition strangers (Lipsky 1968, 1145; see also O'Brien and Li 2004, 86–89). Among a range of potential backers, however, litigants and lawyers often share a common impulse to turn first to the media. Those familiar with the Chinese legal system know that media exposure often

31 Unpublished document on file with the author.
32 Unpublished document on file with the author.

catalyzes concessions (Liebman 2005).[33] Although the local media, overseen by the local propaganda department, is often barred from covering stories regarding politically powerful polluters (Interviews 34, 37, 40, 101, 128; Halliday and Liu 2008, 28; Human Rights Watch 2008, 84), the national media is generally free to report on any story that does not implicate officials above the county level (Interviews 59, 94). At the provincial level and above, environmental reporters say it's best "not to touch a tiger" (Interview 94). In the Pingnan case, plaintiffs believed "the central media were our best allies" (Interview 58). The day after a particularly influential news segment aired on China Central Television's *News Probe* (*Xinwen Diaocha*), for example, the EPB sent an inspection team to Rongping Chemical.[34]

Local governments may not be afraid of lawsuits, but they are afraid of the spotlight.[35] As Yan Yiming, a self-termed public interest lawyer, explains: "In so far as possible, [I] draw in the media as a strategic participant... Among public interest lawyers, the cases I handle are relatively hard, but the result is pretty good every time. Why? I don't handle them alone, but with a lot of media working hard with me" (quoted in Xu 2009). Or, as another lawyer put it, "if the media didn't exist, public-interest litigation wouldn't be possible" (Interview 33). Yet even as litigants and lawyers court domestic coverage, most are more reluctant to talk to the international media. While foreign attention can intensify pressure and bring results, it can also give complaints an unwanted radical cast (Interviews 10, 37, 73, 94). At the very least, involving the foreign media calls for caution. One well-known lawyer advised environmental NGOs at a 2007 conference not to take money from international reporters or pass on government documents because those actions could later be interpreted as leaking state secrets.

---

33 On how media coverage also helps protesters win concessions, see Cai (2008, 168–172).

34 Ironically, the villagers were unable to watch the segment because the electricity suddenly went out during the broadcast (Caijing 2006; Lai 2006, 30).

35 For more on media coverage as a litigation strategy, also see Fürst (2008, 98–102).

Above all, external scrutiny heightens accountability and, in so doing, imparts a degree of power to those who lack it. In China, as elsewhere, complaints easily go unheard unless "perceived and projected" (Lipsky 1968, 1151). Media reports, often submitted as evidence or mentioned in lawyers' closing statements, remind judges of a wider audience and broader social responsibility. Sympathetic coverage also lends litigants a measure of protection by informing opponents that they are being watched (Interview 69). Sometimes, the identity of the observer matters less than bearing witness. An anonymous Internet letter, written by a Beijing lawyer and printed out by local complainants, successfully pressured the government in one Shanxi town into taking a land dispute seriously. No one in the town had Internet access, so officials knew that an online letter indicated outside support (Interview 146).

Ad hoc alliances between journalists and litigants reflect the broader rise of the green media and advocacy journalism.[36] The late 1990s and early 2000s saw the emergence of self-identified environmental journalists at mainstream newspapers like *China Youth Daily* and *Legal Daily*. Encouraged by a monthly environmental journalists salon started by the NGO Green Earth Volunteers in 2001, some journalists began self-consciously using the press to shame local governments and polluters into cleaning up.[37] Their efforts fit into a larger tradition of Chinese advocacy journalism, characterized by frequent use of the first person and a distinct moral position. Even outside the op-ed page, these reports clearly take sides, usually with the powerless. The influential 2003 *News Probe* TV segment on the Pingnan case, to take one example, interweaves advocacy journalism with investigative reporting, a common combination. The reporter, dressed in glasses and a business suit, is cast

---

36 For more on advocacy journalism, see Hassid (2011). On environmental journalism in China, see Wang (2005a) and Zhan (2011).

37 In 1986, the State Environmental Protection Administration (SEPA) founded a government-sponsored forum for environmental journalists. This official organization had less of an impact on environmental journalism, however, than the salon run by Green Earth Volunteers.

as a big-city intellectual fighting rural injustice. In standard Mandarin, which connotes a high level of class and education (somewhat like public school British English), he juxtaposes the plant's emphatic denials of illegal pollution with images of suffering villagers and barren countryside. He even dons a pair of gloves at one point to collect wastewater for testing and to heighten the drama.[38] This is compelling television, replete with villains, underdogs, and heroes. As the Chinese media is now largely reliant on advertising rather than government subsidies, popular appeal is important to even hard-boiled editors (Interview 57; Zhan 2011, 116). For their part, green journalists are happy to help report stories that, as one lawyer put it, "help fulfill their ideals" (Interview 72). It helps too that polluters often lack public-relations skills. In the Sun Youli case discussed in the next chapter, for example, a history of environmental fines did not stop one of the polluters from this credibility-staining sound bite: "We are definitely one of Hebei's pollution standard-abiding companies. We've gotten all kinds of honors ... and think that we are already perfect [so] when this happened, we thought it was unbelievable" (Tianjin Television Station 2004).

Of course, soliciting media coverage is not easy. When litigants and journalists do not share a social circle, contacting the media is challenging. Letters and e-mails are likely to go unanswered, and traveling to news bureaus in major cities is time-consuming and expensive (Fürst 2008, 101). Nor do even sympathetic journalists necessarily see the newsworthiness of yet another pollution case. Media-savvy lawyers brainstorm fresh angles before calling press contacts or simply do not bother pitching run-of-the-mill cases (Interviews 101, 110). And recruiting a reporter is only a first step. Journalists can be bought off and stories can be killed by editors under pressure (Interviews 57, 59). Subtler local evasion, like intransigence from polluters, can also limit the depth and

---

38 The *News Probe* segment inspired other examples of advocacy journalism. After seeing the broadcast, one reporter from the area closed a subsequent story with the line "in the distant north, I pray for my hometown" (Lin 2003).

impact of reports. In Hebei province, one court held a hearing on Christmas and released the decision just before Spring Festival to deter media attention (Interview 134).

In addition, media backlash is a real danger. Irritation with headlines-chasing self-appointed heroes can undercut public support as well as engender it (Huang 2006, 157). Rather than face accusations of making a big deal out of nothing (*xinwen chaozuo*), some lawyers avoid the media altogether (Interview 113). Others say "the Internet is the best choice for poor people" because, unlike reporters, the Web never demands money in exchange for coverage (Interview 146). Bloggers can help now too. A list of media contacts distributed at a June 2007 conference for environmental complainants included influential bloggers under the heading "independent journalists" (*duli jizhe*).[39]

Another part of mobilizing personal networks is taking advantage of connections inside the state. Formal and informal ties to state bureaucrats, or political embeddedness, also confer serious advantage to the well connected (Michelson 2007a, 356). Well-placed backers ease the work of case preparation and protect lawyers from harassment (Michelson 2007a; Halliday and Liu 2008, 32–33; Liu and Halliday 2011, 844). Contacts can help with specific favors, such as providing access to environmental data and serving as character references. One Beijing lawyer, for example, asks friends in government to spread the word that he is a good guy when he is working on a sensitive case (Interview 85). Lawyers also use personal ties to persuade courts to take a case (Interviews 96, 130, 156, 159; Li 2010, 213) or convince judges of their point of view (Interviews 42, 94, 98; Michelson 2007a, 363 and 384). Cases can turn on the opportunities provided by personal access, and those who know the right people – often because of social class or education – benefit. Yet networking is not everything. Principled insiders occasionally slip

---

39 Some independent journalists, although perhaps not those on this specific contact list, solicit fees in exchange for coverage. Strictly speaking, all freelancers are supposed to have a press card issued by the General Administration of Press and Publication in order to practice journalism. In practice, this restriction is often ignored.

key evidence to lawyers or litigants because their conscience demands it (Interview 51). As one official told a lawyer in Zhejiang province, "Working for the government is temporary, but you are a person for your whole lifetime" (Interview 121).

The Long Haul

Even as litigants tally contacts and weigh strategies, most struggle with the far more basic problem of maintaining unity. In the months and years leading up to a mass lawsuit, plaintiffs often fracture over both their understanding of the problem and the best solution. Anthropologist Anna Lora-Wainwright, for example, shows how residents of one Sichuan village were paralyzed by competing explanations for high cancer rates including farm chemicals, hardship and anxiety, and diet (2009, 63). Without a consensus about who to blame, resignation and apathy dominated over anger and action. Commitment can also dissipate over the course of a lawsuit, rupturing once-solid coalitions. The spatial dynamics of pollution, in particular, generate tensions among plaintiffs unequally affected by the problem. A compensation offer viewed as reasonable by villagers living relatively far from a factory, for example, can be seen as entirely unreasonable by villagers living closer by (Fürst 2008, 83; Interviews 26, 65). In mixed-income communities, class also affects plaintiffs' ability to escape pollution. In an air pollution case in Hebei province, richer residents moved away, leaving their poorer neighbors to sue on their own (Interview 40). For all of these reasons, it is sometimes easier for lawyers to work with associations than ad hoc collections of complainants. A fisherman's association or a homeowner's association typically has leaders in place and existing relationships with government bureaus that lend credibility to the complainants.

Staying unified is a problem not only for plaintiffs, but also for the broader legal team. Lawyers and clients, as elsewhere, are separated by a gulf of "knowledge, assurance, and social standing," and the resulting relationship can be tense (Ellmann 1986–1987, 719). Lawyers complain that plaintiffs are uneducated, grasping, and "blind" (*mangmu*) to the law (Interviews 37, 40, 53, 110, 121, 128). Lack of legal knowledge, they say, leads to unrealistic demands and frustration if compensation is not quickly forthcoming (Interviews 37, 97, 128). The hand-holding sometimes demanded by litigants can be especially irritating. As legal scholar Martha Minow observes, "The client's case is the most important one to them, but one of many for the attorney," and this alone generates tension (1990, 723). High-maintenance clients call frequently to check on the status of their case, report new developments or, in one case, just to talk about family problems (Interviews 37, 40, 110). Sometimes, clients even show up at law offices uninvited. My conversation with a Zhejiang lawyer in November 2007, for example, was interrupted by the unexpected arrival of three villagers who traveled an hour and a half to follow up on the previous day's phone call. The displeased lawyer (possibly also embarrassed in front of a guest) told them their behavior was "unbelievably irritating" (*fan si le*) and to go away and stop wasting his time. "Sometimes," he later confided, "I just can't help getting angry" (Interview 121). In this case, as in many others, language marked the class and power differential in the dialogue. The Zhejiang lawyer spoke Mandarin whereas the visiting villagers, like many lower-class plaintiffs, spoke only their local dialect. Mandarin implies expertise and education and, as one lawyer told me, "embodies professionalism" (Interview 131).[40]

This is all to say that deep power inequalities underlie lawyer-client relationships. Most commonly, clients quietly comply with lawyers' instructions. As one plaintiff described his relationship with his lawyers, "They told me what to do, and I did it" (Interview 58; see also Interviews 41, 60). Although some lawyers are tightly integrated into local communities, legal authority can also shade into neglect or casual condescension as differences in social standing sharpen. In 2007, I observed a group of Beijing lawyers ask a villager who had traveled more than twenty-four

40 Speaking the local dialect and having close ties to the community can also help lawyers get business. Outside your hometown, one lawyer told me, "[Potential clients] think you are a crook!" (Interview 46).

hours for legal advice to leave the room while they met to draw up a strategy for his case. Even more telling, we were several minutes into lunch after the meeting before someone noticed that the client was not there. "Maybe he got arrested on the way over here," a lawyer joked as he left the restaurant to look for him.[41] Over the long course of a case, initial deference can also shift to resentment. Disagreements over strategy or fees can form deeper antagonisms, especially once trust is lost. While lawyers expect that some clients will renege on fees, refusal to pay can still be infuriating and hurtful.[42] One lawyer's story of being burnt by a client after a five-year lawsuit finished with the conclusion that lawyers and clients "don't completely trust each other" (Interview 110).

Certainly in major cases, intense pressure cannot help but exacerbate tension between lawyers and plaintiffs. Litigation takes money and emotional stamina, and anxious plaintiffs often want results. Although lawyers usually warn potential clients of the difficulties ahead, many lawyers still worry about disappointing their clients. "I'm embarrassed," one lawyer confided, "because their hopes are on me, and I can't get any money for them" (Interview 73). Nor are successful clients necessarily grateful. "After hearing the verdict," another lawyer said, "I was so happy that we had won. However, my clients were unhappy that they had not been awarded as much compensation as they had hoped for. Had I lost, they would have blamed it on corrupt court officials, but now that we had won, they blamed it on me" (quoted in van Rooij 2010, 71).

One way to look at the journey from dispute to decision is as a wide-ranging quest for allies. Outside help features prominently in litigation stories, and winning compensation often seems to require assistance from an articulate lawyer, a sympathetic EPB official, or a

---

41 This was not an unrealistic possibility as the client's traveling companion, another potential plaintiff, had been taken into custody the previous night. The client was not arrested, however, but had gotten lost between the law office and the restaurant.

42 For more on how Chinese lawyers encounter difficulty collecting fees from clients, see Michelson (2006). In a 2009 online survey of lawyers, respondents averaged 77,000 RMB (US$12,222) in unpaid bills (Michelson and Liu 2010, 319).

crusading journalist. When lawyers and litigants talk about past cases, another common theme is the difficulty of environmental litigation. Many of my interviews turned into a litany of obstacles, some of which are endemic to environmental litigation (like proving causation, maintaining unity, and managing lawyer-client tensions), and some of which are more specific to China (like getting a case into court and leveraging personal networks). Yet despite consensus that environmental cases are a long shot, they are not a lost cause. Sometimes, just barely, the process creaks forward such that appraisals are conducted on time, allies recruited, and compensation won.

3 Frontiers of Environmental Law

MOST PEOPLE PREFER NOT TO GO TO COURT. FROM Chicago to Chongqing, common sense holds that lawsuits are a hassle and, when possible, it is easier to settle disputes outside of court. Barriers to litigation, such as cost, time, and legal knowledge, contribute to what legal sociologists call a "dispute pyramid" in which only a fraction of grievances enter the legal system (Miller and Sarat 1980). A 2010 survey of rural households in six Chinese provinces shows that lawyers, courts, and legal agencies were involved in just 2.2 percent of grievances those surveyed experienced that year. Most of the time, villagers gave up on their complaints (34.9 percent) or pursued informal, bilateral negotiations to resolve the problem (38.4 percent).[1]

Environmental disputes fit this pattern too. The All-China Environment Federation (ACEF), a government-backed non-governmental organization (NGO), estimates that no more than 1 percent of environmental disputes reach courts (Li 2008).[2] Given the obstacles discussed in the last chapter, from finding a lawyer to getting a case accepted by the court, it makes sense that most people first turn to solutions that seem

---

1 Ethan Michelson, Indiana University, personal communication. This is comparable to 2002 survey data in which 1.8 percent of rural disputes were resolved through legal channels (Michelson 2007, 467).

2 In 1999, the State Environmental Protection Agency (SEPA) came up with a similar ballpark estimate: no more than 5 percent (Sha 2003).

easier, such as requesting help from the Environmental Protection Bureau (EPB). Many complainants also pursue multiple strategies to increase the odds that one approach will pay off (van Rooij 2010, 61). If nothing works, conflicts over pollution can escalate. As one self-described "law-abiding" villager explained, "Before the pollution, I had not even been to the township government. But as our problem remained without a solution, I have had to petition everywhere" (quoted in van Rooij 2010, 60). Protest and litigation occupy the top of the dispute pyramid, by which point pollution victims are desperate enough to invest time, spend money, and potentially weather political risk.[3]

Through the stories of four environmental disputes, this chapter peers beneath the tip of the dispute pyramid to chart the potential and limits of legal solutions. The first two cases are landmark environmental lawsuits from the early and mid-2000s that were seen as success stories within China. They illustrate the limits of even a big win, especially in view of ambiguous legacies. In contrast, the second two cases never became lawsuits at all. They point at areas worth watching and hint at future possibilities. After all, the legal frontier is moving quickly: recall that as recently as the late 1990s most lawyers worked for the state, and plaintiffs nearly always shouldered the burden of proof. As the Chinese government rapidly writes new environmental laws and revises old ones, paying attention to which grievances are taken up by courts (and which are not) reveals much about where China's environmental problems lie and how useful the law can be in solving them. But above all, these cases offer an intriguing glimpse into China today. They remind us that behind the legal filings and bureaucratic wrangling are individuals – determined, stubborn, and in some instances, extremely courageous.

---

3 Especially in poor areas, protest is sometimes perceived as easier than litigation. Dachuan village's decades-long fight against a fertilizer factory, for example, never turned into a civil lawsuit because county and township officials advised villagers that litigation would cost too much and it would be hard to win against a major, politically connected enterprise (Jun 2000, 206–207).

Rural Industrialization: *Zhang Changjian et al. v. Pingnan Rongping Chemical Plant* (Fujian, 2005)

One common cause of environmental lawsuits is rural industrial pollution. In the 1980s, many township and village governments invested in low-tech, labor-intensive factories. Rural industry became a vital part of China's economic growth, and local officials often depended on factories to meet economic targets. Local governments were also allowed to retain most tax revenues, a policy which made taxes paid by industry an important part of local budgets and a critical source of funding for public goods like roads, schools, water, and electricity (Tilt 2010, 40–41). By the early 2000s, rural factories employed more than 135 million workers and provided one-third of national GDP. They were also responsible for up to two-thirds of air and water pollution (Tilt 2010, 3).

As in the case discussed below, harm to agriculture and human health are two frequent byproducts of heavy industrial pollution. In 1998, China Central Television (CCTV) broke one of the first stories on the connection between water pollution and abnormally high cancer rates (Liu 2010). By the 2000s, reports of "cancer villages" (*aizheng cun*) were common, reflecting both a real phenomenon and increased awareness of pollution. Rural residents vary, however, in their willingness to accept pollution as a normal part of life. In some places, cancer is blamed on negative emotions, smoking, or consumption of alcohol or preserved vegetables rather than industry (Lora-Wainwright 2010). Occupation affects risk perception, too. A survey of 700 households in rural Sichuan found that factory workers were the least likely group to agree that "pollution affects people's health," likely because their jobs require them to overlook potential harm (Tilt 2010, 99).[4] In other similar villages, however, it might be common knowledge that pollution harms health. Once warned

---

4 Tilt calls this "strategic risk repression," a nice turn of phrase (2010, 103). For an account of another village that ignored pollution because of economic dependence, see van Rooij (2006a, 196–200).

by a TV report, or perhaps the local doctor, villagers deploy whatever mitigation strategies they can. This might mean using well water for irrigation instead of polluted river water or turning down a well-paid factory job (Chen and Cheng 2011).[5] And after awareness of physical and monetary harm sinks in, villagers can become furious about pollution.

That is what happened in Pingnan county, where Rongping Chemical was built in 1994 in a place described on the county government's Web site as a typical mountainous agricultural area. At the time, Pingnan was one of the eight poorest counties in Fujian province. It was so poor that a 1990 survey of seventy households revealed that only three owned sofas (Li 1999, 109). The county government bought a 30 percent stake in the factory in the hopes of spurring the economy (Caijing 2006). As a local cadre later explained, "From the perspective of a villager, you could wish that we'd done a bit better of a job preserving the environment... [but] at the time we built the Pingnan factory, the place was secluded" (quoted in News Probe 2003). Indeed, Rongping quickly became an integral part of the economy and was providing a quarter of the county budget by 2002.

Over the next ten years, however, local enthusiasm dissipated as crops, fish, fruit trees, and forests started dying. People seemed to be getting sick more often, too. Rising rates of nausea, abdominal pain, rashes, and cancer attracted the attention of Zhang Changjian, the village doctor who later led the environmental lawsuit against Rongping. According to Zhang's records, just 7 percent of deaths in Pingnan between 1990 and 1994 were due to cancer compared to 72 percent of deaths between 1999 and 2002.[6] In 1999, Zhang wrote his first complaint letter, and, after acquiring a computer in 2002, he ramped up his writing.

---

5 In their work on rural pollution, Chinese sociologists Aijiang Chen and Pengli Cheng report that villagers get information from the Internet and TV, especially influential national programs like *Focus* (*Jiaodian Fantan*) and *News Probe* (*Xinwen Diaocha*). News travels fast in rural communities, and a fresh understanding can quickly become conventional wisdom, especially if repeated by influential people like the village doctor (2011).

6 These rates are based on a very small sample. There were just thirteen deaths between 1990 and 1994 and twenty-nine between 1999 and 2002.

At peak production, Zhang wrote as many as forty letters and e-mails a day to would-be allies from the top of the Party hierarchy down through local EPB inspectors. A reply from the office of then-premier Zhu Rongji in 2002 boosted Zhang's confidence (Yang 2002; Lai 2006). Zhang started contacting the media, and a sympathetic reporter from *Fangyuan* magazine filed the first major story on Pingnan's pollution in March 2002. More importantly, the reporter also put Zhang in touch with a Beijing-based legal-aid organization that was willing to take the case, the Center for Legal Assistance to Pollution Victims (CLAPV).[7] Although Zhang had previously considered a lawsuit, he had shelved the idea because of the difficulty of finding a lawyer.

The CLAPV lawyers knew from the start that the key to the case was the attitude of the local government (Caijing 2006). "We want to obey the law and maximize our profit," a local official told students from Xiamen University in 2004.[8] In practice, however, money tended to trump law. For years leading up to the lawsuit, strong government support for Rongping made environmental enforcement difficult. As a member of the Standing Committee of the Pingnan County People's Political Consultative Congress (CPPCC) complained to the press, "Why is it that every time there's an inspection inside the factory they know about it and can prepare? This clearly shows that someone inside tipped them off. This kind of collusion ... is a form of corruption" (quoted in Yang 2002).

Indeed, the Pingnan villagers' journey through the courts shows how thuggishly local power holders can behave when their interests are threatened. Some villagers were afraid to join the lawsuit because they were afraid of being beaten up, and government employees were forbidden from participation entirely. When the villagers started raising money for litigation in 2002, the county government confiscated the collection box (He 2004). Subtler intimidation tactics were on display too. A

---

7 At the time of the Pingnan lawsuit, CLAPV was the only national organization offering legal aid in environmental cases. CLAPV also runs training programs for environmental judges and lawyers, discussed in Chapter 7.

8 Transcript on file with the author.

mysterious electricity outage in 2003, for example, prevented residents from watching a national TV segment on pollution in the village (Lai 2006, 30). Later on, Zhang Changjian would suffer the most serious repercussions as the most visible leader of the lawsuit. The county government shut down Zhang's medical clinic in 2004, leaving him without a source of income.[9] "Because of this lawsuit," Zhang told a reporter three years later, "I've thoroughly offended the county government. The result is that my wife has left, I've lost my job, and the NGO that I spent so much effort to establish [in 2007] – Pingnan Green Home – has been banned by the government" (quoted in Wei 2007).

Despite these scare tactics, 1,721 villagers joined the 2002 lawsuit against Rongping. They requested 10.3 million RMB (US$1.6 million) in compensation for economic damages and 3 million RMB (US$476,190) in emotional damages (*jingshen sunhai peichang*), along with a court order to clean up chromium-containing waste and stop pollution before further economic losses and emotional distress occurred. Faced with a politically controversial case, the Ningde Intermediate Court stalled for over two years before issuing a decision in April 2005. The decision required Rongping to "stop the infringement" (*tingzhi qinhai*), a vague, unenforceable pronouncement, and mandated 249,000 RMB (US$39,523) in compensation. It was less than 2 percent of what the plaintiffs had requested, in part because the court threw out the bid for emotional damages.[10] Disappointed, Zhang and the other villagers vowed to appeal. Indeed, the intermediate court decision provided

---

9 According to the government, the clinic was shut down because Zhang did not pass the medical licensing exam (*yisheng zige kaoshi*). Zhang sued the Pingnan Bureau of Public Health in an effort to reverse the decision, but lost the lawsuit (Wei 2007).

10 The decision states that the plaintiffs' claim for emotional damages did not meet the requirements of the 2001 Interpretation of the Supreme People's Court on Problems Regarding the Ascertainment of Compensation Liability for Emotional Damages in Civil Torts (Supreme People's Court 2001). Although the decision does not elaborate, the judges may have been thinking of Article 8, which instructs courts only to award economic compensation if emotional distress has "serious consequences" (*yanzhong houguo*). Confusion over how to fairly calculate emotional damages may have been another issue. The logic behind the villagers' back-of-the-envelope calculations – 10 RMB per month per person between 1994 and 1999 and 30 RMB per month between

grounds for doing so. The court, possibly emboldened by Rongping's appearance on a 2002 SEPA list of China's top fifty-five polluters, clearly acknowledged excessive pollution and correctly shifted the burden of proof to the defendant.[11]

In November 2005, sixteen years after Zhang Changjian wrote his first complaint letter, the Fujian High Court upheld the Ningde Intermediate Court decision and increased compensation to 684,178 RMB (US$108,599) or roughly 397 RMB (US$63) per plaintiff.[12] This payout represented about a month of income for most of the plaintiffs.[13] It was remarkably little, and it took nearly another two years for Zhang and the other villagers to receive any money at all. Although the five designated plaintiff representatives should have been legally empowered to receive and distribute the money on behalf of the group, county officials demanded the villagers submit a new disbursal plan and check for public objections. Under the combined pressure of media attention, further visits from CLAPV lawyers, and petitions to provincial officials, the court finally released some of the money in September 2007.

The outside world deemed this partial win a success. A consortium of judges, including representatives from *Legal Daily* and the All China Lawyers' Association (ACLA), named the case one of the ten most influential lawsuits of 2005. Media accounts framed Pingnan as a David versus Goliath story, in which determined villagers wrested concessions from powerful opponents. It was seen as a triumph against the intractable problem of local protectionism and especially noteworthy because of the number of plaintiffs involved. Indeed, given the grip of the economic-growth-at-all-costs mindset, the media accounts themselves were an

---

1999 and 2002 – may well have been unclear or unpersuasive. See *Zhang Changjian et al. v. Pingnan Rongping Chemical Plant*, Ningde Intermediate People's Court (2005).

11 One of the judges was a graduate of CLAPV's environmental law training program in Beijing, an experience which the CLAPV lawyers thought helped the panel apply the law accurately (Wang 2007, 219).

12 See *Zhang Changjian et al. v. Pingnan Rongping Chemical Plant*, Fujian Provincial High People's Court (2005).

13 This is an estimate based on the average annual income of a Pingnan county farmer in 2005, 3,523 RMB (Pingnan Statistical Bureau 2006).

achievement. National headlines brought attention to rural environmental problems, discussed the reversed burden of proof, and sparked debate about how to improve environmental law. Back in Pingnan, litigation also led to further environmental activism. Zhang Changjian became a full-time environmentalist after losing his clinic and eventually managed to legally register his NGO, Pingnan Green Home (*Pingnan Lüse Zhi Jia*) in 2009. In his words, "Environmental protection has become part of my life, and I absolutely can't let go of it. Even if I let go of my life, I still must protect the environment. Even if I have no job, I still must protect the environment" (quoted in Wei 2007). China Dialogue, a bilingual Web site covering environmental issues in China, picked Pingnan as one of eight cases of the first decade of the 2000s that mattered most (China Dialogue 2011).

At the same time, the Pingnan villagers' pyrrhic victory also highlights the limits of the law. Although the villagers received some money for economic losses, they got nothing for emotional damages or for health-related claims. Moreover, pollution in Pingnan continues. Pingnan Green Home's pamphlets, blog posts, and petitions chronicle a post-2005 history of continued complaints, including a 2009 trip to Beijing to protest a proposed expansion to Rongping Chemical Plant. Rongping's approach to waste disposal also remains an ongoing problem, and villagers claim that the factory is still discharging pollutants directly into the river. In 2010, nine people were detained for blocking the entrance to a newly opened landfill containing chemical waste. "We tried to persuade the villagers to be rational," an official from the Public Security Bureau told the press after the arrests, but it was no use in a community already convinced of the dangers of pollution (quoted in Hu and Peng 2010).

Pollution Accidents: Sun Youli et al. v. Qian'an Number One Paper Mill et al. (Hebei, 2002 and 2003)

Few consumers think much about fish farming beyond the occasional moment at the fish counter spent weighing the costs and benefits of farm-raised fish against wild-caught fish. But in China, fish farming is big business. More than 4.5 million Chinese fish farmers produce about 70 percent of the world's farmed fish (Barboza 2007). Fish farms inhabit thousands of lakes, ponds, rivers, and reservoirs which are vulnerable to water pollution, particularly from industrial emissions and agricultural runoff. Many lawsuits involving fish farms, however, emerge from industrial accidents that abruptly kill large numbers of farmed fish, shrimp, and crabs rather than routine pollution. To give a sense of scale, there were 474 pollution accidents in 2008 (euphemistically called "pollution incidents" in Chinese) and $26.7 million of economic damages (China Statistical Yearbook on Environment 2009, 653). In fact, fish farmers are one of the groups most likely to bring forth civil environmental lawsuits because of the relative frequency of pollution crises and documentable economic losses.

In 1997, Sun Youli and seventeen other fishermen received local government permission to start farming fish and, in so doing, joined what had become a local economic trend. Fish farming was a popular enterprise on Hebei province's Bohai delta in the late 1990s, partly because learning the ropes was relatively straightforward. As a fish farmer in Fujian province explained, "This doesn't take a lot of technology ... you just learn it as you go along" (quoted in Barboza 2007).[14] Fish was also a promising export product. In 2008, the United States would import $2.1 billion of fish and seafood from China (Gale and Buzby 2009). Some fish farmers, especially in export-oriented provinces, learned to minimize uncertainty by signing advance-purchase agreements with middlemen willing to freeze and process fish for export (Einhorn 2010).[15]

In October 2000, a major pollution accident disrupted what would have been the fall fish harvest. One of the laborers for the harvest noticed thousands of fish and shellfish floating dead in water that appeared black

14 Farming fish in the sea is riskier and requires more capital than inland fish farms (Interview 165).
15 The combination of rising labor costs, increased rents, and static export prices made fish farming less profitable in the late 2000s. In 2009, 10 percent of Zhejiang province's tilapia farmers stopped farming the fish (Einhorn 2010).

and red. Sun Youli and the other fish farmers immediately reported the incident to county officials who, in turn, quickly closed down two sluices channeling water from the nearby Luan River to the Bohai Sea. Shutting the sluices reflected widespread suspicion that factories along the river were the most likely source of an industrial pollution accident. This later turned out to be right. The nine paper and chemical factories eventually named as defendants were located in Qian'an city, more than 1,000 kilometers upstream from the sluices.

As is often the case, the Bohai fish farmers were initially reluctant to initiate a lawsuit. Even seven years later, one of the plaintiffs still felt that "if we could have gone through a government bureau, that would have been better" (Interview 51). Instead, their first impulse was to take photos of the damage and petition the government for compensation. Only after a fruitless month did they start looking for lawyers willing to represent them in exchange for a contingency fee, a cut of potential future compensation. The fish farmers found a law firm located a two-and-a-half-hour drive away, the Zhongzi law firm in Beijing. Members of the nearby Tangshan fishermen's association who had worked with Zhongzi law firm on earlier pollution disputes recommended the firm to the Bohai fish farmers. In 1999, a time when few lawyers were thinking about environmental issues, Zhongzi had set up an environmental law department. There was a sense of long-term strategy, insofar as environmental law might develop into a lucrative business, combined with a desire to take cases for a good cause.

In retrospect, the legal team's decision to file the case in the Tianjin maritime court was a brilliant move. The plaintiffs' Beijing-based legal team would later ascribe success to their choice of court, writing that using maritime courts can "remove the administrative interference that accompanies local protectionism, bring the advantage of specialized courts and expert judges into play, increase the efficiency of the case, and guarantee justice."[16] At the time, however, venue shopping was

16 Zhongzi Law Firm, unpublished document on file with the author.

an unproven strategy. The Tianjin maritime court was not accustomed to pollution cases, and, before taking the case in May 2001, judges double-checked with the Supreme People's Court (SPC) to confirm the court had jurisdiction. Environmental monitoring data was also critical. Although one of the Zhongzi lawyers would later recall that "the hardest thing in this case was the lack of evidence," it helped that one of the Zhongzi lawyers was a former EPB employee, a real "insider" (*zaihang*), who knew what kinds of records should exist and who inside the bureau might be able to provide them (Interview 42). Convincing judges to request reports from the Tangshan EPB exposed an unflattering record of law breaking, fines, and dumping. In addition, the fish farmers raised money for independent monitors to collect water samples from fourteen spots near Qian'an city for analysis (Workers' Daily 2002).

As always, linking pollution and damages was an additional challenge. One key piece of evidence was a January 2001 joint investigation by the Hebei Province Fishery Bureau and the Laoting County Fishery Bureau that pinned pollution on paper and chemical factories in Qian'an (Workers' Daily 2002). Then, the Tianjin Maritime Court asked the Bohai Area Monitoring Station (under the Ministry of Agriculture's Fishery Environmental Monitoring Center) to appraise damages. The monitoring station came back with an estimate of 13.6 million RMB (US$2.1 million), almost three quarters of a million RMB (US$119,000) per plaintiff.

The Tianjin Maritime Court saw this appraisal as "objective" (*keguanxing*) and "reliable" (*kekao*) and relied on it heavily in its April 2002 decision. Citing the 2001 SPC explanation on the reversed burden of proof, the court held the nine defendants jointly liable for the entire 13.6 million RMB. The decision also held the nine polluters responsible regardless of whether emissions met environmental standards. Judicial re-affirmation of this principle was a significant breakthrough. In the 1990s, government approval to exceed pollution standards was easily attained and, even when environmental enforcement tightened in the

2000s, courts still frequently imposed a litmus test in which compensation depended on proving illegal behavior.[17] This affirmation of accountability, combined with a sizable payout, attracted national media attention and a few endorsements. Just afterward, a Beijing-based official at the Ministry of Environmental Protection (MEP) told *Legal Daily* that he supported the fish farmers' attempts to protect their rights (Qie 2002).

As the case dragged on, however, the sheen of this initial win started to fade. During the appeal to the Tianjin High Court, many of the fish farmers had to take out loans to pay for basic necessities. In the spring of 2002, Sun Youli could not even fish off his boat because he had no money to pay workers. As one reporter wrote during this period, "Now [Sun's] only hope is that this lawsuit will conclude so that he can get some money to pay his debts" (Workers' Daily 2002). The outcome of the appeal was disheartening too. Although the High Court upheld the earlier decision, the March 2003 decision reduced compensation by 47 percent to 6.5 million RMB (US$1.03 million). First, the decision re-calculated losses based on wholesale value rather than retail value. Second, the Tianjin High Court judges recognized the defendants' long history in the area and penalized the plaintiffs for failing to consider the risk before establishing a fish farm. After the decision, the fish farmers struggled to get even this reduced sum. Finally, after much delay and significant judicial pressure, they received 3.5 million RMB (US$555,555) in September 2004, less than half of what the High Court mandated sixteen months earlier.[18]

But even this partial win gave plaintiffs and lawyers a "feeling of success" (*chengjiu gan*), possibly because they started off with such low expectations. As one plaintiff recalled in 2007, after time smoothed the most unpleasant memories, "The most important thing is that we won"

---

17 Article 41 of the Environmental Protection Law states that polluters should be liable for losses even if emissions are legal.

18 As discussed in Chapter 5, reducing compensation through shared liability or creative accounting is common, especially when the bench is sympathetic to local industry.

(Interview 51). Much like veterans of labor disputes, 80 percent of whom said they would sue again in one study (Gallagher 2006, 804), the Bohai fish farmers were also ready to head back to court. During my 2007 visit, they discussed several potential environmental cases with the lawyer who accompanied me, at least one of which came to fruition. They said they understood the court's need to balance their claims against the broader imperative for economic growth, even if reduced compensation was disappointing. One of their lawyers, who would later become one of China's most experienced environmental litigators, agreed the decision was "fair" (*gongping*). Just after the case, he wrote: "for now, most enterprises face a number of difficulties reliably meeting [environmental] standards... lightening industry's civil liability can contribute to their enthusiasm for environmental protection."[19] Taking a long view, he saw the Sun Youli case as just a beginning.

When I returned to the area in 2011, the fish farms were gone entirely. The government had shut them down as part of a bizarre five-year plan to transform an area known for industry into an eco-tourism destination. Government press releases envision the beaches of Laoting as the future "rear garden" of Beijing and Tianjin, after 10.5 billion RMB (US$1.66 million) in investment builds high-speed roads, a slew of tourist facilities, and a national park with an oxygen bar. The plan is a bold attempt to attract the wealth of the Beijing-Tianjin metropolis and hitch Laoting county to the tourist economy of better-known nearby beach towns like Beidaihe (Laoting Tourism Bureau 2011; Laoting County Government 2012). Remembering the Sun Youli case suggests that controlling pollution will be an ongoing challenge. The seaside is still downstream from Qian'an city and just 45 miles from Tangshan city. Both are major industrial centers known for cement factories, steel plants, and chemical projects, and there is always a danger of another pollution accident that will drive tourists away.

19 Unpublished document on file with the author.

Pushing Boundaries: *Chinese Sturgeon et al. v. PetroChina Company Limited* (Beijing/Heilongjiang, 2005)

Like the previous two cases, most civil environmental lawsuits in China are tort cases, which is to say that they center on winning compensation for economic losses. However, the dispute pyramid reminds us that lawsuits are a small part of a vast landscape of environmental enforcement, grievances, and activism. Shanghai EPB officials, for example, spend more time triaging nuisance complaints about noise pollution or odors from a nearby restaurant than investigating more serious violations of the law (Warwick and Ortolano 2007). Before returning to courts, the next two cases look at environmental activism outside of them. In the first case, a group of Beijing-based academics used the threat of litigation to provoke discussion about public interest litigation. In the second case, Shanghai homeowners did not turn to the law at all. Petitions and protest were easier and proved just as effective as litigation.

Using litigation as a publicity stunt means courting controversy and it is not a common tactic even among Chinese activists. One of China's few such lawsuits started on November 13, 2005, when an explosion at a petrochemical plant owned by PetroChina released 100 tons of toxins into the Songhua River. Within two weeks, the spill was international headline news because of the scale of the accident and because the Songhua River flows north through northeastern Jilin province and over the border into Russia. For the first five days, factory management and local government officials tried to fix the crisis without alerting higher-ups, even dumping reservoir water into the river to dilute contaminants (Green 2009). Secrecy continued even after the central government was notified on November 18. When the 50-mile benzene slick started approaching Harbin, a large city dependent on the river for running water, city officials cut off the municipal water supply and claimed a sudden need for repairs. Few believed them. Rumors began circulating, including reports of an earthquake as people started to stockpile food and leave the city (Yardley 2005). Amid rising public panic, the Harbin city government finally announced the spill eight days after the initial incident (Wang, Duan, and Wang 2005).

More than seven hundred miles away, a group of six Peking University professors and graduate students saw the Songhua spill as an opportunity to push forward environmental public interest law. Driven by a desire to call attention to the issue of standing – allowing a wider range of groups or individuals to sue over environmental harm – they drew up an unusual legal response to the pollution accident in just two weeks. Rather than suing on their own behalf, the academics chose to list themselves as "representatives" (*daibiao ren*) for the real plaintiffs: the Chinese sturgeon, Songhua River, and Taiyang Island. In compensation for harm, they requested 100 million RMB (US$15.8 million) to establish a fund to clean up the Songhua River. 100 million RMB is a large number – certainly large enough to make people pay attention – but the Peking University team thought it was reasonable considering the length of the river and PetroChina's deep pockets.

As discussed further in Chapter 7, the decision to sue on behalf of an animal species, a river, and an island reflected the influence of American environmental law. Some members of the group were working on a translation of American environmental law decisions at the time, and their lyrical brief explicitly draws on U.S. precedent. In keeping with Justice Douglas's minority view in the 1972 case *Sierra Club v. Morton*, the brief argues that "woodpeckers who eat wood, coyotes and bears, lemmings and river salmon should all have their day in court." Furthermore, "Countries with an advanced conception of environmental protection have already started to put this new legal idea into practice...In America, for example, it is firmly established that endangered species and environmental NGOs can team up to bring litigation."[20]

---

20 See *Chinese Sturgeon et al. v. PetroChina et al*, legal suit prepared December 6, 2005. Copy on file with the author.

This is radical language and no one involved ever thought the case would go to trial. Rather, they conceived of the case as a performance. It was an opportunity to illustrate an academic argument and in so doing, bring attention to public interest law at a moment when both the administrative and civil procedure laws were under revision. As a result, it came as no surprise when judges at the Heilongjiang High Court case-filing division refused to even read the legal brief on December 7, let alone accept the case.[21]

Up to the point when the case was refused, the Peking University academics kept the impending lawsuit quiet. Afterward, however, they put the legal brief up on a university Web site where it sparked online discussion. Two weeks later, Peking University hosted a standing-room-only panel on the lawsuit to discuss whether using animals as plaintiffs was creative or crazy. Despite outside interest, however, the protagonists decided to limit their audience and avoid the media. As one person involved later explained, "We wanted to make clear that this wasn't a political activity," and staying out of trouble also meant staying away from the press (Interview 44).

This kind of innovative, boundary-pushing litigation is risky, and, to a large extent, it was only possible in this case because of the protection afforded by the Peking University name. Peking University is one of China's most prestigious universities, sometimes called the "Harvard of China." This reputation, along with a history of campus political activism, helped cast the six legal representatives as respected academic provocateurs rather than threatening radicals. As a judge at the Heilongjiang High Court told one of the Peking University professors, "Only you Peking University people could do this" (Interview 39). Even more important, the professors' professional and social connections propelled the would-be lawsuit into the public eye even without much news

---

21 The judges at the case-filing division orally turned down the case without issuing a written reason for refusal. Privately, some judges admitted that they had been ordered to steer clear of the Songhua River controversy (Interview 44).

coverage. In 2006, this question appeared on the 2006 national judicial examination:[22]

> Four teachers and students from a certain university jointly sued Company A over pollution along a certain river. They asked the court to mandate that Company A pay compensation to take care of the pollution. In addition to the four teachers and students, the plaintiffs included a famous island in the river. The court refused to take the case. Which of the following explain the relevant points of law?

One of the correct answers (there were several) was the Civil Procedure Law does not allow public interest litigation.[23] Although the test endorsed the court's decision to turn down the case, it is notable that public interest litigation turned up on the exam at all. For academics struggling on behalf of an idea, bringing public interest litigation into the consciousness of more than 200,000 test takers certainly constitutes a degree of validation.[24] Considering that the case never even enjoyed a hearing, this national ripple effect reflects the prestige of the Peking University professors and law students involved. A veneer of legal scholarship can lend respectability to potentially radical experiments, especially when prestigious institutions or well-known individuals lend social capital to a cause.

In the end, however, the sense of crisis that so often accompanies environmental accidents called far more attention to pollution problems than did the failed lawsuit. The head of SEPA, Xie Zhenhua, was forced to resign over the spill and resulting cover-up (Duan 2005). PetroChina was fined the highest fine possible for pollution, one million

---

22 Both lawyers and judges are required to pass the test. Contrary to the wording of the question, there were actually six teachers and students involved in the lawsuit. Copy of the question on file with the author.

23 This changed in 2012. Revisions to the Civil Procedure Law that go into effect on January 1, 2013 allow lawful authorities (*falü guiding de jiguan*) and relevant organizations (*you guan zuzhi*) to initiate environmental public interest lawsuits (Standing Committee of the National People's Congress 2012).

24 Between 200,000 and 260,000 people per year take the national judicial exam (Peerenboom 2009, 1).

RMB (US$158,730), and the State Council passed a five-year plan to improve water pollution along the river (State Council 2006; Qie 2007). Environmental protection, at least for a time, was more of a priority in the heavily industrial northeast. In Beijing, the new head of SEPA credited the Songhua crisis with "initiating fresh progress on the cause of environmental protection" (State Environmental Protection Agency 2006). And on the ground in Jilin province, an EPB official noticed his bureau "suddenly had status" (*diwei mashang shang lai le*) following the spill (Interview 87).

By itself, however, the Songhua spill was not enough to reprogram attitudes toward preventing pollution accidents or solving them.[25] Xie Zhenhua, the sacked chief of SEPA, reappeared in 2006 as a vice-chairman at the powerful National Development and Reform Commission (NRDC), a post that might well count as a step up from his old job. He also led the Chinese delegation at the Copenhagen climate-change talks in 2009. Meanwhile, environmental crises continue to make headlines, including major oil spills near the Yellow River in 2009, in Dalian in 2010, and in Bohai Bay in 2011. Although reports from the MEP say water quality in the Songhua River is improving, the deeper lessons of the Songhua spill have yet to sink in.

NIMBY Disputes: the Shanghai-Hangzhou Magnetic Levitation (Maglev) Train (2007–2008)

While environmental accidents were making headlines in the 2000s, not-in-my-backyard (NIMBY) environmental disputes were clearly on the rise as well.[26] By the early 2000s, about 70 percent of urban residents in China owned their home, and the media was full of accounts of

25 For more on China's recent spate of environmental accidents, see Wang (2010).
26 Burningham (2000) argues that researchers shouldn't use the term NIMBY because it is "so firmly associated with limited and self-interested responses to local environmental change" (60). Although I agree that the term has some negative connotations, I've used it here because it so clearly evokes a certain type of collective action.

homeowners banding together to oppose unwelcome neighborhood developments (Cai 2005, 779). Well-known incidents included opposition to a power plant in Chongqing (2002), a major highway linking Hong Kong and Shenzhen (2004), high-voltage electricity transmission towers in Beijing (2004 and 2007), a chemical plant in Xiamen (2007), and a nuclear power plant in Shandong (2007). China's upwardly mobile middle classes were demanding a voice in how their neighborhoods were transformed, and these protests brought new issues, passion, and people to Chinese environmentalism. Even if middle-class protesters cared more about protecting property values than conserving nature, as was often the case, the arrival of NIMBY disputes opened a new arena of environmental rhetoric and claims. Yet few NIMBY protests have turned into lawsuits, even though middle-class claimants seem likely to have the education to understand the law and the money to hire a lawyer. The 2007–2008 dispute over the extension of the Shanghai-Hangzhou maglev train, discussed below, illustrates why: litigation does not measure up to the perceived efficacy and cost of other tactics.

Shanghai's maglev train has always been a symbol of the city's high-tech modernity. Amid much fanfare, Shanghai opened the world's first high-speed commercial maglev train from the Pudong airport to downtown Shanghai in 2004, and, despite the fact that the Pudong maglev was losing money, the central government approved plans in 2006 to extend it 37 kilometers to the Hongqiao airport and 175 kilometers to the nearby city of Hangzhou. Initial plans indicated that the Hangzhou extension would cost 35 billion RMB (US\$5.5 billion) and that trains would reach 450 kmph (Xinhua 2007). The idea was to complete the new line in time for the 2010 World Expo to reinforce visitors' impression that, as celebrity socialite Paris Hilton put it, "Shanghai looks like the future!" (quoted in Associated Press 2007).

Controversy arose because the Shanghai-Hangzhou line was slated to pass through a densely populated residential neighborhood in the Minhang district. Although residents heard rumors about the new maglev train as early as 2006, they were not officially notified until just before the Chinese new year in 2007 (Qian 2007, 64). The initial 'Notice of Demolition and Resettlement' posted around the neighborhood was vague. There was no map of the proposed line, and it did not specify which residents (if any) would be moved to make way for the new track. On February 25, 2007, a group of concerned residents went to various government offices to investigate. They discovered that the Shanghai-Hangzhou line would pass within 22.5 meters of their community, but there were no plans to demolish the buildings near the line or compensate the residents (Qian 2007, 65).

This particular section of Minhang district had long been cursed by transportation planners. Several major transportation lines already criss-cross the area, including a subway, train, and elevated highway. Since Shanghai's southern train station opened in 2006, upward of 100 south-bound trains pass by each day (Interview 63). The Shanghai-Hangzhou maglev would run parallel to these tracks, a plan with the advantage of limiting the noise and visual impact of trains and highways to one forsaken stretch of the city. For the people living in the area, how-ever, news of the maglev was a final indignity at the end of a decade of transportation-related bad news. As one resident said, "If they add a maglev train, it will just be one disaster after another" (quoted in Qian 2007, 65).

Residents were particularly concerned that the maglev plans included only a 22.5-meter safety zone. Living so close to the tracks, they argued, would mean increased noise pollution and exposure to dan-gerous electromagnetic radiation. Residents also claimed that the plans violated 2003 Shanghai city planning regulations that call for a minimum 50-meter safety zone on each side of any maglev line. Rumors were rife that initial plans included a 50-meter safety zone, which was later changed to 22.5 meters in the interest of expediency (Qian 2007, 66). This was a credible possibility because a 50-meter non-residential zone flanks the Pudong maglev on each side, a project that was the product of the same government planning process. Residents complained that they were "the world's lab rats" (*shijie de bailaoshu*) and that this was a clear case of "one line, two systems" (*yixian liangzhi*).[27]

But despite assertions that "the state is breaking the law" (*guojia shi zai fan zui*), residents did not sue the government (Interview 107). In our conversations, they offered a battery of justifications, including the limited scope of existing laws ("there is no maglev law on radiation") (Interview 63), conviction that the courts would refuse the case (Interview 107), and difficulty finding a lawyer (Interview 65). A Guangzhou homeowner involved in a similar NIMBY dispute summed up the prevailing sentiment well: "The law is so feeble. Law is a weapon of citizens. But it is just like a bullet. Sometimes it hits the target, sometimes it misses it, and at other times it does not come out the barrel at all" (quoted in Cai 2005, 795). Nor did legal professionals in the community advocate for legal solutions. As in other instances of Shanghai homeowner activism, most protest organizers were retired, self-employed, or worked for foreign companies, all professions that enjoy some insulation from government pressure (Chen 2006, 9–11). Lawyers and judges were more circumspect, likely because judges are government employees, and lawyers apply annually to the local justice bureau to renew their license.

In lieu of law, the organizers turned to tactics they perceived to be cheaper and easier. First, the communities closest to the proposed line began petitioning the government and reaching out to the media. They wrote to the district government, the city government and the central government expressing their concerns. Premier Wen Jiabao and the National People's Congress also received letters. At first, there were very few domestic media reports because the story was so sensitive. Word on the street was that the maglev train was a pet project of the Shanghai government's Jiang Zemin clique and enjoyed high-level support in Beijing (Interview 107).

27 Jinhong Community, document entitled "Our living environment is getting worse by the day, we want to be further from the maglev! (*Juzhu huanjing riyi ehua, women yao yuanli cixuanfu!*)," 2007. Copy on file with the author.

When efforts to attract national attention stalled, the residents went international. In this solidly middle-class community, residents had Internet access, relatives abroad, and a strong sense of being part of a global world. Just as some activist NGOs seek international allies to pressure their home government (Keck and Sikkink 1998), this group of Shanghai citizens started looking for pressure points outside China. Germany was a logical first step because German companies Siemans and ThyssenKrupp were part of the maglev-construction consortium. The residents wrote to German chancellor Angela Merkel requesting intervention: "You know perhaps more than us about the noise caused by the Transrapid [maglev train] and the damage caused by the electronic magnetic field. We hope with all our heart that you can help us" (quoted in Spiegel Online 2007). Others suggested using the Olympics to attract attention. When the Olympics arrive, an online-forum post suggested, "We should all hang English signs."[28]

In March and April, residents became more proactive in their efforts to gain public attention. They hung giant banners with slogans such as "We want environmental protection" (*yao huanbao*) and "We want a public hearing" (*yao tingzheng*) from the top of their apartment buildings. This was a clever tactic, as the banners were nearly impossible for public-security officials to rip down and easily visible from the nearby elevated highway. Unlike Web sites and blogs, which are routinely blocked by city authorities, the banners got the message out. Journalists from state news agencies and the international media started covering the dispute.

At the same time, residents began weekly demonstrations in front of government offices. They worked out a schedule where they would gather one week at the city government and the next week at the district government. According to reports from Xinhua news agency, the Minhang district government received more than 5,000 petitioners in a

---

28 Shanghai Maglev Dispute, anti-maglev BBS board (1,327 posts). Accessed May 27, 2007. Copy on file with the author.

single day in March 2007. These alternate-week protests lasted from the end of March through the end of April. Participants estimate that there were more than 500 people at some of the demonstrations, including more than 100 people on the day that they delivered a petition to the city government in People's Square (Interviews 63, 64, 107). During this period of intense activism, many residents would log on to QQ, a popular Chinese instant-messenger service, after work to discuss the dispute (Interview 65). One housing complex also organized nightly gatherings from 8–9 PM in the lobby of one of the buildings (Interview 63).

The Shanghai government's first response was to organize a series of meetings in April 2007 (Interview 107). The main purpose of these meetings was to "work on the residents" so that they would understand that maglev train "wouldn't be any more dangerous than using a microwave oven" (Interview 107 and 65). As a Shanghai EPB official explained to me, "Economic development has to move forward, and it may influence ordinary people." Officials must help residents "do thought work" (*zuo sixiang gongzuo*) to accept the outcome of government planning (Interview 105). Although residents were not allowed to see the complete text of the 2006 Environmental Impact Assessment, they were reassured that the report did not foresee undue noise pollution as long as the train did not exceed 200 kmph in residential areas (Qian 2007, 66). Residents were also invited to visit the Pudong maglev in the hopes that seeing a working train would assuage their fears (Interview 105).

None of these clumsy attempts at public relations convinced the community. In mid-May 2007, the government suspended construction of the Shanghai-Hangzhou line pending revisions to the plan and new approval from the central government. The residents decided to also take a break from activism until new developments occurred or the weather cooled down and the seventeenth Party Congress was safely past (Interview 107).[29] The maglev project then spent four years on hold before the

---

29 In January 2008, there were additional anti-maglev demonstrations in People's Square and along Nanjing Road. According to news reports, protestors were angry about lack

central government shelved the plan in January 2011 (Chenzhong 2009; Shanghai Daily 2011). No explanation was given, but an unnamed source from the Shanghai Municipal People's Congress said that concerns raised by residents were a major reason for the initial suspension of the project (Xinhua 2007). Later on, the 2010 opening of a Shanghai-Hangzhou high-speed rail line also lessened the need for a similar, high-speed maglev train. In the end, it is hard to know whether economic arguments or people power ultimately changed government plans, although it is likely that both factors mattered.[30] At a minimum, the outcry prompted a critical pause. That pause gave planners time to recognize problems like duplication of existing infrastructure and the possibility of cost overruns, a real danger if further activism forced construction underground.

Taking Stock

At the close of the first section of the book, what can be said about patterns of success and failure in environmental lawsuits? This is certainly a question of great practical interest to anyone hoping to win a case, as well as a line of inquiry for future researchers interested in explaining variation in outcomes. Above all, the last three chapters suggest that the economic clout of the polluter, measured by jobs provision and contribution to local tax revenue, matters a great deal. Polluters like Rongping Chemical Plant are often seen as too big to fail, especially in towns dominated by a single company or industry. At the same time, however, cases against smaller polluters with less access to special protection are also common. The nationwide rise in the number of enterprises – from 165,080 in 1998 to 323,793 in 2007 – also increased the number of targets available for litigation (van Rooij and Lo 2010, 28).

---

of transparency and public input surrounding recently released plans to extend the train to the Hongqiao airport as well as Hangzhou.

30 On a trip to Shanghai in August 2012, I heard another explanation as well: that the project lost political backing after former Shanghai Party Chief Chen Liangyu was dismissed from office in 2006 on corruption charges.

Nor do major enterprises always win. There are many mitigating factors, especially local government attitudes toward newly binding pollution targets. If pollution reduction is a serious goal, lawsuits may provide a welcome opportunity to crack down on long-time law breaking and deter future offenses. Official support for pollution victims, or at least neutrality toward them, also shapes plaintiffs' dealings with the EPB. The EPB is a major source of evidence, and an obstructionist bureau can seriously hinder a lawsuit. Expert allies can also tip the success of a case, especially lawyers and appraisers. And popular pressure can change local dynamics entirely, transforming a first impulse to protect GDP into a need to defend the vulnerable. Courts can be swayed by media reports as well as by petitions and protest (Liebman 2011, 176–177).

As more detailed data become available, patterns of regional variation will also become rich ground for research that builds on and complicates the account presented here. It is clear that some places have more environmental lawsuits than others, and it is worth exploring how the volume of litigation in a county or province relates to the level of economic development, the number of lawyers, the severity of pollution, and other factors. Interesting anomalies may also emerge. Several people, for example, suggested that Shanghai has fewer environmental lawsuits than Beijing (Interviews 50, 108, 174). If true, why would that be the case?

For now, the two "wins" profiled in this chapter, the Pingnan and Sun Youli lawsuits, underscore the limits of what courts in the early 2000s stood ready to deliver: minimal to moderate compensation for economic losses. Judges chose to monetize damages at a level that would ensure the continued operation of keystone industries without overburdening polluters. Neither lawsuit was followed by lasting environmental improvement and, along the Bohai coastline, it took a government fiat to re-orient the economy toward the greener alternative of eco-tourism. The real legacy of both cases was the media attention and public sympathy they drew. News reports forged a mainstream understanding that local government and industry had acted badly and, in so doing, brought scrutiny to the growth-at-all-costs mantra that amplified the impact of the case beyond those directly involved. National coverage of major lawsuits brought the price of industrialization into the public consciousness, costs that had gone unquestioned during China's long economic boom.

With landmark wins as ambiguous as these, it is no wonder that most environmental complainants steer clear of courts in favor of semi-legal tactics that, as one Chinese sociologist described it, "Step on the line but don't cross it" (*caixian bu yue xian*) (Zhang 2010, 118). The triad of public relations, petitions, and protest can be highly effective too, as the Shanghai maglev case shows. At the same time, the increasing frequency of NIMBY disputes represents a potential cache of environmental cases. NIMBY disputes could be the next frontier of environmental litigation, should government attitudes change or urban residents come to see courts as fairer, cheaper, or more efficient. This is not impossible to imagine. At least in some places, officials may well decide that channeling disputes into courts is a better way to maintain stability than rewarding a ruckus.

Of course, there is no guarantee that the scope of environmental litigation will expand. Legal evolution is rarely so neat or teleological. Rather, the idea of a moving legal frontier helps us map the landscape of environmental litigation by filling in where the law is now and sketching the interstices where it is not. From NIMBY complaints in Shanghai to industrial accidents along the Songhua River, many of China's most pressing environmental problems never enter the legal system. Scanning a wider range of environmental complaints reveals the narrow bandwidth bracketed by legal solutions and, in an area of law that is changing rapidly, indicates where we might tune in for tomorrow's groundbreaking cases.

4 Political Ambivalence

The State

A GREAT MANY AUTHORITARIAN STATES HAVE FAIRLY autonomous courts that are expected to follow the law in routine criminal prosecutions and civil disputes. While this may initially seem surprising, a reliable legal system has many advantages. For the state, predictable law can help attract foreign investment, maintain social order, and divert blame for unpopular policies (Moustafa 2007, 33–37). For its leaders, legal constraints on powerful interests like police departments, local governments, and major taxpayers can also help ensure that national policies are consistently implemented. And insofar as dispute resolution is seen as efficient and fair, well-run courts can shore up citizen support and give legitimacy to governmental authority. (Shapiro 1981; Nonet and Selznick 2008).

What authoritarian leaders often want, of course, is the appearance of an independent judiciary rather than the reality. Political authorities have special interests and important allies that can be threatened by truly independent courts. As a result, authoritarian regimes often turn to what legal sociologists Philippe Nonet and Philip Selznick call repressive law, or law subordinated to the requirements of the government. The hallmark of repressive law is political intervention in particular cases (2008, 39). Such intervention can be done on an ad hoc basis, as when officials transmit instructions directly to judges, a system dubbed "telephone justice" in the former Soviet Union (Hendley 1996). Or it can be systemic, as when leaders divert politically sensitive cases to special courts that are reliably subservient to their concerns (Toharia 1975).

Direction can be less overt, too. In many authoritarian regimes, lawyers and judges are attentive to the limits of tolerance because straying beyond it risks punishment. Both groups are aware that the state is keeping a close watch, especially when authorities give signs they are attuned to the historical association between legal professionals and political upheaval. From eighteenth-century France to contemporary Pakistan, lawyers, judges, and legal academics have often been at the forefront of calls for an independent judiciary, limits on executive power, and basic civil rights (Halliday and Karpik 1997; Halliday, Karpik, and Feeley 2007).[1] This is the crux of the authoritarian dilemma over courts: on the one hand, autonomous courts burnish and legitimatize authoritarian rule. But on the other hand, a truly independent judiciary carries the threat of subversion. This chapter explores the implications of this dilemma from two vantage points inside the state: first from the commanding heights of leadership, and then from the point of view of city officials responsible for implementing policy goals.

The view from the top of the state, where the chapter opens, explores the relationship between law and ambivalence and outlines the control strategies designed to keep litigation in check. The chapter then shifts perspective to look at the pinnacle of the state from below, as glimpsed through confusing (if not outright contradictory) signals gleaned from official speeches, regulations, or actions. This approach reflects the point of view of my sources, most of whom were not officials, but instead political outsiders struggling to make sense of an opaque political system. Mixed signals from the central leadership are also visible from a rung down the state hierarchy, among the mid-level bureaucrats responsible for the explosive growth of environmental courts in the late 2000s. The final section discusses the new courts as examples of innovation shaped

---

1 Note that this is different from calls for democracy. As Karpik points out, it is possible to have political liberalism without democracy, as in Hong Kong, and democracy without political liberalism, as in Egypt (2007, 469).

by ambivalence, particularly conflicting pressures to address pollution, keep up economic growth, and maintain stability.

Political Ambivalence

Ambivalence is part of the human experience. As psychologists have long known, people often experience mixed feelings or contradictory ideas about something or someone.[2] Sociologists write about ambivalence too, particularly the tension between opposing values in certain professions and social relations (Merton and Barber 1976). Yet ambivalence is not a word much used in accounts of politics, perhaps because, as sociologist Neil Smelser writes, it is "such a powerful, persistent, unresolvable, volatile, generalizable, and anxiety-producing feature of the human condition, [that] people defend against experiencing it in many ways" (1998, 6). At the very least, actions born of ambivalence often occur "beyond the range of consciousness and calculation," making ambivalence hard to see and even harder to study (Smelser 1998, 6).

But ambivalence can apply to states too. After all, as political scientist Joel Migdal points out, states are both "the powerful image of a clearly bounded, unified organization" and "a heap of loosely connected parts" (2001, 22). This paradox, between the state as a unified symbol and the real-life divisions within, simultaneously creates opposing preferences and disguises them. Behind the façade of a unified front, states often behave *as if* they are ambivalent. Up and down the chain of command, far-flung collections of individuals, factions, and bureaucracies routinely send mixed signals about any number of issues, from policy priorities to the best way to win a claim.

Still, it is awkward to keep referring to a state that behaves *as if* it is ambivalent. To get around this clumsy phrasing, this book treats the

2 The Swiss psychologist Eugen Bleuler first introduced the term "ambivalence" in 1910. It was picked up by Sigmund Freud, among others, who used the idea to explain sadomasochism and oedipal relations (Smelser 1998, 6).

as if as implied and discusses the phenomenon of political ambivalence instead. The risk lies in using a phrase that, at first glance, might seem to treat the state as a coherent (if ambivalent) whole. Nothing could be further from the truth. As Migdal underscores, bureaucracies are rarely capable of coordinating a homogenous response. Political ambivalence reflects state incoherence and the reality that political signals are as likely a mishmash as a "harmonious mesh" (Migdal 2001, 117). The word ambivalence is chosen carefully, too. Ambivalence is different from arbitrariness, which depends solely on discretion, or ambiguity, which is calculatedly vague. Although any given signal might well be random or unclear, underlying conflict in values, pressures, and commitments produces the conflicting cues characteristic of ambivalence.

Law and Political Ambivalence

Environmental Litigation in China: A Study in Political Ambivalence limits itself to a single arena of intense ambivalence: litigation through courts. Although courts defuse conflict and build support for leaders, they can also siphon power and legitimize dissent. The historic project of building a legal foundation, discussed in Chapter 1, is also the story of one state's attempt to reap the benefits and avoid the dangers of law.

China's turn toward law reflects three reasons even autocrats sometimes prefer a well-functioning legal system: the need to promote economic growth, control local government officials, and convince citizens they inhabit a well-governed, modern state.[3] From the start, legal reforms were linked to plans to reduce central planning and develop a "socialist market economy" (O'Brien 1990, 158–159). Law was necessary to enforce contracts, break up monopolies, and crack down on fraud. To take an egregious example, there was no law in the early 1980s against filling up empty soda bottles with brown liquid and selling it as Coca-Cola (Vogel 2011, 706). Particularly after Deng Xiaoping's 1992 southern tour

---

3 For more on the general logic of the first two reasons, see Moustafa (2007, 21–32).

calling for further economic reform, the idea that "a market economy is a rule of law economy" gathered momentum in both political and academic circles (Peerenboom 2002, 55). To this way of thinking, law needed to come in line with international practice in order for China to join the world economy. Laws covering topics from taxation to property rights would free domestic initiative while also reassuring foreign investors that China was a credible, predictable place to do business (Lee 2007, 176). An uptick in foreign investment, first in the 1990s and then following China's 2001 accession to the World Trade Organization, deepened the appeal of a legal system capable of inspiring commercial trust. There was also pressure to match what others could offer. As countries compete for investment, "It is difficult to find any government that is not engaged in some program of judicial reform designed to make legal institutions more effective, efficient and predictable" (Moustafa 2007, 24).[4]

Courts can also help solve one of China's biggest problems, monitoring local officials (O'Brien and Li 1999; Edin 2003). In a large, decentralized country, it is difficult for Beijing to know about local problems, let alone solve them. Information is the most basic tool of environmental enforcement, and, due to limited resources, local Environmental Protection Bureaus (EPBs) often lack it. Recall, for example, that the Shanghai EPB does not collect environmental information from more than 70 percent of registered small-scale enterprises (Warwick and Ortolano 2007, 244). Except for citizen complaints and litigation, these enterprises go unmonitored. Environmental lawsuits, then, can serve as a "fire alarm" to attract higher-level attention to the worst abuses and rein in local power holders (McCubbins and Schwartz 1984, 250; see also

---

4 It is not clear how well the Chinese government has succeeded in building investor confidence through legalization. Peerenboom and He (2008) report that commercial cases are more effectively resolved than socio-economic cases, but others suggest that Chinese courts still do not effectively guarantee property rights (Liebman 2007, 637). Foreign investors may also be willing to overlook weak courts because of the allure of China's market size and the speed with which Chinese partners can make decisions (Vogel 2011, 710).

Interview 135). As implied by the creation of the 1990 Administrative Litigation Law (ALL), which allowed lawsuits against government agencies, "Having citizens as watchdogs makes sense even to dyed-in-the-wool Leninists who . . . need on-the-ground sources of information if they are to uncover and stop misconduct" (O'Brien and Li 2005, 13). In this way, environmental lawsuits can find and discipline the worst polluters and, in so doing, help the Chinese government fulfill basic responsibilities toward its citizens (Interview 11; Xu 2005, 27; Jiang 2006).

Of course, there are many ways the state can control local officials and stop pollution besides citizen-initiated environmental litigation. In 1960s Japan, for example, the central government responded to four major pollution lawsuits by strengthening the environmental protection bureaucracy and creating a state-run compensation system for environmental damage claims (Upham 1987). Or in 1980s Brazil, leaders empowered national government prosecutors to sue polluters and local environmental agencies for not doing their job (McAllister 2008). The politics of institutional choice, or why one solution wins out over another, depends a great deal on how officials perceive costs, especially the costs of using courts. In contemporary China, where we know little about how leaders think, observers are often left to deduce intent from outcomes. As decentralization and the decline of communist ideology increased local discretion in the 1990s and 2000s, for example, the ALL was interpreted by many as an attempt to rein in local officials and, in so doing, extend the legitimacy of the Chinese Communist Party (CCP) (Ginsburg 2008, 67–71). Still, litigation is not China's sole strategy for environmental improvement. Citizen lawsuits fit into an array of state initiatives, including bigger EPB budgets, environmental targets, and new laws.

Finally, "ruling the country by law" (*yifazhiguo*), the legal principle written into the constitution in 1999, connotes both good governance and modernity. As part of efforts to appear more modern in the early 2000s, Chinese courts underwent reforms to bring them in line with perceived international standards. Judges, for example, started donning a black gown and keeping order with a gavel during hearings.[5] There was also a construction drive, culminating in claims that 70 percent of courts were renovated or re-built between 2000 and 2006 (Balme 2010, 168). Certainly, Chinese courtrooms felt surprisingly Western by the time I was doing fieldwork in the mid-2000s, from the state seal on the wall to the court recorder typing in the middle of the room. A State Council white paper sheds light on the logic of these visual changes: "The rule of law signifies that a political civilization has developed to a certain historic stage." It is the "crystallization of human wisdom" that is "desired and pursued by people of all countries" (State Council 2008). Law, in this formulation, reflects the evolution of China's entire political civilization. It is a universal value – the very crystallization of human wisdom – and an integral part of what it means to be a modern state.

To be clear, China's turn toward law and litigation is not a sign of political liberalization, but of authoritarian responsiveness. The CCP is increasingly searching out public feedback in order to draft sound policies and encourage political loyalty (Cai 2004; Gilboy and Read 2008).[6] The Ministry of Justice (MoJ), for example, solicited external comments on the 2007 amendments to the Lawyers Law, a first for the agency. Even civil rights lawyer Li Heping, a well-known government critic, acknowledged the request for outside opinions marked a significant improvement.[7] As public participation in decision making gains currency, lawsuits are seen as a way to hear and solve citizen problems. Environmental complaints rose significantly in the 2000s, and from the CCP's perspective, litigation is far preferable to protests (Gu 2008, 275). As leaders admit, extreme environmental degradation is already affecting social stability: pollution-related mass incidents (the official term for

---

5 There were interesting local attempts to indigenize these Western symbols. For example, the embroidery on judges' robes shows socialist motifs like a stalk of wheat and a gear wheel (Michelson 2005).

6 For more on the move toward pluralism within one-party rule, see Mertha (2008) and Leonard (2008, 66–67).

7 See Heping Li, The river turns eastward to the sea: My views on the amended law on lawyers, November 27, 2007, Stacy Mosher trans. Copy on file with the author.

protest) rose an average of 29 percent annually between 1996 and 2011, with more than 60,000 incidents in 2006 (Pan 2006; Plumer 2008; Caijing 2012).[8] Lawsuits are not a panacea, but they can be combined with complaint hotlines, public hearings, and mediation to stimulate responsiveness to citizen needs and provide the state with a safety valve to head off unrest.

Everyday Control

Harnessing the law to serve state goals is a risky strategy. Despite widespread agreement at the top of the state that legalization can be combined with one-party rule, world events in the mid-2000s increased leaders' skittishness about citizen power. In particular, they watched the color revolutions in the former Soviet Union and the Balkans with a careful eye on China's own NGOs, lawyers, and other potential rabble-rousers.[9] According to several sources, President Hu Jintao was reported to have asked officials at an internal party conference in May 2005 to guard against Chinese imitation of these uprisings (Spector and Krickovic 2007, 18; Wilson 2009, 372). In 2008, lower-level court and police officials received a similar message from a state-sponsored documentary titled "Lessons From the Color Revolutions" (Lam 2008, 3). As top leaders increased their vigilance, litigation came under special scrutiny because it is inherently adversarial and politicized. No one wanted the demonstrations over court decisions that are standard fare in most legal systems or, worse still, lawyer-led protests against state assaults on judicial independence, like those in Pakistan in 2007.

Long-term ambivalence over law and courts is a sustained balancing act. Although China aspires to predictable, efficient law, similar to

---

8 Pan Yue, the outspoken deputy director of the MEP, openly talks about how local government officials looking for "quick achievements" condone pollution, infringing on local rights, and sparking instability (Liu 2007).

9 The color revolutions include the Rose Revolution (Georgia, 2003), the Orange Revolution (Ukraine, 2004) and the Tulip Revolution (Kyrgyzstan, 2005). For more on the Chinese response to the color revolutions, see Spector and Krickovic (2007), Wilson (2009), and *The World* (2007).

Singapore, there is always the lurking danger that courts will support complaints against the regime. At a time when tamping down protest is a top concern and spending on internal policing exceeds the army budget, how does China keep the legal system in line? How can Shanghai mayor Han Zheng tell protestors opposed to extending the maglev train that the government "welcome[s] citizens to voice complaints through legal channels" and remain confident that litigation will not launch a broader political challenge? (Xinhua 2008a).

In other countries, crisis tactics are a common solution to this dilemma. When courts threaten political power, leaders often intervene to reverse decisions, limit judicial review, or reshuffle key personnel (Tate 1993, 318–19). After the 1988 *Chng Suan Tze* decision released several dissidents from prison, for example, the Singapore government passed constitutional amendments limiting judicial review over similar cases in the future and abolishing almost all avenues of appeal for those arrested under the Internal Security Act (Silverstein 2003). Or when supreme court decisions started impinging on Zimbabwe president Robert Mugabe's political priorities in 2001, he replaced the chief justice and added another three judges (Widner and Scher 2008, 249–51). In these moments, there is usually little official attempt to cloak heavy-handed tactics in legal language. The cost of averting a crisis is credible commitment to the law. However expedient, this makes the government look repressive and iron-fisted. As a result, direct confrontation is usually a last resort. Day-to-day, subtler forms of everyday control keep authoritarian legal systems in check.

Many accounts of everyday control focus on judges, particularly the indoctrination and incentives designed to ensure they prioritize state interests (Hilbink 2007; Moustafa 2007, 46–50). In China, judges are also key. The vast majority of judges are CCP members, and all judges are appointed and approved by the state (Landry 2008a, 209). Once on the bench, directives from the Supreme People's Court (SPC) and policy statements help judges read key political priorities. Decisions that are reversed on appeal and judged wrong by court administrators can lead to fines, demotion, and transfer.[10] Everyday control also requires the state to pay close attention to lawyers. Often, violence and intimidation coerce lawyers to drop individual cases and abandon networks capable of sustained and strategic litigation (Moustafa 2007, 54; Widner and Scher 2008, 235). Indeed, in mid-2000s China, well-known political lawyers such as Gao Zhisheng and Chen Guangcheng were beaten up, interrogated, and imprisoned (Fu 2006; Human Rights Watch 2008, 32–51). At the same time, however, most of China's lawyers never experience this kind of hard-line social control. As some voices inside China acknowledge (Gu 2008, 285), resorting to harassment, prison terms, and violence runs the risk of radicalization. Even states with a strong police presence often try to discourage contention before it starts and regulation is one of the most important tools keeping Chinese lawyers in check.

To start, the Chinese government controls the number of accredited lawyers. Beginning in 2002, passing the national judicial exam became a pre-requisite for a lawyer's license. The test is abysmally hard to pass and less than 10 percent of applicants succeed. The number of lawyers increased an average of just 13.1 percent per year from 1981 to 2004, despite the growing financial appeal of the profession (Zhu 2007, 340). In addition to a license, renewed yearly by the Justice Bureau, lawyers must also join the local lawyers association and retain employment at a registered law firm in order to practice. These three requirements, especially the yearly license renewal, give officials a great deal of leverage over individual practitioners. "The first warning," one Shanghai lawyer explained, "is that someone at the Judicial Bureau will give you a simple phone call to invite you to 'have a chat'" (quoted in Human Rights Watch 2008, 87). The next step is making trouble for recalcitrant lawyers. As two Beijing lawyers discovered, intransigence can lead to delayed license renewal (Interview 116) and pressure on law firms to find a new employee (Interview 70). Finally, lawyers (like everyone else) are subject

---

10 Several judges discussed penalties for "wrong cases" in their courts (Interviews 74, 88, 93).

to broad state secrets laws that can be deployed against the truly defiant (Peerenboom 2002, 351).

Overall, China's approach to everyday control seeks a balance between allowing litigation and controlling individuals. Lawsuits can serve official goals as long as everyone in the courtroom maintains allegiance to the state. The oath introduced by the Ministry of Justice in 2012 makes this bargain explicit. As a condition of practice, lawyers must swear loyalty to the country and allegiance to Party leadership (BBC 2012). Loyal lawyers like these can help clients see the government's perspective and drop irrational demands (Gu 2008, 292). Even President Hu Jintao says that "strengthening lawyers' ranks" can combat corruption and improve law enforcement (Li 2004a). Indeed, state belief in the usefulness of lawyers lends the profession a degree of freedom. Lawyers and observers agree that control is "ad hoc, reactive and not omnipresent" and that lawyers are generally left alone (Fu 2006, 19). At least in Beijing, one lawyer explained, the Justice Bureau simply "can't keep track of all of us" (Interview 110).

Inside the Central Bureaucracy

Day to day, the authoritarian dilemma over courts plays out in private policy battles among bureaucracies, factions, and interest groups jostling for power. Although most bargaining occurs in private, occasional public signals suggest the general contours of commitment surrounding environmental litigation. Drafts of the 2007 revisions to the Civil Procedure Law and the 2008 Water Pollution Prevention and Control Law included provisions for public interest environmental litigation. Although these provisions were later cut, their initial inclusion suggests the idea had some political traction as early as the mid-2000s, well before it was written into the 2012 amendments to the Civil Procedure Law.

Throughout the decade, two supporters of public interest environmental lawsuits were the Ministry of Environment Protection (MEP) and the Supreme People's Procuratorate. In both cases, new public interest provisions would boost the agency's profile and counterbalance the powerful, economic growth-oriented National Development and Reform Commission and Transportation Bureau (Interviews 12, 19, 135, 140). In a 2005 submission to the State Council, the Supreme People's Procuratorate wrote that rising pollution levels made "the establishment of a system for civil and administrative environmental lawsuits both necessary and feasible" (quoted in Bie 2007, 457). The hope behind those words was that legal reforms would grant the agency the high-profile power to sue in the public interest. At the same time, some reformers at MEP continue to favor recruiting citizen, NGO, and journalist allies to help pressure polluters (Interviews 2, 135). Finally, there are signs that the courts are starting to see beyond their initial fear that any sign of welcome would cause the volume of environmental lawsuits to skyrocket (Interview 140). As discussed below, a number of cities have opened environmental courts and SPC judges in Beijing judges also express concern that court authority might be undermined if the "final line of defense" refuses to accept cases (Interview 104).

Still, this tentative association of interests is far from a solid coalition. Even the MEP is not unequivocally in favor of change. Insiders report that the agency is divided between reformers, notably in the Legal Affairs Department, and warier divisions (Interview 135). Some also see the sidelining of Vice-Minister Pan Yue, China's most outspoken and well-known environmental bureaucrat, as a signal that the agency is taking a more conservative turn. Pan was passed over for promotion at the 2007 Party Congress and lost his post as agency spokesperson in 2008 (Interview 147; Watts 2009). In addition, reformers face serious opposition from officials concerned about loosening Party control over the legal system. Top court officials, including SPC president Wang Shengjun, echo former Politburo Standing Committee member Luo Gan's statement that "there is no question about where legal departments should stand. The correct political stand is where the party stands" (quoted in Kahn 2007; see also Tang 2007; Lam 2008). Often, belief in a correct political stance is accompanied by worries about the negative influence of Western rule of law. Warnings against "infiltration and disruption activities by Western countries," as the president of the Jilin High Court put it, suggest wariness about lawsuits brought by citizens, let alone NGOs (quoted in Lam 2008, 3).

Mixed Signals: Signs of Encouragement from the Central Leadership

Although bureaucratic power struggles help explain the origins of mixed signals, they give little idea of how plaintiffs, lawyers, or even low-ranking judges read the political winds. As others have also observed (O'Brien and Li 2006; Hassid 2008; Wright 2008; Cai 2010; Stern and O'Brien 2012), people in China are highly attentive to cues from the state, especially when they are lobbying for change. Observable indications of official preferences, which I call signals, came up routinely in interviews, particularly in discussing trends or sketching the broader political context. The signal most frequently mentioned was the fate of lawsuits elsewhere. Those I interviewed discussed successful and unsuccessful cases in roughly equal measure and saw these outcomes, at least in part, as an indication of political preferences. Many were also attuned to the evolving priorities of top leaders, as expressed in speeches, regulations, and policies. Looking up at the state from below, they reported a range of mixed signals surrounding the desirability of environmental litigation.

What follows is an overview of the most significant of these signals. Although the central government appears more interested in stopping pollution than empowering courts, it is unequivocal about neither. Pro-environment rhetoric and policies mask unease about public involvement, just as disquiet about lawyers and large-scale litigation co-exist with efforts to make the law more accessible. On the positive side of the ledger, signs of central support help explain why some see environmental cases as less risky than other types of rights-related litigation (Huang 2006, 155; Interviews 3, 27, 72, 110, 116, 124). At the same time, negative signals reinforce the popular understanding that environmental cases remain politically sensitive and hard to win.

The most visible sign of encouragement was the increased attention to environmental protection discussed in Chapter 1.[11] During the first decade of the 2000s, top leaders' speeches often referenced sustainable development and the importance of environmental protection. At the seventeenth Party Congress in 2007, President Hu Jintao introduced the term "ecological civilization" in a particularly influential report that also called environmental protection a "vital interest" of the Chinese people. The elevation of environmental rhetoric was not lost on observers. Citing Hu's report and a 2005 State Council decision, SPC vice-president Wan E'xiang found it "evident that the Communist Party Central Committee and the State Council have raised the issue of China's environmental protection to a higher level" (Wan 2011; see also Chen 2009, xiii). The Chinese media also helped magnify awareness of the leadership's pro-environment turn. Environmental slogans were widely reported and, at least inside some state-run media outlets, interpreted as encouragement to cover more environmental news. The Chinese documentary *Mouthpiece (Houshe)*, directed by Guo Xizhe and released in 2009, contains a telling scene in which an editor at a state-run TV program coaches reporters on how to turn themes from the seventeenth Party Congress into news:

> If we push forward this emphasis on environmental protection, it will be a good manifestation of our adherence to [the principles of] harmonious society (*hexie shehui*) and scientific development (*kexue fazhan*) from the seventeenth Party Congress...For example, we promote clean gas. So many years after it was introduced, what has been the impact of clean gas on Shenzhen's air quality?

11 Many interviewees talked about the greening of the state (especially see interviews 7, 23, 30, 36, 72, 78, 81, 87, 94, 105, 122, 127, 135, 137, 145, 166, 175).

By 2009, one staff member at an environmental NGO felt "like we have the luxury of having so much rhetoric in support of what we're doing ... it can't be that sensitive" (Interview 145).

High-level attention to the environment also translated into increased interest in using courts to help solve environmental problems. In 2005, political elites started publicly calling for environmental public interest litigation as one way to fix a situation in which "polluting enterprises are local heroes" for providing jobs and tax revenue (Liang 2005). Liang Congjie and Chen Xunru brought up the topic at the Chinese People's Political Consultative Conference (CPPCC), a political advisory body, in 2005 and 2006 while a group led by Lü Zhongmei raised the idea at the 2006 NPC (Bie 2007, 449–56). Around the same time, academics and journalists also began writing about environmental public interest litigation, particularly the idea that a wider range of groups and individuals should be allowed to bring environmental lawsuits on behalf of the public interest. By 2007, researchers at Zhongnan University of Economics and Law could claim a "consensus among scholars" that some combination of the procuratorate, the EPB, NGOs, and citizens should be allowed to initiate public interest environmental litigation. Experiments with environmental public interest litigation started to pop up in China's environmental courts in the late 2000s, and, by 2012, the Civil Procedure Law had been revised to allow lawful authorities (*falü guiding de jiguan*) and relevant organizations (*you guan zuzhi*) to initiate environmental public interest lawsuits (Standing Committee of the National People's Congress 2012). Although not yet clear how "lawful authorities" or "relevant organizations" will be defined in practice, the change indicates growing support for the idea that China should "give law greater clout in [the] battle against pollution" (Jiang 2006).

Tentative support for environmental litigation is also visible in national laws. Most important, a 2001 SPC explanation – a document that instructs lower courts how to deal with unclear areas of the law – shifted the burden of proof to the defendant in pollution cases (SPC 2001a). In effect, polluters are responsible for disproving any link between their behavior and plaintiffs' losses. Shortly thereafter, the shifted burden of proof was written into the 2004 Solid Waste Law, the 2008 Water Pollution Law, and the 2009 Tort Law.[12] By the end of the first decade of the 2000s, the principle was entrenched. In Japan, in contrast, it took the "moral momentum" of four major pollution cases to shift the burden of proof through court opinions (Upham 1987, 44). At least on paper, the new rules make it far easier for plaintiffs to win in court as well. Just after the revisions to the Tort Law, an American law firm commented that a literal interpretation of the standard would set "a very high bar for defendants," especially because of the difficulty of proving a negative (Freeman and Feng 2010).

As part of a larger revival of "justice for the people" (*sifa weimin*), other central policy documents also stress the importance of legal aid for environmental cases.[13] In the 2000s, litigation on behalf of "weak and disadvantaged groups," usually defined to include the handicapped, women, juveniles, the elderly, the poor, and laid-off, unemployed, or migrant workers, became an officially sanctioned way to help those left behind in China's economic transition. There was a dramatic expansion of the legal aid system, from 132,097 cases and a budget of 27.5 million RMB (US$4.4 million) in 1999 to 727,401 cases and a budget of 1 billion RMB (US$158 million) in 2010 (Zhu 2007, 404; China Law Yearbook 2011, 1069). There were also efforts to make civil claims easier, including a State Council decision to lower litigation fees in 2007.

General interest in making courts accessible spilled over to environmental issues too. A State Council decision called for improvements to environment-related legal aid in 2005 and the Ministry of Justice listed environmental protection as a legal aid priority area in 2008 because "places and work units (*danwei*) that harm the masses'

---

12 Although a SPC notice shifted the burden of proof in environmental cases as early as 1992, the change went largely unnoticed until it was re-affirmed by the 2001 explanation.

13 The SPC re-introduced this phrase in 2003, accompanied by encouragement to reach out to petitioners (Liebman 2011, 20–22).

environmental rights" should be held responsible (State Council 2005; Ministry of Justice 2008). Encouragement for environmental legal aid was written into the 2008 Water Pollution Law, the same year that the state-run China Legal Aid Foundation established a "green action legal aid" fund (Ministry of Justice 2008a). By the time I attended the opening of an environmental rights protection center in Hebei province in June 2007, it was already a ribbon-cutting platitude to say that China "needs lawyers and the law" to protect weak groups, support environmental protection, and preserve stability.

Mixed Signals: Signs of Discouragement from the Central Leadership

In the 2000s, these signs of encouragement were matched by strong indications of unease. Despite unprecedented national attention to energy and environmental targets, economic performance indicators often take local precedence, especially in China's many indebted townships. A typical story from People's Daily reveals ongoing pollution at a factory in Liaoning province, despite orders from the MEP and the provincial EPB to stop production. According to a local government official, the decision to subvert orders from higher-ups reflects a "holistic plan to realize social stability, economic growth and environmental protection" (*People's Daily* 2010).

In the local parlance, environmental litigation is "a little bit politically sensitive" because in the past, concern over degradation has sometimes masked a political agenda. In the 1980s, green movements in Eastern Europe helped overthrow communist regimes in countries including Bulgaria, Poland, Hungary, and Czechoslovakia (Jancar-Webster 1998, 73–76; Economy 2004, 249–252). A decade later, political scientist Jane Dawson found that protests over nuclear power in the former USSR gave local nationalists a way to demand regional self-determination (1996). In China, environmental NGOs and lawyers rarely publicly mention democracy because they are well aware of official fears that

China will follow Eastern Europe.[14] Still, even if activists avoid the "d" word, environmental lawsuits can be politically sensitive. Even a seemingly straightforward monetary compensation case can touch on volatile issues such as land-use policy, urbanization, subsistence, and citizen rights. Some Chinese academics and governmental officials lump environmental complaints with other "irregular disputes" that reflect "relatively high danger to the society" and "directly or indirectly show confrontation with or revolts against the existing social order" (Gu 2008, 258).

Official discomfort with environmental lawsuits is visible in the lack of litigation stemming from major pollution incidents. The kind of oil spills and chemical leaks that hit headlines rarely become court cases. Rather, standard operating procedure is to pay off victims with a small amount of compensation, fine the company, and punish a few responsible individuals. Many believe confidential orders from the SPC sometimes instruct courts to turn away high-profile environmental cases (Interviews 13, 29, 56, 126). Certainly, local regulations governing environmental disputes often make it clear that lawsuits are an unwelcome last resort. In Shandong province, for example, regulations lay out a course of action that brings complainants to the courts only when administrative bureaus cannot resolve the problem (Shandong Province 1994).

A final sign of concern about litigation is the increasing numbers of regulations designed to keep lawyers apolitical and disputes small-scale. In 2005, an SPC notice mandated that all collective lawsuits go through Basic People's Courts (BPCs), regardless of the size of the claim. Among lawyers, this notice suggested strong political unease over collective action as well as a desire to keep complaints as local as possible. Just a year later, in 2006, the All China Lawyers Association (ACLA) passed

---

14 There are a few exceptions. In an interview with Elizabeth Economy at the Council on Foreign Relations, one activist made an explicit link between democracy and environmental activism: "Environmental work may lead to greater democracy in China. In fact, environmentalism and democracy are related. Many NGO leaders are hesitant to say [this], but I believe that the NGO movements are creating democracy" (Economy 2004, 169).

new guidelines indicating further disquiet over collective cases. The guidelines require lawyers in cases with more than ten plaintiffs to seek the local Justice Bureau's "supervision and guidance;" new reporting requirements that some lawyers see as yet another opportunity for interference (Interview 96).[15] Other recent regulations ban contingency fees in cases involving more than five plaintiffs, effectively limiting class-action representation to those who can afford up-front payment (National Development and Reform Commission 2006). And finally, Article 40 of the 2007 Lawyers Law (which some call the Law to Control Lawyers) bars lawyers from "inciting or abetting parties to engage in disturbing public order, threatening public security, and other illegal methods to resolve grievances" (Standing Committee of the National People's Congress 2007). In combination, these rules serve as effective boundary markers, warning the risk-averse majority to stay well away from fractious mass cases, especially those involving the down-and-out.

Environmental Courts and Cautious Innovation

For local officials peering up the chain of command in anticipation of changing priorities, there is more than one logical response to mixed signals. Most of the time, bureaucrats play it safe and steer as far clear of environmental lawsuits as possible. On occasion, however, mixed signals can be read as an opportunity to risk the rewards of innovation. One of the best examples of this kind of ad hoc innovation is the opening of more than sixty city- and district-level environmental courts between 2007 and 2012 (Zhang 2012). Innovators included Dalian (2004), Shijiazhuang (2004), Nanjing (2004), Shenyang (2006), Guiyang (2007), Changzhou (2008), Kunming (2008), Wuxi (2008), Beijing (2010), and Jiujiang (2010).[16] These environmental courts took various forms:

---

15 The lawyers' reports to justice bureaus that I've read straightforwardly summarize court decisions, media reports, and progress in the case to date.

16 This follows a first wave of experimentation with environmental courts. China's first environmental court was established in Wuhan in 1989, followed by similar experiments in Shenyang in 1996 and Harbin in 1999.

stand-alone environmental tribunals (*renmin fating*), environmental trial divisions (*shenpan ting*), green collegiate panels (*heyiting*), and environmental circuit courts (*xunhui fating*).[17]

This rapid burst of nearly identical experimentation reflects a tradition of local experimentation in policy making as well as career incentives to innovate. From rural de-collectivization to stock market regulation, Party authorities have a long history of encouraging local officials to try out new approaches so that the best ideas can be adopted nationally (Heilmann 2008). For ambitious officials, good press about successful experiments attracts the attention of higher-ups and can lead to promotion. Experiments with public participation in Chongqing, for example, triggered more than 60,000 news articles and won local officials a high-level presentation at the government's headquarters in Zhongnanhai (Leonard 2008, 68–71). At the same time, the penalties for failure are typically manageable or low. Projects are rarely directly terminated, but rather lapse into inactivity when political support falters or fades (Heilmann 2008, 27). To some extent, there is also ongoing pressure to come up with new ideas (*chuangxin*) (Interviews 149, 154). New institutions like environmental courts can be listed as achievements on annual evaluations and may trigger a prestigious visit from a central government delegation, as happened in Wuxi (Wuxi Intermediate Court Work Report 2011). As a Kunming lawyer pointed out, "Even President Obama needs political achievements! [The environmental courts] are like his efforts to improve health care or solve unemployment. You need to solve problems that real people face" (Interview 155).

In public, the rationale for environmental courts is decidedly green. Pro-environmental signals from the central government, particularly the

---

17 I use "environmental courts" as an umbrella term to cover freestanding environmental courts as well as environmental divisions within courts (sometimes called green chambers) and designated panels of green judges. In many cases, institutional choice was constrained by court level. Only basic-level courts can establish tribunals and circuit courts while trial divisions can only be set up at (or above) the intermediate court level. All levels of court can create collegiate panels, a slate of judges detailed to environmental cases.

seventeenth Party Congress and increasing emphasis on environmental targets, incentivized local officials to make real calls for an "ecological civilization" (Interviews 167, 173). Echoes of central rhetoric often surface in government documents that frame environmental courts as part of efforts to promote sustainable development and "build up an ecologically civilized city" (Guiyang Municipal Government 2009; see also Kunming Intermediate Court et al. 2008). Judges agree that environmental lawsuits will deter polluters and help EPBs manage cross-district pollution (Interview 173; Shu 2008; Qie 2009). The head of the Guiyang environmental tribunal went as far as to tell reporters in 2008 that judges should "break through neutrality" and encourage government agencies to cut off electricity, loans, and cheap credit to polluters (Wang 2008). As an article in *Kunming Daily* optimistically summed up, Kunming's environmental court is "a sharp sword hanging above the heads of polluters" (2010).

But even if court officials later claim credit for transforming the city from an industrial civilization to an ecological civilization, as they did in the 2011 Wuxi Intermediate Court Work Report, the record suggests that environmental commitment is often born of crisis. At a minimum, the establishment of the three most high-profile environmental courts, Wuxi, Kunming, and Guiyang, was also a response to extraordinary pollution. In 2007, Guiyang set up two environmental tribunals in an unusually fast sixty-eight days because of fears that pollution would jeopardize drinking water for 3.9 million city inhabitants (Interview 173; Gao 2010, 3). Likewise, arsenic pollution in Kunming's Yangzonghai Lake in 2008 not only prompted a fishing ban and the suspension of 30,000 residents' water supply, but also accelerated the emergence of Kunming's environmental court (Interview 154; Yuan 2009). And in Wuxi, the head of the environmental court told reporters that record pollution in nearby Tai Lake was a factor in the decision to establish his division (Qie 2008; see also Interview 175).

So far, the early history of environmental courts suggests ambivalence about the enterprise. After all, hanging a plaque, reassigning judges, and sending out a press release are innovative moves that also preserve flexibility. There is no guarantee that an environmental protection court will live up to its name by accepting cases, actively pursuing investigations, or making green decisions. As political pressures shift, and officials reorder their goals accordingly, environmental courts can adjust their activity, too. Indeed, environmental courts have shown a mix of experimentation and caution.

On the one hand, there have been a few high-profile moments of innovation. Trial regulations in Wuxi, Guiyang, and Kunming allow social organizations (*you guan shehui tuanti*) to sue in the public interest and the Guiyang and Wuxi environmental courts accepted two cases brought forth by the All-China Environment Federation (ACEF), a government-backed group, in July 2009. After years of academic calls to expand standing, these cases were heralded as a breakthrough (Shieber 2009). In fact, ACEF was best known for bureaucratic inertia and timidity before this case (Interviews 10, 12, 24, 94). Shortly after ACEF was founded in 2006, the legal aid department changed its name from the Center for the Defense of Environmental Rights (*weihu huanjing quanli zhongxin*) to the less strident and less political Environmental Legal Services Bureau (*falü yuanzhu bu*). Despite some progress, such as a legal aid hotline and a lawyer-training program, the department won only three cases in its first two years.

Experiments with government-initiated environmental litigation, which started to pop up in regular courts in the 2000s,[18] have continued in environmental courts, too. In April 2010, for example, the Kunming procuratorate teamed up with the city EPB to sue two pig farms for contaminating the underground water supply (Chu 2010). The government won the case, and officials publicly hoped that the 4.3 million RMB (US$682,540) payout would serve as a valuable deterrent to other polluters. These early forays into government-led public interest litigation

---

18 For example, the Guangdong procuratorate brought two different pollution cases to the Guangzhou Maritime Court in 2008 and 2009 (Deng 2009).

Table 4.1. *Environmental Court Caseloads*

Location	Year established	Number of cases	Main types of cases
Guiyang	2007	524 (through October 20, 2012)	70% criminal[19]
Wuxi	2008	More than 300 (through May 2009)	95% non-litigation administrative execution
Kunming	2008	17 (through April 2010)	41% criminal

Sources: Gao (2010); Lei (2010); Guiyang Qingzhen Environmental Court, personal communication, October 23, 2012.

won national attention and support. An SPC judge told *Legal Daily* that "this kind of innovative environmental enforcement coordination mechanism . . . is increasingly urgent and necessary" (Yuan 2009). Would-be imitators showed interest as well. In an award-winning essay posted on the Jiangxi Court Web site, judges from the Nanchang High Tech Industrial Zone Basic Court discuss the advantages of opening an environmental court in the Poyang Lake Ecological Economic Zone (Kuang and Xu 2010).

But at the same time, others have been disappointed by slow pace of change and an embarrassing (*ganga*) lack of cases (Interview 159; Lei 2010; Sun 2010. As Table 4.1. shows, one issue is the type of case filed. In Kunming and Guiyang, court caseloads are dominated by criminal cases brought forth by the procuratorate, many of which involve illegal logging. In Wuxi, meanwhile, close cooperation between the environmental court and the EPB has translated into high numbers of non-litigation administrative execution cases (NAECs) (*feisu xingzheng zhixing anzi*), a type of administrative litigation in which government agencies seek court enforcement of administrative decisions. Among this array of criminal cases and NAECs, what is missing is civil environmental lawsuits, especially high-profile, important cases.

19 The 70 percent figure refers only to 2007 and 2008. In 2012, the Guiyang court reported a slowdown in criminal cases. That year, they handled 39 percent fewer criminal cases than in 2008.

Moreover, critics say that the handful of public interest lawsuits too often tackle easy targets rather than the most important sources of pollution (Interviews 147, 154, 164). Nor does public interest litigation necessarily boost judicial authority. Cases brought to court by government agencies require so much intra-governmental consultation that the hearing can feel like a show (*biaoyan*) followed by a preordained decision (Interviews 159, 164). Along these lines, Kunming's first public interest lawsuit, the 2010 case in which the procuratorate and the EPB jointly sued two pig farms, was especially controversial. Environmental lawyers complained that the case was too small-scale and insignificant to have lasting influence. In their words, the lawsuit is like "using anti-aircraft guns to kill a mosquito" (Chu 2010) and "a breakthrough can't come from no where" (Interview 149). Others saw the EPB's dual identity – as both enforcers and public interest plaintiffs – as unfair.[20]

In keeping with the courts' cautious approach, litigation brought by NGOs has inspired particular unease.[21] The Kunming environmental trial division, for example, never replied to a 2010 request to file the first environmental public interest lawsuit brought forth by a grassroots NGO, an attempt by Chongqing Green Volunteers to sue a coal-fired power plant over failure to operate desulfurization equipment. The lawyers who drafted the complaint knew the case was unprecedented and might be turned down but hoped that officials would explain their logic (Interview 149). When asked about the case in March 2011, a Yunnan judge called it "a declaration of war (*zhandou xiwen*), not a case with a basis in law" (Interview 153). However, the court kept silent, preferring to let the issue die rather than publicly debate the legality of the claim.[22] Even cases brought forth by the government-backed

---

20 One lawyer involved in the lawsuit believes future cases should be brought by NGOs because they will have an easier time winning public trust (Interview 155).

21 Environmental courts are cautious about litigation brought by citizens, too. Only Guiyang allows citizen-initiated environmental public interest litigation.

22 Hydropower production was down more than 80 percent in Yunnan province in the first quarter of 2010, so the case may have arisen at a moment when continued operation of the power plant was essential to meeting energy demand (Moser and Sovacool 2011, 17).

All-China Environment Federation (ACEF) have been contentious. The head of the Wuxi environmental court describes the court's most daring moment, accepting a ACEF-initiated case in July 2009, as a "foolhardy" decision made without input from higher-ups. In his retelling, the case ended in meditation rather than a legal decision because of fears that progressing too fast would be counterproductive (Meng 2010).

In addition to political caution, inexperience has slowed down courts too. At first, an environmental lawyer recalled, Kunming government agencies "had no idea how to bring a lawsuit or what to do" (Interview 155). Even several years after the environmental trial division opened, judges were still wrestling with practical issues like how much evidence should be required to file a lawsuit and how to commission a scientifically informed appraisal (Interview 153).[23] City officials are likewise still pondering how to distribute money from Kunming's environmental public interest litigation fund, established in 2010 to provide eligible NGOs and government agencies with up to 200,000 RMB (US$31,745) for litigation fees.[24] With no role model to follow, officials have yet to fix fair lawyers' fees or set up a reimbursement process. Of course, there are advantages to moving slowly as well. Future priorities may well change and, much like environmental courts themselves, the fund can support environmental claims or lapse into inertia accordingly. Judges themselves express concern that environmental courts might be disbanded if support from the leadership falters or if they fail to define a clear mission and attract more cases (Interviews 153, 172; ACEF and NRDC 2011, 15).

Another possibility is that political risk may lessen over time if routine practices numb political sensitivities or local experiments win central approval. Recent signals from top court officials certainly seem encouraging. After several years of letting environmental courts operate in a legal grey zone, a 2010 SPC notice granted courts permission

---

23 These practical problems are present in all environmental lawsuits, but are usually resolved on an ad hoc basis because environmental cases comprise such a small percent of a court's docket. For more on issues with appraisals, see Chapter 2.

24 For more on the fund, see Chu (2010). As of March 2011, no money from the fund had yet been distributed (Interview 153).

to open specialized tribunals in areas with lots of environmental disputes (SPC 2010b). SPC president Wang Shengjun also proudly cited efforts to "promote the establishment of local environmental courts" in his 2011 work report to the National People's Congress, a statement all the more remarkable because Wang is hardly known as a reformer (Supreme People's Court 2011). Much like the slow start of administrative divisions in the 1990s, environmental courts may yet uncover a steady supply of cases and become a permanent institution.

5 On the Frontlines

The Judges

AT THE PINNACLE OF THE STATE, CHINA'S TOP LEADERS
agree that law should serve the Chinese Communist Party
(CCP). Down in the trenches, at the frontlines of decision
making, Chinese judges in civil environmental cases decipher this dic-
tum and attempt to diffuse local discontent.[1] But why do judges make
the decisions they do? This chapter looks at legal decisions as a window
to how political ambivalence over courts shapes judges' political logic.
Amid official rhetoric about public participation, lifting up the poor and
abating pollution, the question of how judges interpret competing state
signals remains open. Whether goals are implemented or quietly aban-
doned depends a great deal on judicial decision making, particularly how
closely judges hew to the law or exercise autonomy in making decisions.

This chapter draws on forty-two decisions in pollution compensation disputes (*huanjing wuran sunhai peichang jiufen*) from 2000–2007.[2]

---

1 The image of the commanding heights of leadership and the trenches of political decision making comes from political scientist Joel Migdal's anthropology of the state
(2001, 116–124). Environmental inspectors, of course, interact daily with polluters and
are also on the frontlines of environmental protection in a different way.

2 This sample of decisions comes from the database *Beida Fayi* (http://www.lawyee.net).
In December 2007, my research assistant downloaded all cases from 2000–2007 containing the search terms "environment" (*huanjing*) or "pollution" (*wuran*). I discarded
three decisions because they lacked basic information about the facts of the case, which
left me with forty-two decisions. An independent company since 2003, *Beida Fayi* is
one of several national legal databases aiming to become China's version of Lexus-
Nexis or Westlaw. Many of the cases on *Beida Fayi* are publicly available – either

Chinese legal decisions are not public documents, and this selection, which was downloaded from a Beijing-based legal database, is almost certainly not a random sample. Conversations with database employees lead me to believe that there are too many cases involving major losses, especially from rich areas of the country, and too few class actions. Still, even if not representative, the cases recounted below illustrate how judges think about pollution disputes and the kinds of solutions they deem appropriate. Both Western and Chinese socio-legal research on Chinese courts rarely looks carefully at decisions, probably because they are largely seen as uninformative, pro forma recitations of the facts (Zhang 2003, 88).[3] Yet legal decisions are getting more interesting. In 2005, the Supreme People's Court (SPC) issued a notice telling lower-level courts that written decisions should include legal reasoning (Liebman 2007, 626).[4] In my sample, this is clearly starting to happen. Three pages, the average length of the decisions I examined, is long enough to at least hint at the court's concerns and rationale. While these opinions do not offer groundbreaking legal insight, they reflect what political scientist Martin Shapiro calls "the popular element" in judging (1981, 56).[5] Even courts in one-party states are often compelled to offer public justification, however glancing, for their actions.

published on the Internet or in case compendiums compiled by courts and publishers – although the database also obtains some decisions through "cooperative relationships" (*hezuo guanxi*) with individual courts. Courts sometimes publish decisions online or through a court publishing house because they have reference value (*cankao de zuoyong*) as correct applications of the law in typical (*dianxing*) cases.

3 For an example of recent work looking at legal decisions, see Liebman (2013).

4 On how legal decisions are getting longer and better, also see Peerenboom (2002, 287).

5 A *Southern Weekend* profile of one of China's busiest courts reported a caseload of 7,540 cases split among 13 judges (Zhao 2008). Under these circumstances, one judge explained, if a decision "explains the case clearly, you can write it succinctly and that's fine" (quoted in Zhao 2008). American judges face similar pressure to get decisions out fast. Patricia Wald, a former judge on the United States Court of Appeals for the District of Columbia, writes that "thinking great thoughts is…out…[F]inal opinions will usually be committee products with all the obstacles to virtuoso performance that entails" (1992–1993, 178).

My starting point in analyzing these decisions is a typology based on two key elements of judicial decision making in one-party states: 1) the degree of *legal formality* (how closely judges adhere to the letter of the law) and 2) *individual autonomy* (judges' power to make decisions rather than follow instructions from political elites). Thinking along these two dimensions highlights variation in judicial strategy. While Chinese judges typically comply with clear political instructions regardless of the legal merits of those orders, a combination of shifting incentives, uneven application of the law, and political ambivalence produce a degree of de facto discretion, especially in low-profile, run-of-the-mill cases. Most of the cases in my sample deal with exactly this kind of everyday justice. While researchers tend to focus on high courts[6] and landmark cases[7] rather than the trudge of low-level judicial work (Kapiszewski and Taylor 2008, 755), judges are the "assembly line workers" responsible for negotiating competing state goals and fashioning locally acceptable bargains (Zhao 2008). As others have found (Liebman 2007, 637; Kapiszewski and Taylor 2008, 745), rulings in mundane cases can also display real legal creativity. Everyday pollution disputes show innovation at the margins as courts occasionally offer new legal interpretations or validate new types of claims. Day to day, Chinese judges arbitrate between citizen grievances and state goals to shape the practice of environmental law.

Two Dimensions of Judicial Decision Making in One-Party States

Looking at Chinese judges as strategic actors provides entry into a broader conversation about judicial politics in illiberal states. In America, there is an active debate about when and whether judges strictly follow the law, vote according to their convictions, or strategically nudge along policy change. In strong single-party states, however,

6 Constitutional courts have attracted an especially great deal of attention. See Klug (2000), Jacobsohn (2003), Ginsberg (2003), and Hirschl (2008).
7 For in-depth examinations of groundbreaking Chinese cases, see Shen (2003), Hand (2006), and Kellogg (2007).

less attention has been paid to judges' choices.[8] Researchers often assume that, as in Augusto Pinochet's Chile, judges uphold the status quo because institutional incentives effectively bind their interests to the Party's (Hilbink 2007). This conventional wisdom, although often correct in broad outline, overlooks variation in the dynamics of decision making. Even when law serves the state, the degree of extra-legal interference and judicial attention to legal texts depends on regime, court, and type of case.

Two aspects of judicial decision making are particularly helpful in understanding this variation. The first dimension is judges' degree of *individual autonomy*. In short, who decides cases: individual judges or political elites?[9] While a bench of three judges typically hears civil cases in Chinese courts, there is no guarantee that the judges who try the case will decide it.[10] Important cases are often decided by the court adjudication committee *(shenpan weiyuanhui)*, comprised of top court officials appointed by the local people's congress and approved by the CCP (Zhu 2007, 177). Courts are also officially under the supervision of the political-legal committee of the local branch of CCP, and particular cases can elicit a meeting and instructions. But the demands of scale dictate that these direct orders, or what is sometimes called "telephone justice," is reserved for the most high-profile, politically sensitive cases. Chinese courts handled 6 million civil cases in 2010, and only a small percentage are important enough to warrant external attention (Zhu 2007, 205; Zhu 2010, 68; Peerenboom 2010, 86; Fu and Peerenboom 2010, 125). Observers suggest that criminal cases are most likely to trigger intervention from the political-legal committee, especially when government bureaus disagree (Yu 2009, 63). Judges, at least in most everyday civil cases, are quietly left to the day-to-day work of hearing cases and making decisions.

---

8 For exceptions, see Ai (2008) and He (2009).

9 Talking about "political elites" rather than "the Party" leaves room for the possibility of intra-Party disagreement. The CCP is not a monolithic united front, but a collection of bureaucracies, factions, and individuals.

10 Minor cases are heard by one judge.

The second dimension is adherence to the law, or what law scholars call legal formality. At one extreme, judges apply the letter of the law without consideration for consequences or extenuating circumstances. At the other extreme, laws and regulations give way to wide-ranging judicial discretion. Lower court judges are particularly likely to engage in this kind of informal problem solving to maintain local harmony (Coates 1987; Nader 1990). Keeping both sides happy, even if it means bending the law, makes intuitive sense to local judges concerned with avoiding further conflict and maintaining judicial prestige. As one Australian chief magistrate explained, "It's eighty percent dealing with people [and] twenty percent law" (Roach Anleu and Mack 2007, 191).

Conceptually, both dimensions are a continuum with room for intermediate positions between the two poles. In particular, political elites are capable of influencing individual cases through signaling that stops far short of an official meeting or phone call. When law is officially subordinated to the state, Party values permeate courts. Directions are usually unnecessary when the vast majority of judges are CCP members[11] and all judges are well-steeped in Party priorities. This is true in many large organizations: even absent specific instructions, workers obtain a good idea of what bosses want through general announcements, rumors, and common sense. In investigating the 1986 Challenger explosion, for example, U.S. physicist Richard Feynman concluded that President Ronald Regan had not rushed the space shuttle launch to coincide with his annual State of the Union address. Rather, as Feynman writes, "The people in a big system like NASA *know* what has to be done – *without* being told" (2007, 217).[12]

---

11 Although I have not seen official numbers on the percent of judges that are Party members, small-n surveys by Chinese researchers suggest that at least 80 percent of judges belong to the CCP. In a 1997 article, legal scholar Jerome Cohen also estimates based on personal interviews that more than 90 percent of judges are CCP members (797).

12 Otto Ulc makes a similar observation about courts in 1950s Czechoslovakia: "In about ninety percent of the court agenda, there was not the slightest sign of interference in our decision-making...But the sorry experience with the remaining ten percent and the awareness that someone might at any time inflict his 'suggestion' upon us, conditioned *all* our adjudication" (1972, 61).

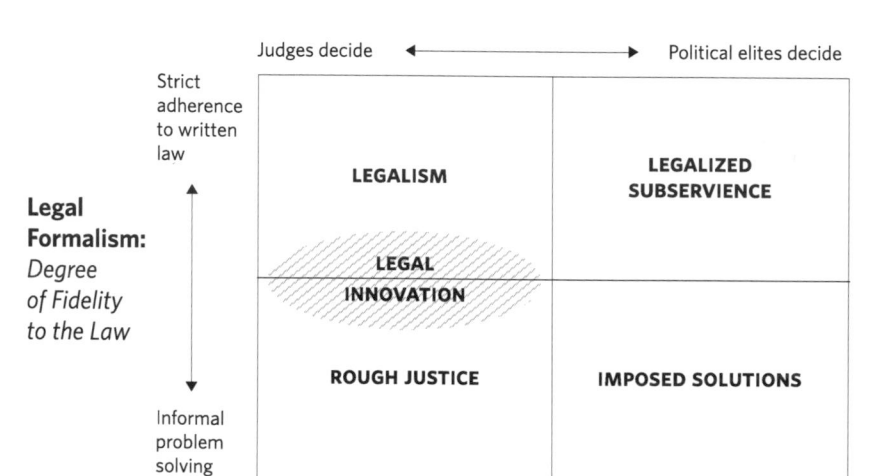

Figure 5.1. Judicial Decision Making in One-Party States

Plotting these two dimensions against each other yields a useful typology of judicial decision making in one-party states (see Figure 5.1).

Legalism, in the upper left-hand corner, is what Philippe Nonet and Philip Selznick call "autonomous law" (2008). This is a "model of rules" that values procedure, regularity and fairness where judges are constrained by statutes and precedents (Nonet and Selznick 2008, 53). In illiberal states, the combination of scrupulous attention to the law and judicial autonomy produces a system like apartheid South Africa (Chaskalson 2003) or Pinochet's Chile (Hilbink 2007). Taboos against political behavior, as Hilbink observed in Chile (2007, 37), or a culture of legal positivism compel adherence to the law, moderated by a small amount of discretion that is both legally permissible and politically tolerated. Laws leave judges some room for personal judgment, perhaps in their interpretation of the law or the penalties associated with breaking it. Apartheid-era judges, for example, sentenced Nelson Mandela to life in prison rather than death, a flash of clemency that changed the course of South African history (Chaskalson 2003, 596–597).

In the upper right-hand corner, which I call legalized subservience, political goals are written into highly specific laws that leave judges little room to maneuver. In East Germany, for example, "innumerable instructions, analyses, inspections, and consultations" helped judges "find the politically correct solutions to social ills whose diagnosis and remedy usually had already been prescribed by the Party" (Markovits 1996, 2293). This kind of legal specificity is an especially common way to deal with political dissent, through Nuremberg-like laws that identify, target, and punish enemies of the regime. Even the most illiberal regimes are image conscious, and legalized subservience obscures repression with flawlessly legal language. Sometimes, one-party states also shunt highly political cases into subservient tribunals while allowing judicial autonomy in ordinary cases. Franco's Spain, for example, preserved the appearance (if not the reality) of independent justice through separate military courts targeted at subversion (Toharia 1975).

When judges diverge from the law, shown in the bottom half of the typology, decisions are likely to either protect the influential or feature a compromise. In the lower left box, termed rough justice, relatively independent judges forge informal solutions. Sometimes, outright corruption or social pressure induces judges to take a side. Absent a personal interest in the outcome, Shapiro's logic of the triad mediates toward compromise (1981). The need to convince losers that both the outcome and the process were fair leads many judges to agree with the Zapotec observation that "a bad compromise is better than a good fight" (Nader 3 1990, 1).

Still, whenever top cadres make their interests known, the reality of a Party-subordinate legal system pushes most judges toward the safety of an imposed solution, shown in the lower right box. As one judge recounted an example of strategic retreat, "The [court] president addressed me at the very beginning of this lawsuit, saying 'the Environmental Protection Bureau (EPB) acted groundlessly; you have to pay close attention in handling this case'" (quoted in Zhang 2008, 146). Imposed solutions means that everyone from old school friends to state-owned enterprises can negotiate special legal treatment, provided that leaders prove willing to extend themselves.

The zone of legal innovation, in which judges push and expand the boundaries of the law, lies halfway between rough justice and legalism and overlaps both. In well-established, independent legal systems, legal creativity often corresponds to what Nonet and Selznick call responsive law. Judges base decisions not just on a legalistic reading of rules, but on substantive concerns about justice. Law is flexible, political, and potentially unstable because judicial interpretation offers a way to change the very substance of the law itself (Nonet and Selznick 2008, 78). Yet legal creativity is deeper and hardier than responsive law. A close reading of Chinese civil environmental cases shows a dollop of innovation where we would least expect to see it: in a one-party state inculcated in a civil law tradition of judges as "a kind of expert clerk" (Merryman 1985, 36). Even in relatively inhospitable environments, there can be room for new inferences and interpretations.

Beyond China, these four ideal types of judicial logic highlight the shifting pressures on judges in illiberal states. Legal systems may not fit neatly into one box because justice varies not only between countries but also within them. Particularly in large, decentralized court systems, judges' individual autonomy and the degree of formalism differ locally. Just as environmental enforcement depends on local circumstances, so too does judicial logic and outcomes. In addition, judges' strategies may shift with the type of case. Certainly, parallel courts for politically sensitive cases – what Tom Ginsburg and Tamir Moustafa call a "fragmented court system" (2008, 17) – show a different approach to judicial decisions than their mainstream counterparts.

More immediately, these two dimensions offer a more precise way to discuss the dynamics of decision making in civil environmental cases. As discussed below, my sample of forty-two cases feature low legal formality and fluctuating autonomy from external pressure. Most of the cases fall under the rubric of rough justice, although imposed solutions are also possible when political elites make a clear preference known.

Fluctuating Autonomy

Judicial choice is hard to see (and even harder to study) because it is frequently concealed. Judges disguise discretion in authoritative decisions "written to look like a standard drill in legal reasoning" (Amsterdam and Butler 2000, 202). The goal is to dispel doubt and dissuade appeal, not to debate the law. However, contrary to the conventional image of Chinese judges as rubber-stamping bureaucrats, pollution lawsuits suggest that judges exercise a fluctuating degree of autonomy. In addition to the practical constraint that political elites cannot possibly weigh in on every decision, discretion stems from uneven application of the law, legal silences, and mixed signals surrounding political goals. Uncertainty about both legal principles and state priorities, in short, lends judges the political and legal cover to plausibly defend the decisions they see fit.

Legally, civil environmental cases hinge on two points. First, the Environmental Protection Law, a 1991 EPB circular, and State Council regulations agree that polluters must pay pollution victims even if discharge meets government standards (Wang 2005, 195). Second, the 2010 Tort Liability Law, the 2008 Water Pollution Law, the 2004 Solid Waste Law, a 2001 SPC explanation, and a 1992 SPC notice shift the burden of proof such that defendants are responsible for proving that pollution did not cause losses. This latter point is particularly important for pollution victims looking for compensation. Environmental cases turn on causation, and it is notoriously difficult to prove (or deny) a connection between pollution and harm.

In practice, the set of decisions discussed here – almost certainly publicly released because court leaders thought the law was correctly applied and the case merited reference[13] – show widespread confusion on both counts. Several courts imposed a litmus test whereby the

---

13 Releasing legal decisions to national databases likely requires the approval of court leaders unwilling to harm the court's reputation by publishing decisions that they know to be wrong.

illegality of emissions is a pre-requisite for court-mandated compensation,[14] and many more did not reverse the burden of proof.[15] Judges, perhaps unaccustomed to pollution cases and unfamiliar with environmental laws, tend to default to the General Principles of the Civil Law. The General Principles, which should be trumped by more specific environmental regulations, limit liability to polluters who do not comply with environmental standards and operate according to the logic of "whoever claims it, proves it." Although this gap between national laws and local implementation is not surprising, the key point is that irregular application of the law gives judges a degree of freedom to diverge from it. Absent a uniform understanding of basic legal principles, ignorance becomes a credible defense for questioned decisions.

The deeper source of discretion, however, is the silence of the law surrounding evidence. To start, evidence is often scarce and hard to collect.[16] A case brought forth by fish farmers in Chongqing, for example, hinged on the village head's willingness to vouch for the number of dead fish. But this was an unreliable proof of damages. It turned out that the village head was too lazy to return to the fishponds after an initial inspection and tallied numbers self-reported by plaintiffs instead (Interview 161). When unclear aspects of a case like this arise, judges are responsible for investigating, although many lack the time or desire to do a good job (Interviews 74, 122). One problem is that soliciting evidence frequently requires wheedling reports out of bureaucrats with little incentive to cooperate. A conscientious Tianjin judge made three

---

14 As the Shanxi High Court wrote in 2000, "Pollution within government standards does not give rise to civil responsibility" (*Qinghianren Village Committee v. Shanxi Luchang*, Civil Division No. 6). See also *Zhang Wenjian v. Deng Guoqiang*, Beijing Second Intermediate Court, No. 9040 (2004). All decisions on file with the author.

15 Again, this is striking because I would expect this sample to reflect national best practices. For examples of decisions that do reference the 2001 SPC explanation, see *Liaohe Youtian Liaohai Jituan Youxian Gongsi v. Xu Ke'an*, Liaoning Liaohe Youtian Intermediate Court, No. 2 (2003); *Yuan Wei Shipin Gongsi v. Lu Kaiwen*, Anhui Bangbu City Intermediate Court, No. 285 (2005).

16 Nor is testimony from witnesses especially common. See Liu (2009, 205) on reluctance to testify in court.

trips to the EPB to obtain pollution data, succeeding only after he went drinking with local officials (Interview 93). Other judges see gathering more evidence as a liability because simple facts and short decisions are easier to defend on appeal (Upham 2005, 1696).

In addition, judges lack guidelines about how to use the evidence that does exist. In one typical case, Ye Hanjia and his family sued a Guangdong chemical company for 950,000 RMB (US$150,793) for medical expenses after he lost work time and suffered emotional distress from poisoning caused by a chemical spill.[17] As evidence, Ye and his family presented medical records from directly after the accident and nine months later as well as photos of the scene. The defendant supplemented this with: 1) a copy of its operation permit, 2) a Public Health Bureau report stating there were no illegal emissions three months after the accident, 3) a pollution control center statement that Ye's family no longer exhibited symptoms of poisoning several months post-accident, and 4) a copy of the initial compensation agreement with Ye. There were no epidemiology reports, competing opinions from groundwater experts, or even pollution data from the day of the accident. The judges, in other words, lacked information about the two most important facts of the case: the severity of the spill and the cause of the Ye family's original illness. Much like nineteenth-century magistrates, they simply had to decide whose evidence to believe and what was fair.

Of course, discretion can also facilitate corruption by giving judges room to overlook evidence, distort the law, or delay enforcement. Judges can be persuaded by people they know, particularly their bosses, or swayed by meals, gifts, and cash. Salaries remain low, even after years of anti-corruption efforts, and supplements can be welcome. In fact, one of the limits of legal decisions as a source is how well they hide behind-the-scenes influence. Even at moments when "incoherent, inconsistent or utterly unconvincing" reasoning sparks suspicion, it is impossible to

---

17 *Ye Hanjia v. Ruidefeng Gongsi*, Guangdong Dongwan Intermediate Court, No. 219 (2001).

know exactly how meddling mattered (Li 2012, 861). As one environmental lawyer cynically remarked, "The big cases are about politics, the
mid-sized cases are about influence, and only the small cases deal with
law" (quoted in Wee 2012).

Still, small cases are plentiful, and countervailing attempts to exert
influence can cancel each other out. Under these circumstances, the
diversity of CCP goals both makes a judge's job more difficult and gives
him or her an additional degree of flexibility. As Chapter 4 recounts,
economic growth is always a top Party priority, but there is increasing
recognition that environmental protection matters, too. Pollution disputes require judges to navigate varied and conflicting state objectives
including economic growth, environmental protection, social stability,
and the protection of vulnerable groups. As anthropologist Anna Lora-
Wainwright observed in a Sichuan village, "The clashing targets put forward by the central state itself pose a challenge to local cadres' ability to
implement central directives" (2009, 62). On the ground, it is not always
easy for judges to figure out what to do. The local government's "tolerance interval" is hazy, especially when cases touch on multiple goals
(Epstein, Knight and Shvetsova 2001). As a result, judges afraid of getting it wrong routinely solicit ideas from other judges in the same division (Interview 74), senior judges (Interview 6), Party committees (Zhu
2007, 183), or higher-level courts (Liu 2006, 93–94) on how to handle
tough cases. Even SPC judges in Beijing receive occasional requests for
advice from judges nervous about environmental cases (Interviews 103,
104). Often, the advice is as much political as legal. Top court officials are
political appointees, vetted by the Party committee of the local government and approved by the local people's congress, who are trusted to
transmit Party priorities.[18] As some environmental decisions openly

18 The court president (*yuan zhang*) is elected and dismissed by the relevant people's
congress. The vice-president, division heads (*ting zhang*) and assistant division heads
(*fu ting zhang*) are appointed and dismissed by the standing committee of the People's
Congress (Zhu 2007, 177). The Party committee of the local government must approve
all names before they are submitted to the People's Congress for approval (Zhu 2007,
179). For more on the importance of court officials, see Peerenboom (2002, 281 and
284–5), Liu (2006, 93), and Liebman (2007, 627).

note,[19] the most important cases are not decided by the judges present at the hearing, but by an adjudication committee of senior judges and court officials.[20]

From a systemic perspective, however, giving advice is a time-consuming burden for higher-level courts already struggling to manage their own caseload. In the mid-2000s, SPC documents and public statements began signaling that judges should ask for advice only in influential cases or cases where there is a dispute about the law (Zhu 2007, 183). Requiring decisions to be made locally, of course, lends local judges de facto power to weigh conflicting government priorities. In response, judges sometimes choose to prioritize moral imperatives over economic ones. Judges talk about feeling responsible for the down-and-out masses (*laobaixing*), occasionally showing visible sympathy for the vulnerable (Interviews 93, 166; Gu 2008, 273). At times, the new national emphasis on environmental protection also surfaces in lower-court decisions. A court in Chongqing found that "water is one of the factors that influence human survival and development ... [and the defendant] must not be allowed to pollute or destroy the environment."[21]

In a far-flung, deeply political court system, this limited degree of judicial autonomy varies. Disputes between citizens, such as noise complaints, rarely trigger the same kind of external pressure as high-profile, politicized cases. While it is difficult to discern the exact tipping point when cases become politically sensitive, judges clearly spend most of their time handling the commonplace. Here, as legal scholar Xin He notes in his work on divorce disputes, judicial discretion depends on the court (2009; see also Liebman 2007, 632). Just as resources and legal knowledge accumulate in some courts more than in others, some judges have more autonomy than others. Research on three Sichuan courts, for

---

19 *62 Lianghexian Hexixiang Damengwucun 62 Hu Nonghu v. Lianhe Xian Yuantong Liuhuangchang,* Yunnan Lianhe County Court, Civil Division, No. 51 (2005).
20 For more on adjudication committees, see Upham (2005, 1682), Chen (2012, 510–12), and He (forthcoming). Although no official statistics are available, the committee reportedly hears less than one percent of all cases.
21 *Gong Changjiu et al. v. Shen Xiang,* Chongqing Basic Court, Civil Division, No. 1045 (2006).

example, found a wide range of judicial decision-making power in criminal cases. Depending on the court, judges (rather than higher court officials or the court adjudication committee) made decisions 89 percent, 68 percent, or 0 percent of the time (Lan 2008).

In large part, the degree of discretion depends on the local specifics of judicial evaluation. Courts issue yearly indicators of decision-making quality (*shenpan zhiliang pinggu zhibiao*), which include the number of appeals, complaints, and retrials (Ai 2008, 106; He 2009, 12). These numbers are used in judges' annual evaluations. Doing a good job leads to raises, better housing, and access to court cars. Doing a bad job might mean fines for "wrong decisions" (*cuo an*) or, in extreme cases, demotion or transfer to a different court or government bureau. Overall, penalties for "wrong decisions" are meant to tackle two of the largest problems facing the Chinese judiciary: corruption and the uneven application of the law. Judicial consistency is an ongoing problem, and, in 2008, the SPC announced an improved tracking system designed to penalize regional judges with a record of misjudgments (Lam 2008, 4). Despite attempts to improve central control, however, rewards and punishments vary a great deal (Yu 2009). In some places, for example, the criteria for a "wrong case" includes incorrect legal reasoning or mere reversal while in other places it is limited to instances of corruption and decisions with no basis in law (Yu 2009, 20).[22] Wrong decisions can, as in Gansu, result in a two to four point loss on evaluations linked to annual bonuses (Yu 2009, 57), or, as in Shanghai, warrant only a minor 100 RMB fine (Interview 74). Variation in local incentives, as political scientist Yu Xiaohong points out, gives some judges more motivation than others to puzzle out political tolerance intervals and position themselves accordingly (2009).

When it exists, judicial discretion influences the tenor of proceedings as well as the outcome. In an environmental hearing I attended

22 The supervisory division of individual courts and the local procuratorate determine "wrong cases" through an investigation of cases that were changed on appeal (*gai shen*), reheard (*zai shen*), or generated complaints.

in Hebei province in January 2008, judges allowed a representative from the Beijing-based Center for Legal Assistance to Pollution Victims (CLAPV) to both sit with the plaintiff's counsel and give a speech even though the NGO had no official role in the courtroom. The representative used the speech to frame the dispute as a typical water pollution case and lend prestige to the plaintiff's cause. Although the head of CLAPV (the representative name-dropped) is busy helping the National People's Congress (NPC) revise the Water Pollution Law, his organization "is here today to help the plaintiff use the law to protect his rights." The court president sat in the front row during the hearing, and the unusual presence of external observers, including me, likely encouraged him and other court officials to carefully consider the plaintiff's case.

Most of the time, however, uncertainty about actors' tolerance guides judges toward conservative, by-the-book decision making. Risk-averse decisions are common sense when, as in one Zhejiang Basic People's Court, annual bonuses equivalent to four months of salary require the court president's signature (Interview 6). And in the instances when elites signal the limitations of tolerance, possibly through a carefully worded comment like "this case needs careful examination," an ad hoc retreat to an imposed solution is the norm. In the end, as legal scholar Ran Hirschl writes about judges elsewhere, courts "hand down decisions that favor the powerless primarily when doing so is consistent with elite values and interests" (2008, 109).

Rough Justice

Writ large, legal systems provide "an echo chamber for conversations about credit and blame" (Tilly 2008, 35). But in individual struggles, like the Henan farmer blaming a paper factory for his dead fish or the Beijing insomniac living next to a noisy bus depot, what does this conversation look like? Here, legal decisions are one way to infer how Chinese judges think about responsibility and fairness. In terms of the typology discussed above, 54 percent of this sample of cases clustered around "rough justice."[23] Decisions aim to defuse grievances by balancing a near overwhelming state imperative for economic growth with concerns about vulnerable groups, pollution, and social stability. As Judge Yang from the Wuhan Intermediate Court writes, the trick in environmental cases is to find a "balancing point between political and judicial wisdom" (2010, 310).

Most immediately, judges hope to leave both parties satisfied. The "biggest headache," one Chinese judge explained, is when decisions trigger complaints to supervisors in the judiciary (Interview 74; see also He 2009, 14). Judges work hard to ensure influential parties retain a positive impression of the court. When Beijing lawyers showed up in a small town in Zhejiang province to handle a pro bono environmental case, for example, the court sent a car to pick them up, and judges took them out to dinner after the hearing (Interviews 70, 116). Balancing interests and keeping both sides happy frequently translates into pragmatism. At least in environmental cases, Chinese judges often follow U.S. judge Patricia Wald's advice to employ "pragmatism that decides cases on the merits...[and] takes all the circumstances, including precedent, real-world significance and institutional relationships...into consideration, tempered on occasion by compassion" (1992–1993, 181). Few judges, in China or elsewhere, have a "visionary or crusading bent," and environmental decisions tend to divide responsibility and split the difference in a way that dents but upholds the status quo (Posner 1993, 3). As one judge wrote in 2007, "The court is just like a 'swill barrel' in which the conflicts of society, like garbage, are stuffed. It is the judge who is responsible for mixing them to balance law, society and politics well" (quoted in Balme 2010, 162).

---

23 As all of the cases in the sample involved requests for monetary compensation, I coded a case as corresponding to "rough justice" if plaintiffs received a portion of the sum they requested. Plaintiffs got more money than they requested in two cases (4.7 percent of the sample), the exact amount they requested in four cases (9.5 percent of the sample), and no compensation in ten cases (23.8 percent). I was unable to classify three cases because the decision did not contain information about the amount of requested compensation.

Balancing and pragmatism are most visible in the way that judges handle compensation. Depending on the number of plaintiffs and the extent of the losses, pollution disputes cases can involve significant damages. The average case in the sample involves a claim of 1.02 million RMB (US$161,904), although there are some big-money outliers like a 2000 case in Shanxi province in which a village sued for 18 million RMB (US$2.8 million) in damages.[24] While these numbers are not representative, each case highlights the difficulty of translating legal credit and blame into cash payouts.

This is often the moment in which judges diverge from the law. Citing "discretion" (*zhuoqing*), judges find a variety of reasons to lower compensation. In a case in Fujian province, for example, the court slashed requested compensation by 30 percent on the grounds that the defendant should not bear full responsibility when noise pollution is the inevitable result of flaws (*quexian*) in national development policies.[25] Courts assess damages, as one decision explained, "from the perspective of justice and reasonableness" (*cong gongping heli de jiaodu*).[26] As in a 2003 dispute in Anhui over air pollution from a neighborhood bathhouse, judicial perception of a reasonable standard often encompasses non-legal factors, like the proprietor's ability to pay (*jingying zhuangkuang*).[27] In

24 *Qinghianren Village Committee v. Shanxi Luchang* (2000). As one would expect, there was a difference between the amount of compensation requested in mass cases (cases with more than five plaintiffs) and non-mass cases. The average request for compensation in mass cases was 2.7 million RMB (US$428,571), and the average request for compensation in non-mass cases was 776,518 RMB (US$123,256). I have full data on the amount of compensation requested and the amount of compensation received for 39 of 42 cases, including 8 mass cases and 31 non-mass cases. I coded one case where the village committee served as a plaintiff as a mass case because compensation claims were made on behalf of the entire village (i.e., more than five people). Under these circumstances, the political logic of the case should be more similar to a mass case than an individual lawsuit.

25 *Yang Hanqiu v. Disan Hangwu Gongchengju Diliu Gongcheng Gongsi*, Fuijian Xiamen Intermediate Court (2002).

26 *Guangzhou Poya Dengshi Zhizao Youxian Gongsi v. Xie Zantian* (2005).

27 *Chen Renxia v. Yin Hongxia*, Anhui Chuzhou Intermediate Court, Civil Division No. 120 (2004).

addition to extra-legal factors, judges also come up with legal reasons to adjust compensation. In the absence of official guidelines detailing how to allocate blame, one common strategy is to divide legal responsibility. Fish farmer Wang Shouxiang's failure to mitigate the effects of pollution, a Zhejiang court found, entitles him to only 56 percent of his requested compensation.[28] Or, as a Shandong panel argued, plaintiffs should have sought out government bureaus to help combat pollution.[29] Lack of due diligence, at least in this interpretation of the law, has financial consequences. Another strategy, as in cases in Shandong and Anhui provinces, is to dismiss compensation requests unaccompanied by a stamped, official receipt of expenditures.[30]

Regardless of judges' rationale, this group of environmental cases shows how frequently judges compromise by granting part, but not all, of a plaintiff's requested compensation. Across all cases, plaintiffs were awarded an average of 29 percent of their claimed losses.[31] Judges were slightly less favorably inclined toward mass cases (those with more then five plaintiffs), granting plaintiffs 24 percent of claimed compensation. In non-mass cases, plaintiffs managed to get orders awarding an average of 42 percent of requested damages. These numbers fit the common perception that judges mandate compensation based on their (not always accurate) impression of what polluters can afford (Interviews 42, 46, 167).

---

28 *Ningbo Beilunqu Baifengshang Yangdianhua Yichang et al. v. Wang Shouxiang,* Zhejiang Ningbo Intermediate Court, Civil Division, No. 440 (2002).

29 *Zhang Pengguo and Li Yuping v. Shengli Youtian Gongyi Xinjishu Shiyou Kaifa Youxian Zeren Gongsi,* Shandong Dongyang Intermediate Court, Civil Division No. 27 (2004).

30 Without more information about these cases, it is hard to know how to interpret judicial demands for an official receipt. This could be a way to show favoritism to defendants or a safeguard against inflated claims. For example, see *Zhang Pengguo and Li Yuping v. Shengli Youtian Gongyi Xinjishu Shiyou Kaifa Youxian Zeren Gongsi* (2004) and *Yuan Wei Shipin Gongsi v. Lu Kaiwen* (2005).

31 Courts often have trouble enforcing their decisions, and I am not making any claims about how much money plaintiffs actually received. Rather, this is the amount ordered by the court. This 29 percent figure includes cases in which plaintiffs lost and were awarded no damages.

Judges' tendency to split the difference, to a large extent, shows a pragmatic impulse to locate a compromise acceptable to both sides. The Sun Youli case discussed in Chapter 3 is a particularly good example of this kind of "split it down the middle" approach. The first decision in that case held nine paper and chemical factories jointly liable for 13.6 million RMB (US$2 million) in damages to fish farms owned by the eighteen plaintiffs. On appeal, however, the Hebei High Court reduced compensation by 47 percent, based on two public justifications. First, the decision re-calculated losses based on wholesale value rather than retail value. Second, the judges recognized the defendants' long history in the area and penalized the fish farmers for failing to consider the risk before starting business. Those involved in the case, however, recognized that the bench primarily wanted to lessen the burden on industry, a goal that even the plaintiffs' lawyer found fair (*gongping*). As he later wrote, "For now, most enterprises face a number of difficulties reliably meeting [environmental] standards ... lightening industry's civil liability can contribute to their enthusiasm for environmental protection."[32]

Sometimes, judges also trim compensation because they think plaintiffs are inflating claims. Judges, according to one Beijing lawyer, frequently ask questions like "How can farmers make so much money?" (Interview 146). To combat these kinds of stereotypes, one lawyer encouraged his client to showcase his wealth by driving an expensive car to the court (Interview 165). At times, though, suspicion is warranted. One Guangdong court caught a farmer cheating when back-of-the-envelope calculations revealed that the number of dead fish he claimed could not be conceivably packed into a pond the size of his fish farm.[33] Or in Yunnan province, farmers planted trees difficult to cultivate under the best conditions and demanded pollution-related compensation when they failed to grow (van Rooij 2006a, 153).

32 Unpublished document on file with the author.
33 *Ping Zao v. Zhongnan Shiyouju*, Guangdong Foshan Intermediate Court, Civil Division No. 3 (2005).

Faced with uncertainty about the facts, the law and overlapping political priorities, judges in environmental cases often take refuge in common sense. In a moment of transparency, a Guangdong court wrote out
a checklist for environmental cases in a 2005 decision: 1) whether there
is pollution, 2) whether there is harm, and 3) whether there is causation
between pollution and harm.[34] When these determinations prove difficult, as they frequently do, judges and lawyers often fall back on assumptions about how an average person would see the case. A Shanghai court,
for example, sided with a plaintiff in a 2004 light pollution case because
the brightness "exceeded what a normal person can stand."[35] Or in a
2001 case in Hebei, the defense argued that noise and vibrations from a
railroad couldn't possibly cause cracks in neighboring houses. According to the defense, the plaintiff's claim was not even worth discussing
because "there's no need to prove common sense."[36]

Common sense, as invoked in these cases, is an extension of local
knowledge. Judges are enmeshed in local communities, and, as a result,
frequently come to the case with a preexisting understanding of the
situation.[37] Industrial pollution, at least for one Henan court, does not
need proof because "everyone knows about [it]."[38] In another case in
Inner Mongolia, industrial discharge into the Yellow River reduced Baotou city's water supply to a single back-up reservoir (Jiang 2006b). Baotou judges, like all city residents, were angry about the water crisis and
favorably predisposed to a large settlement (Interview 118). At other
times, local ties sway judges toward the polluters' perspective. Dealing
with social suasion from friends and relatives, in addition to pressure
from officials, lawyers, plaintiffs, and defendants, is part of most judges'

---

34 *Guangzhou Poya Dengshi Zhizao Youxian Gongsi v. Xie Zantian* (2005).
35 *Lu Yaodong v. Shanghai Yongda Zhongbao Qiche Xiaoshou Fuwu Youxian Gongsi*,
   Shanghai Pudong Basic Court (2004).
36 *Yin Bingquan et al. v. Beijing Tieluju*, Beijing Railway Court, No. 23 (2001).
37 For more on how basic-level courts are rooted in local communities, see Upham
   (2005).
38 *Zhumadianshi Suyahu Shuiku Guanliju v. Zhumadianshi Yicheng Hongyuan Waleng
   Banzhichang*, Henan Runan Basic Court, Civil Division No. 30 (2003).

job (Peerenboom 2002, 315–16). Isolated objectivity is rarely worth the cost of loneliness and even local ridicule (He 1999, 234).

Judges' deep local roots also help them identify and handle cases that might escalate (*keneng naoshi de anzi*). Pollution lawsuits can shade into protest, especially when the financially desperate are certain they have been wronged. This on-the-streets anger occasionally surfaces in written decisions, an implicit judicial acknowledgement of the permeable boundary between law and justice by other means. Judges noted that Mr. Ye, the Guangdong man whose family was diagnosed with pesticide poisoning, originally received compensation only after he was arrested for digging up the road leading to the chemical factory.[39] Or, in a 2005 case in Yunnan province, a village halted factory production for almost a year by blocking delivery of raw materials.[40] Volatile cases, one judge explained, "are urgent and it's important to get a decision out quickly" (quoted in Zhao 2008). When emotions are running high or when there are a lot of plaintiffs involved, courts frequently refuse to hear cases altogether. Local connections help risk-averse judges manage the critical extralegal work of avoiding intractable cases and fashioning acceptable bargains.

Innovation at the Margins

One advantage of reading forty-two legal decisions is that the cases collectively offer a sense of the limits of the law, or the legal frontier. As environmental lawyers know, Chinese courts are much more comfortable with some kinds of grievances than others. In general, judges are inclined to treat pollution cases as private economic disputes, solvable via negotiated monetary settlement. Non-monetary claims and rulings, such as a request for an apology,[41] moving a factory,[42] or recognizing

---

39 *Ye Hanjia v. Ruidefeng Gongsi* (2001).
40 *62 Damengwucun 62 Hu Nonghu v. Lianhe Xian Yuantong Liuhuangchang* (2005).
41 *Lu Yaodong v. Shanghai Yongda Zhongbao Qiche Xiaoshou Fuwu Youxian Gongsi* (2004).
42 *62 Damengwucun 62 Hu Nonghu v. Lianhe Xian Yuantong Liuhuangchang* (2005).

herdsmen's land rights,[43] are usually ignored. Lawyers were still struggling to draw a legal connection between illness and pollution during my fieldwork in the mid- and late-2000s, a tough sell because courts fear a landslide of similar cases (Interviews 110, 122). As one prominent environmental lawyer told *The New York Times* in 2007, "No previous [mass] lawsuit has proved the link between pollution and cancer, but I am optimistic that we can be successful" (quoted in Mackey 2007).[44]

Yet despite strong incentives to avoid controversy, Chinese judges occasionally innovate. When they do so, they tend to bypass the bold rhetoric of landmark decisions in favor of understated innovation at the margins. Nine decisions, or 21 percent of the cases in the sample, show this kind of bounded creativity. First, some decisions quietly validated new types of claims. Compensating cancer villages may fall beyond the current legal frontier, but some courts recognized the link between pollution and health.[45] Others awarded compensation for emotional distress caused by noise,[46] and in 2004, a Shanghai court accepted China's first light pollution case.[47] Other decisions stood out as innovative because of the presence of rights language, a significant rhetorical turn as none of China's environmental laws mention rights at all (Wan 2011). By talking about rights associated with environmental protection, as when a Beijing court claimed that "the environment is a basic condition of human

43 *Damu Linzhabu et al. v. Dongwu Zhumu Qinqi Dianhua Jiangbanchang et al.* Inner Mongolia High Court, Civil Division No. 6 (2004).

44 Courts have supported individual plaintiffs on occasion. A 2009 decision from the Qingxian People's Court in Hebei province, for example, connected a lung cancer death to air pollution from a nearby factory and awarded 83,105 RMB (US$13,191) to the surviving spouse (Qie 2009).

45 *Wan Hongxiang et al. v. Lianshui Xianchanglin Bingbangchang*, Jiangsu Lianshui Basic Court, No. 1117 (2000); see also *Lu Yaodong v. Shanghai Yongda Zhongbao Qiche Xiaoshou Fuwu Youxian Gongsi* (2004).

46 *Wan Hongxiang et al. v. Lianshui Xianchanglin Bingbangchang* (2000); *Yang Hanqiu v. Disan Hangwu Gongchengju Diliu Gongcheng Gongsi*, Fujian Intermediate Court (2002); *Shi Meizhu v. Nanjing Aihua Zhuangshi Youxian Zeqian Gongsi*, Nanjing Gulou Basic Court, No. 208 (2002).

47 *Lu Yaodong v. Shanghai Yongda Zhongbao Qiche Xiaoshou Fuwu Youxian Gongsi* (2004).

existence and development," courts also validate them.[48] A court in Shanxi province, for example, found that pollution infringed on "residents' right to health, leisure, and property"[49] while other judges connected pollution disputes to the "right to use your house normally"[50] and "the right to live peacefully and the right to health."[51] In 2005, a Guangzhou court went as far as to write "environmental protection is a basic national policy because behavior that infringes on environmental rights not only endangers our health and living environment, it also causes incalculable harm to the environment of future generations."[52] As one judge explained, "Rights that are not written in the text of the law, but are hidden between the lines, can be discovered" (quoted in Kellogg 2007, 180). The appearance of rights talk in lower-court decisions shows how deeply it has penetrated the Chinese state.[53] Certain circumscribed rights, at least, may edge toward entitlements by dint of official repetition.

Taken individually, each appearance of rights language or support for a new claim is not of great significance, especially because the Chinese legal system has neither judicial review nor binding precedent. Yet these moments of divergence are significant because they show judges pushing the boundaries of the law. Taken together, they indicate systemic tolerance for modest innovation, especially in cases that do not touch powerful local interests (Liebman 2007, 632). Being a Chinese judge can be a creative enterprise for those who subscribe to Judge Yang's view that "judges should not only be the executor of laws, but also the discoverer, explainer and creator [of them]" (2010, 312–313; see also Interview 167).

---

48 *Xiong Wansheng v. Beijingshi Zonghe Touzi Gongsi et al.* Beijing Second Intermediate Court, Civil Division No. 5696 (2000).

49 *Qinghairen Village Committee v. Shanxi Luchang* (2000).

50 *Chen Renxia v. Yin Hongxia*, Anhui Chuzhou Intermediate Court (2004).

51 *Yang Hanqiu v. Disan Hangwu Gongchengju Diliu Gongcheng Gongsi* (2002).

52 Guangzhou Basic Court, quoted in *Guangzhou Poya Dengshi Zhizao Youxian Gongsi v. Xie Zantian*, Guangdong Guangzhou Intermediate Court, Civil Division No. 1770 (2005).

53 For more on the importance of rights-based claims, see O'Brien and Li (2006).

Isolated instances of innovation may also ripple through other courts, slowly shifting the mainstream interpretation of environmental law. Law professors Benjamin Liebman and Timothy Wu document a trend toward soft precedent in which lower courts look at other decisions for guidance in handling difficult cases (2007; see also Kellogg 2007, 171; Interviews 74, 93, 166).[54] In my sample, a 2002 Guangxi High Court decision discusses the legal implications of a similar case while the Zhejiang High Court looks even further afield toward "principles commonly used by every country in the world in handling environmental pollution rights infringement cases."[55] The groundbreaking 2004 Shanghai light pollution case was also written up in the *Supreme People's Court Gazette*, a clear indication that higher-ups thought the case merited widespread attention and reference (SPC Gazette 2005, 40–42). Sometimes, lawyers even observe movement in the legal frontier as a set of local judges becomes accustomed to new types of claims. Zhou Litai, one of China's best-known labor lawyers, recalls a four-year progression from losing almost every labor case to winning 40 to 50 percent of the time (Zhou 2005, 201).

A single successful lawsuit can also inspire imitators. After the Sun Youli case made national headlines, for example, one of the lawyers involved started receiving inquiries from would-be plaintiffs as far away as Guangxi province. On a trip to Hebei province, I also observed one of the plaintiffs in the Sun Youli case quietly pull aside a lawyer to solicit advice on a new set of pollution-related losses. Having once won compensation through litigation, he was ready to sue again.[56] Local word of mouth can inspire copycat litigation, too. A Beijing property lawyer's

---

54 Competition among legal databases over the next several years should put more cases online and make it much easier for judges to research cases. In addition, a 2010 directive asks lower courts to consider "guiding cases" selected by the SPC in making decisions (SPC 2010).

55 *Zhejiang Jianchayuan v. Jiaxingshi Buyun Ranhuachang*, Zhejiang High Court No. 17 (2000).

56 I later heard from the lawyer that he did bring another lawsuit.

2003 decision to sue a real-estate developer over toxic levels of ammonium, for example, convinced many of his neighbors to follow suit. And, of course, winning a novel lawsuit can legitimate similar claims and pave the way for successors. Lawyers in the Sun Youli lawsuit thought that the Tianjin Maritime Court decision "created an example" (*chuangzao le dianfan*) because it was one of the first high-profile cases to correctly shift the burden of proof to the defendant.[57]

Incursions beyond the legal frontier occur because judges, much like the local officials discussed in the last chapter, have incentives to innovate. Local government is a common testing ground for economic and legal reforms, and the most successful innovations are adopted nationally.[58] This is career-making stuff and some ambitious judges angle for attention from higher-ups. Officials from the innovative administrative division of the Pingdingshan Intermediate Court, for example, have been invited to national-level SPC conferences – public recognition that is both immediately gratifying and holds the promise of possible future promotions (Yu 2009, 57). Some judges also subscribe to the "no action, no authority" approach to judicial decision making and believe that courts need to take bold action to increase their influence vis-à-vis other government bureaus (Yu 2009, 39). Other innovative decisions are obliquely aimed not at government officials, but at a peer group of judges and academics. Taking a stand for social justice and pushing the boundaries of the law wins accolades among reform-oriented legal elites (Yu 2009, 50–52). Nudging forward social change can be personally satisfying too. As one Guangdong judge told the newspaper *Southern Weekend*, "Ever since I found out that [labor] decisions can change a few things, I've felt that this work is really meaningful" (quoted in Zhao 2008). Moreover, the risks of modest innovation are typically low. Local

---

57 Unpublished document on file with the author.

58 For more on the importance of decentralized experimentation, see Heilmann (2008) and O'Brien (2009, 134).

experiments can quietly lapse into inactivity, judges can recant, and the tiny minority of not-forgiven mutineers can find new jobs.[59] In recent years, publicly chastised judges have left courts to study law in top graduate programs or to become lawyers (Yu 2009, 73).

When law exists to serve the Party, or any powerful clique, what can we learn from the ways in which judges choose between politically circumscribed solutions? First, taking judicial choice seriously compels an "anthropology of the state" that charts the gap between central intention and local interpretation instead of skimming over it (Migdal 2001, 97). While regimes may aspire to a single standard of justice, decisions often depend on the political signals surrounding either a type of case or a specific lawsuit. Nor are these signals necessarily clear cut. In China, judges sometimes find themselves responsible for interpreting competing priorities and even occasionally edging forward new understandings of the law. Indeed, as the next chapter explores in regard to lawyers, political ambivalence often leads to unintended consequences. Grassroots attempts to remember the past, interpret the present, and see the future can prompt actions quite different than what a centralized and coordinated five-year plan might have envisioned.

Second, litigation can make visible one of the hidden transcripts of politics: the competing values and commitments that divide the state against itself.[60] Controversial lawsuits bring the fault lines of politics into high relief, such as Supreme Court decisions over abortion in America or dismantling settlements in Israel. In places where political disagreement is frequently swept under a façade of unity, such as China, judicial decision making can offer much-needed insight into the underlying political spectrum. Mapping cases onto the four profiles of judicial logic sketched

---

59 On how local experiments quietly fade away, see Heilmann (2008, 27).
60 The phrase "hidden transcripts" is borrowed from political scientist James Scott. Scott's hidden transcripts refer to "a critique of power spoken behind the back of the dominant" and I have borrowed the term here to evoke a slightly different kind of hidden political conflict (1990, xii).

here promises a better understanding of where official priorities lie and when they conflict. Indeed, scrutinizing the political pressure that judges face (and how it varies by issue and court) can help answer the question of where the boundary between law and politics lies and why it shifts.

6 Heroes or Troublemakers?

The Lawyers

FOR LAWYERS, ENVIRONMENTAL CASES ARE LOSERS. THEY are seen as unprofitable, difficult to win and, sometimes, politically sensitive. So why would any sensible lawyer take one on?[1]

Returning to the theme of political ambivalence, this chapter explores this question. Although routine practitioners handle most environmental cases, a minority of environmental lawyers are motivated by a cause rather than cash. Legal reforms lent Chinese lawyers a degree of freedom to find "something to believe in" and pick cases accordingly (Scheingold and Sarat 2004, 2). In so doing, they drew on seemingly conflicting visions of lawyers as socialist crusaders and as international professionals.[2] Recognizing the importance of the socialist law tradition underscores the degree to which moral commitment can serve authoritarianism as well as subvert it. Some idealistic lawyers provide pro bono help for "weak and disadvantaged groups" (*ruoshi qunti*), not to nudge

---

1 My focus here is on licensed lawyers who have passed the state bar exam. Other kinds of legal advocates and representatives include basic-level legal workers (*jicheng falü gongzuozhe*) and legal advisory agencies (*falü zixun jigou*). In addition, there are unauthorized black lawyers (*hei lüshi*) and barefoot lawyers (*chijiao lüshi*). For an excellent overview of how these different groups relate to each other, see Liu (2009, especially chapter 3). On how lawyers pick cases, see Michelson (2006). On the lack of environmental lawyers in China, see Ferris and Zhang (2002, 598).

2 I am indebted to Sida Liu for crystallizing this distinction in my mind (see Liu 2009, 110).

forward democracy, but in the hopes of building a better, more egalitarian China under the Chinese Communist Party (CCP). As sociologists Terence Halliday and Lucien Karpik note, lawyers are neither necessarily "liberal actors-in-waiting" nor the "perpetual creators of rule of law regimes" (1997, 60).

This is especially true because the possibility of activism co-exists with routine self-censorship. In response to uncertainty, lawyers often decide that sticking to well-trodden areas makes sense. In particular, stories about repression, which I call "control parables," harden limits on activism by assigning meaning to seemingly random repercussions. The rules for daily behavior are not handed down from the pinnacle of the state, but jointly written (and rewritten) by Chinese lawyers and their government overseers.

Routine Practitioners[3]

Environmental lawsuits are relatively rare, and, at any given moment, most lawyers are not involved in one. In a 2007 survey of 1,337 lawyers, 4.8 percent of respondents reported working on an environmental case in the previous twelve to fifteen months.[4] This translates into fifty-five environmental lawyers, 81 percent of whom had handled just one or two environment-related cases. Only seven lawyers reported five or more environmental protection cases, although this tiny group collectively

---

3 The term "routine practitioner" is borrowed from Liu and Halliday's typology of criminal defense lawyers (2011).

4 There were fifty-five environmental lawyers among the 1,145 who provided data on their civil caseload. Of these fifty-five lawyers, 83 percent were men and 16 percent were women. All had at least some college education, and 84 percent were between thirty and fifty years old. The survey interviewed lawyers in eight locations: Beijing, Shanghai, Guangzhou, Jilin, Zhejiang, Jiangsu, Qinghai, and Shandong. Lawyers were asked how many environmental protection and pollution cases (*huanjing baohu he gonghai fangmian de anjian*) they handled between January 31, 2006, and the time of the survey (which was administered between February and April 2007). Many thanks to Ji Weidong at Shanghai Jiaotong University for generously allowing me to analyze survey data collected by him and his team, as well as to John Givens for his advice.

handled nearly 60 percent of the total volume of environmental cases. Still, there were only four exceptions to the general rule that environmental work never exceeded 20 percent of any lawyer's portfolio.[5] Even the seven superstar environmental lawyers also accepted many other types of work.

Lack of specialization suggests that environmental cases are an occasional part of ordinary lawyers' work. Despite complaints that pollution cases are poorly paid, lawyers say they will sometimes take one if they have time (Interviews 67, 76, 97, 130, 161). Water pollution cases are especially appealing because of large losses to clients and the relative ease of demonstrating causation (Interview 15; Ma 2003; Caijing 2006). Prior to 2006 regulations banning contingency fees in mass cases, lawyers also used to sometimes gamble on a 20 to 30 percent payout in collective cases.[6] When lawyers lack the financial freedom to be choosy, environmental lawsuits can also be "thrust upon them as a condition of practice and survival" (Liu and Halliday 2011, 845–846; see also Interview 52). As a lawyer in Qinghai province explained, "In developed cities like Shanghai or Beijing, lawyers are highly specialized. Here, lawyers must be generalists and take all kinds of cases.... if a lawyer only wanted to specialize, he would starve. There simply aren't enough cases" (quoted in Wu 2008, 195). An environmental lawyer located in a mid-sized city in Zhejiang province agreed: "It's like being a doctor in an isolated place where you see all kinds of illnesses; I'll handle whatever case comes my way" (Interview 76).

In addition to generalist lawyers who occasionally encounter an environmental case, a small, specialized group of maritime lawyers frequently handle claims surrounding oil spills (Interviews 60, 68, 84). Oil spills are more lucrative than run-of-the-mill pollution cases because

---

5 Of these four lawyers, three reported that between 20 and 23 percent of their cases were environmental. For the fourth lawyer, over half (53 percent) of his caseload was environment-related.

6 For the full text of the notice banning contingency fees in mass cases, see National Development and Reform Commission and the Ministry of Justice (2006).

damages are relatively easy to prove and because all legally registered oil tankers carry insurance to cover claims (Interview 68). "You know from the start that there's going to be compensation," one maritime lawyer said, "it's just a question of how much" (Interview 68). A case with multiple parties will involve most well-established lawyers in the field, and professional pride dictates that no one wants to sit a major case out (Interview 60).

The other advantage of environmental cases is publicity. Because regulations limit advertisements to a dry recitation of qualifications and basic biographical facts, lawyers rely on referrals to find new work (Qiu 2006, 15).[7] Lawyers who are less well-connected, often younger lawyers or those from a lower-class background, are always looking to expand their network (Interviews 97, 161; Liu and Halliday 2011, 847). High-profile environmental cases, especially those with lots of plaintiffs, can help attract new clients by multiplying social ties and drawing media coverage (Interviews 12, 130). Indeed, environmental lawyers stand out in the 2007 survey as hard workers. On average, each environmental lawyer was juggling 134 cases, compared to an average workload of just 29 cases among lawyers without an environmental case. Lawyers with a high-volume caseload are less likely to be choosy about the cases they handle, such that a handful of environmental cases that might otherwise seem obscure or risky meld into their daily workload.

Do-Gooders

Other environmental lawyers are recognizable cause lawyers: activists motivated by a cause rather than financial reward. The existence of this group is interesting as the conventional wisdom so often links cause lawyers with democracy (Scheingold 2001, 384).[8] At first glance, values-driven litigation seems to exemplify a peculiarly democratic "diffusion

---

7 Article 127 of the All China Lawyers Association's 2004 "Code of Conduct for Lawyers" states that individual advertisements should be limited to basic biographical data like the lawyer's name, photograph, place of birth, educational background, name of law firm and scope of legal services.

8 I use the terms "activist lawyer" and "cause lawyer" interchangeably here.

of power that stands in stark contrast to how one-party systems tightly control legal confrontations" (Zemans 1983, 692). Legal scholar Inga Markovits, writing about East German lawyers, concurs: "Socialism did not like individual challenges to state authority. It liked even less for such challenges to be articulated and sharpened by professional squabblers" (1996, 2297). Yet "cause lawyers in an authoritarian state" is not a contradiction in terms.[9] Despite the affinity between cause lawyers and political liberalism,[10] litigation neither requires nor masks stirrings of liberalization. Socially committed lawyers can diminish the worst excesses of inequality and improve governance regardless of who is in power.

Sometimes, Chinese lawyers are drawn into de facto pro bono work by personal entreaties such as helping out a friend (Interview 106) or representing their hometown (Interview 127).[11] Other times, they are compelled by compassion and a sense of shared humanity.[12] As one lawyer put it, "Chinese people have it really tough, so I'm willing to make a bit less money or take the case for free" (Interview 98). These lawyers talk about helping people (Interview 161), following their conscience (Interview 161), and pursuing something meaningful (Interview 33). They frequently mention a strong sense of responsibility to society and a desire to make a contribution.[13] Conceptually, these do-gooders do not fit the mold of cause lawyers as self-aware moral crusaders (Scheingold and Sarat 2004). Yet in the shadow of a socialist legacy, lifting up the

---

9 For other work on cause lawyers in illiberal states, see Michalowski (1998), Bisharat (1998), and Sidel (2008). On activist lawyers in China and Hong Kong, see Pils (2007), Halliday and Liu (2008), Fu and Cullen (2008), and Tam (2010).

10 See Halliday and Karpik (1997) and Halliday, Karpik and Feeley (2007).

11 The term "de facto pro bono" is borrowed from Kritzer (2002, 1945). On de facto pro bono work in China, see Michelson (2006, 21).

12 For people who discussed human sympathy, see Interviews 34, 47, 73, 96, 98, 116, 122, and 127. For more on this kind of de facto pro bono work in Qinghai province, see Wu (2008, 196).

13 Chinese-speaking readers may be interested in the exact phrases lawyers used to make this point. They talked about a desire to contribute to society (*dui shehui you gongxian*) (Interview 46); serving society (*wei shehui fuwu*) (Interview 79); a sense of responsibility to society (*dui shehui you zeren gan*) (Interviews 89, 161); societal responsibility (*shehui zeren*) (Interview 97), and doing something good for society (*dui shehui huozhe dazhong zuo yixie haoshi*) (Interview 106).

disadvantaged blurs the boundary between charity and activism. Even carefully parsing the language of the most self-reflective lawyers, it is difficult to tease apart the pull of human sympathy from a deeper egalitarian commitment to a more just society.[14]

Beyond intermittent altruism, a significant minority of environmental lawyers are recognizable cause lawyers. These are the lawyers dedicated enough to scan the news looking for pollution victims to represent in court (Interviews 72, 90, 126), spend 10,000 RMB (US$1,587) of their own money on a case (Interview 70), or set up a local hotline for pollution victims (Interview 53). Although a few describe themselves as environmentalists (*huanbao zhuyizhe*) (Interviews 89, 127), most reject the label and prefer to call themselves a person who appreciates nature (Interviews 53, 125), or someone who appreciates the severity of China's environmental problems (Interviews 9, 46, 113, 174). Some of those most concerned about environmental degradation are former Environmental Protection Bureau (EPB) employees (Interviews 46, 73). At the same time, the wide scope of environmental cases attracts lawyers who care little about pollution.

The environment is a flexible cause, broad enough to encompass concerns about inequality and an overbearing government as well as pollution and nature conservation. Cases attract a collection of lawyers driven by disparate beliefs and lawyers see environmental cases as one way to push forward a number of causes including homeowners' rights (Interview 91), fishermen's rights (Interview 98), rule of law (Interview 72), and checking state strength (Interview 116). As one of China's best known environmental lawyers put it, "I firmly believe that every lawsuit I conduct helps rebuild people's confidence in the system ... every environmental case, even if the lawsuit itself is unsuccessful, is an advancement of the rule of law in China" (quoted in Mackey 2007).

---

14 As Shamir and Chinski point out, causes are not objective facts, but constructed and articulated by lawyers themselves (1998, 231). So far, China's most articulate legal activists have converged around rights protection without an accompanying eloquent defense of egalitarianism.

Mixed ideological and financial motivation is also common, even among lawyers who self-consciously take environmental cases because of personal values. Some say that environmental litigation offers a way to turn concern about the environment into a marketable expertise (Interviews 28, 73, 108, 118, 134). Climate change and pollution are headline news, and future-oriented lawyers sense business opportunities in clean-development mechanism projects and corporate advice on environmental standards (Interviews 47, 82). The more intellectually inclined also enjoy learning about a new area of law (Interviews 106, 121) even if a short-term financial payoff is unlikely.

Across causes, the Chinese environmental lawyers I met believe in both the necessity and the promise of incremental change. Like moderate rights protection lawyers who "limit their advocacy to legal issues," or grassroots criminal defense lawyers who seek to spread "ideas of the rule of law, locality by locality, across the vastness of China," they see individual cases as a way to slowly change society (Fu and Cullen 2008, 116; Liu and Halliday 2011, 849). These cases, in the words of one lawyer, are "not just a way to get compensation, but to change the legal system and slowly expand the space for action" (Interview 110). Environmental lawyers' overriding orientation is toward nudging an agenda forward, one uncontroversial step at a time. Although they admire the courage of lawyers more inclined to political criticism, like dissident lawyer Gao Zhisheng, they worry about backlash from doing too much too fast (Interviews 14, 25, 37). Even the most political environmental lawyers – the ones who talk about environmental cases as a "breakthrough point" (*tupokou*) for democracy (Interview 123) – are not advocates for regime change or even deep liberalization. Rather, they are talking about democratization with a "small d:" a gradual expansion of public participation to increase state responsiveness to citizen needs.

To some extent, this scaled-down political agenda reflects the influence of Tiananmen and the other protests of 1989. For at least one cohort of activist lawyers, youthful participation in the democracy movement marked a biographical moment, a point in time that divides lives into 'before' and 'after' terms (McAdam 1989, 758). After the government crackdown, some turned to law to make a living, and later, as a lower-profile way to push forward political change (Interviews 85, 148).[15] As one lawyer writes:

> In 1980, China opened up to the world again. Western philosophy, politics and legal theory all started flooding in. These completely new, strange ideas strongly affected Chinese citizens, hastening the 1989 student democracy movement that so transfixed the world. As a sophomore in college, I went to Tiananmen Square and saw my class-mates block the tanks with their flesh and blood.... at that moment, I knew I was destined to spend my life in the struggle for liberty. The flame of that conviction never went out, even when the aftermath of Tiananmen forced my ideals to the bottom of my heart. I became an environmental lawyer, committed to the fight for rights.[16]

In the post-Tiananmen era, rights litigation became a way to mount a "critique within the hegemony" significant enough to satiate at least some desire for change (Scott 1990, 106). As de facto restrictions on internal migration relaxed in the 2000s, like-minded lawyers started converging on China's big cities, particularly Beijing, to find clients and community.

The Emergence of Legal Activism

The existence of a small coterie of environmental cause lawyers intersects a larger story about the emergence of activist lawyers who "take law and the legal process seriously while realizing the 'outer limits' of law in an authoritarian state" (Fu and Cullen 2008, 112; see also Hand 2006; Pils 2007; Kahn 2007a; Lü 2007). In the 2000s, terms like rights defense lawyer (*weiquan lüshi*), public interest lawyer (*gongyi lüshi*), and

---

15 Pu Zhiqiang is one example of a lawyer willing to talk publicly about his experiences in 1989 (Pan 2008, 274–77). Liu and Halliday make a similar point about criminal defense lawyers (2011, 852).

16 Unpublished document on file with the author.

impact litigation (*yingxiang xing susong*) broke into the Chinese media and public consciousness. An active discussion ensued about what these labels meant and whether public interest law was a good thing. As a June 2009 headline in the newspaper *Southern Weekend* (*Nanfang Zhoumo*) bluntly asked: "Public Interest Lawyers: Heroes (*Yingxiong*) or Trouble-makers (*Diaomin*)?" (Meng 2009). As recounted below, changes in the bar opened up new room for legal activism. Cause lawyers arrived in the 1990s and 2000s because a combination of reforms, diversification, and new affluence gave some lawyers the political space and financial free-dom to pick and pursue a cause.

Outside of China, research on Vietnam (Sidel 2008), Hong Kong (Tam 2010) and the Occupied Territories (Bisharat 1998) suggests that would-be cause lawyers benefit from the authoritarian dilemma over courts. When illiberal governments invest in the trappings of law, activist-minded lawyers can find ways to bend the system to their ends. Even litigation in courts that are perceived as rigged can be worthwhile, especially when new regulations and rhetoric about the importance of law create handholds to hold the powerful accountable for their promises. As Chinese legal academic Jiang Ping writes, Chinese "lawyers [can] rely on the law's small openings and contradictions as well as its authority" (Jiang 2005, 28). Equally important, law serves what is sometimes called an expressive function: it sends a signal about what the state considers to be acceptable and unacceptable claims.[17] Shortly after the Chinese constitution incorporated new language about protecting human rights in 2004, for example, one self-identified human rights lawyer proclaimed that:

> Time is progressing. It is not like before when people were pun-ished for speaking out...clauses on human rights are written into the constitution and the concept of human rights is already deep in peo-ple's hearts...Why would lawyers need to be concerned if we only

---

17 Law serves a dual expressive function: it reflects social norms as well as state prefer-ences.

act within the framework of the law, make our activities public and act with justice in mind? (Guo 2005, 105)

For lawyers like this, constitutional cover lent official validation to human rights-related claims. It became possible to cast oneself as a patriot with justice in mind.

In China, activist lawyers started emerging in force only after the privatization of the bar gave lawyers the professional freedom to pursue their personal passion.[18] After the Cultural Revolution, lawyers worked as civil servants in legal advisory offices (*falü guwen chu*) modeled after Soviet law offices. Lawyers were part of the state bureaucracy and simultaneously expected to serve socialism and the masses. This changed in 1996 when the Lawyers Law transformed them into "professionals providing legal services to society" (Michelson 2003, 59). From the state's perspective, turning government employees into private professionals offered a way to expand lawyers' ranks without paying for it. A series of similar cost-cutting initiatives in the 1980s and 1990s culminated in a 2000 State Council-mandated drive to convert all remaining state-owned law firms to partnerships (Michelson 2003, 59–65). The campaign was largely successful. By 2004, only 14 percent of law firms were state-owned, down from 98 percent in 1990 (Zhu 2007, 332).

By the mid-2000s, most of China's lawyers were working for partnership law firms.[19] Outside elite law firms in big cities, most work on a per-case commission basis instead of drawing a salary (Michelson 2006, 11). Lawyers then turn over a fixed percent of billed income, typically between 30 and 50 percent, to the firm in exchange for office space and a staff position. This setup generates intense economic pressure in an already competitive market. Many law firms have minimum annual

18 For a more complete history of lawyers in post-Cultural Revolution China, see Michelson (2003, 59–83), Peerenboom (2002, 345–350), Liu (2008a), and Liu (2011).

19 As Michelson (2006, 12) points out, lawyers have the same tax status as individual enterprises (*geti hu*). During my fieldwork, I also frequently heard lawyers refer to themselves as *geti hu*. By 2007, however, *geti hu* seemed to be a relatively neutral description rather than the self-deprecating reference to a marginalized social group that Michelson heard in 2000 (Michelson 2003, 81).

billing quotas, forcing lawyers to hustle commissions to stay employed (Michelson 2006, 13).[20] In addition, lawyers are responsible for taxes, annual fees to the All China Lawyers Association (ACLA), and the day-to-day expense of cultivating connections in the bureaucracy. Most lawyers undoubtedly worry about personal solvency far more than social change.

Still, in the short time since lawyers became private professionals, many have also joined the upwardly mobile middle class. While there are no national statistics on lawyer salaries, a 2007 survey found a median income of 100,000 RMB (US$15,873) per year (Liu 2008).[21] Even among Chinese urban professionals, this is a good living. Drawing on data from 2004 and 2005, Chinese legal scholar Zhu Jingwen estimates that lawyers make at least twice as much as those employed in other white-collar jobs including finance, real estate, and information technology (2007, 362–3). As one Jilin lawyer put it, "We've solved the problem of getting enough to eat. This is a prosperous society now!" (Interview 89). Prosperity, in turn, imparts financial freedom for occasional pro bono work. "Once you are dressed and fed," one lawyer told me, "you can do environmental work" (Interview 46; see also Interviews 5, 72, 82, 89, 116, 121, 125, 161, 168, 175). With the exception of a few lower-class lawyers driven by the strength of their beliefs, Chinese cause lawyers are middle- and upper-class recruits.

It has been less than twenty years since Chinese lawyers left the government bureaucracy, and, to some extent, legal activism simply reflects diversification. The jump from 63,088 lawyers in 1995 to 195,170 lawyers

20 Minimum annual billing quotas are meant to prevent lawyers from billing their clients directly and underreporting their gross income to the firm. This, of course, only partly solves the problem because lawyers can still underreport income after meeting the quota (Michelson 2006, 13).

21 Zhu estimates average annual income at a roughly comparable 80,000 RMB (US$12,698) (2007, 362). Income is also correlated with level of education. A 2009 online survey found that median annual income among lawyers with junior college degrees or less, bachelor's, master's, and doctoral degrees was 50,000 RMB (US$7,936), 88,000 RMB (US$13,968), 138,000 RMB (US$21,904), and 231,000 RMB (US$36,666) respectively (Michelson and Liu 2010, 316).

in 2010 brought a wider range of concerns and motivations to the bar (Zhu 2007, 30; China Law Yearbook 2011, 1067). Just as growing numbers of Jewish, Catholic, and black lawyers introduced civil rights litigation to America after World War I, pockets of an increasingly heterogeneous Chinese bar are now debating the public interest, and who lawyers should serve. Some see civic commitment as a way to resuscitate the reputation of a denigrated profession (Interview 14). Lawyers, as one saying puts it, "Just take money and don't do anything" (Interview 8; see also Michelson 2003, 20–24). If people admire lawyers, one op-ed in *Legal Daily* complained, "it is because they make a lot of money, not because they uphold law and justice" (Zhang 2006b). In this environment, some are understandably drawn to an alternative identity where lawyers are intellectuals and social activists who use their expertise on behalf of society.

As terms like public interest lawyer (*gongyi lüshi*) and rights-protection lawyer (*weiquan lüshi*) entered the Chinese lexicon in the 2000s, some lawyers also found an idealistic professional identity to be a refuge. Forgoing financial reward brings judicial respect, as one lawyer said, "not only for our morality but for our professionalism" (Interview 115). Pro bono work can allow relief from the sometimes expensive and sometimes unpleasant task of cultivating good relationships with judges (Interviews 115, 131).[22] Others find winning a case without relying on connections – just "because of your skill and because of the law" – to be tremendously satisfying (Interview 121). By the mid-2000s, a few public interest law firms and NGOs had opened in Beijing, including the Open Constitution Initiative and Dongfang Public Interest and Legal Aid Law Firm, both established in 2003, and Impact Law Firm, which started in 2006.[23] Often cast as "heroes who pursue justice," China's activist lawyers are now regular features in both the domestic and international

22 On how some lawyers dislike using connections (*la guanxi*), see Lo and Snape (2005, 450) and Wu (2008, 198).
23 The Open Constitution Initiative was first registered as *Yangguang Xianzheng* in 2003 before changing its Chinese name to Gongmeng in 2005.

press (He 2005, 1). These lawyers pursue causes from consumer rights to religious freedom, sometimes acting as plaintiffs and sometimes drawing clients from a society increasingly concerned with protecting legal rights. At least a few Chinese lawyers, like their American counterparts, see "litigation in much the same way athletes see the Olympics – a vivid showcase for their talents and proof of both their social importance and their selfless endeavors" (Schuck 2000, 36). In so doing, this nascent community of legal activists has drawn inspiration from two very different historical traditions, one home-grown and the other international.

Two Visions of Law

When Qiu Jiandong filed the case later dubbed China's first public interest lawsuit, he was not even aware of the term public interest litigation. In 1996, Qiu sued a branch of the Post and Telecommunications Office over a 1.20 RMB (US$0.19) overcharge on his bill owing to a failure to account for nighttime and holiday phone discounts (China Labour Bulletin 2007, 4). The "one RMB and twenty cents case," as it was called in the media, opened a series of consumer rights lawsuits over unfair or hidden fees. In fact, as public interest litigation gained currency in the early and mid-2000s, consumer rights cases (which are often considered the least sensitive type of public interest litigation) became a mainstream way for lawyers-turned-plaintiffs to protest unfairness (Huang 2006, 155). Yet back in 1996, Qiu Jiandong filed his first case before he had a label for his actions or knew of like-minded comrades. As he once commented to me, "This is a case of theory lagging behind practice."

The story of Qiu's first case reminds us that relatively isolated lawyers also take up the law for a cause. Without the spur of external networking, encouragement and exchange, local lawyers often draw on closer-to-home traditions to find and justify pro bono work. In particular, many draw on a socialist and revolutionary tradition of virtuous lawyers helping the poor. Cause lawyers can have socialist as well as democratic aspirations, especially because there is nothing inherently democratic about "a struggle on behalf of egalitarian values and redistributive policies" (Scheingold 2001, 383). On the contrary, egalitarianism places Chinese cause lawyers squarely in the socialist mainstream. Just as Cuban lawyers committed to the revolution voluntarily formed law collectives to give the poor access to justice, fighting for the rights of China's disadvantaged can help meet state goals (Michalowski 1998).

Many occasional cause lawyers fit comfortably within a tradition of state-sponsored legal aid. Back when they were government employees, lawyers had an official obligation to represent the poor, and many are accustomed to reducing fees in poor and rural areas (Liebman 1999, 238). In 1994, the Ministry of Justice announced plans to establish a national legal aid system. The budget and scope of the program reflect growing official emphasis on access to justice. In 1999, the legal aid system handled 132,097 cases on a budget of 27.5 million RMB (US$4.4 million) (Zhu 2007, 404). Eleven years later, in 2010, the numbers were up to 727,401 cases and a budget of 1 billion RMB (US$158 million) (China Law Yearbook 2010, 1069). In addition to government-run legal aid centers and legal aid offices inside government bureaus, China is also one of the few countries in which the local justice bureau assigns legal aid cases to lawyers (Liebman 1999, 214).[24] Although lawyers report variation in how many cases they handle, mandatory legal aid work helps plant the idea that lawyers should help deserving clients on behalf of society. Cause lawyers, at least in their egalitarian, socialist incarnation, can push for social transformation without advocating democracy.

Activist lawyers also draw inspiration from iconic images of revolutionary lawyers that pre-date the current legal aid system. While lawyer bashing has a long history in China, popular depictions of virtuous lawyers also surface amid jokes and complaints. The 1947 Shanghai movie *Bright Day*, for example, features a heroic lawyer who "acts for causes" (Conner 2007, 210). Lawyer Yin is a pro bono defender of old

---

24 Even lawyers in private practice are required to handle a certain number of legal aid cases per year. This regulation is implemented more stringently in some places than others.

ladies and rickshaw pullers as well as a self-aware crusader against class exploitation. In the character's didactic summation:

> It's shameful that good people are oppressed again and again but don't feel their oppression. No, that's not right, it's good people like us who don't rise up to fight evil, to struggle to death with those bastards. That's the disgrace!" (quoted in Conner 2007, 206)[25]

For some lawyers, revolutionary zeal far outlasted the 1949 Communist Revolution. Discussion on the ACLA Web site in the mid-2000s still showed lawyers invoking revolutionary rhetoric and casting themselves as heroic defenders of the masses (Halliday and Liu 2007). As one lawyer wrote, "I have adopted the practice that the more unjust the case, the more it is the kind of case where common people are eager to receive legal aid, the more willing I am to undertake [it]" (quoted in Halliday and Liu 2007, 99).

Tracing sympathy for the poor and oppressed through twentieth-century Chinese socialist and revolutionary history helps explain the appearance of twenty-first-century activist lawyers in an ostensibly hostile setting. Local historical exemplars, both recent and not so recent, simultaneously inspire action and help counter accusations of foreign influence. In fact, one American foundation representative believes that "indigenous cause lawyers get more bang for their buck" because they have less need for staff and overhead (Interview 86). At the very least, a gloss of historical continuity can help make rights litigation look like a natural extension of post-Mao communism. In this way of thinking, environmental litigation can ameliorate the wealth inequality and corruption that accompany capitalism and usher in "an equal and just society" (Xu 2005, 25). Environmental lawsuits are not a scary manifestation of rights consciousness and human rights, but exemplify moments when

---

25 For more on the film, see Conner (2007). Conner suggests that *Bright Day* is a typical 1940s "left-wing" film concerned about class and poverty. These films were both socialist and realist without necessarily being connected to the Chinese Communist Party.

the "national and societal good aligns with citizen interests" (Song 2006; see also Pan 2004). Sometimes invoked strategically and sometimes sincerely, historically resonant language casts activist lawyers as state allies in a glorious tradition.

At the same time, however, many of China's most vocal promoters of leveraging the law for social change are drawn to and inspired by international example. For these lawyers and academics, the 1996 Lawyers Law re-oriented the Chinese bar toward international standards of professionalism. He Weifang, one of China's superstar law professors capable of packing a room both on and off campus, sees lawyers as "a new type of profession influenced by foreign culture" (2005, 1). In particular, discussions of public interest law often touch on the concept's foreign origins. In most versions of the retelling, public interest law originated in ancient Rome and took off in the West in the 1960s and 1970s (Lü and Wu 2007, 20). This abbreviated history overlays an implicit teleology that public interest law is an inevitable part of how legal systems develop. In a 1997 speech, China's Minister of Justice explicitly equated the ability to provide legal aid with the country's overall level of legal development (Liebman 1999, 223).

In Chinese law schools, academics also bring international experience into the public consciousness. Books and articles like *Frontline Research on Handling Environmental Disputes: Chinese, Japanese and Korean Scholars Discuss* (Zhang 2007) or *Citizen Lawsuits in American Environmental Law and Their Inspiration for China* (Jiang 2006a) translate and interpret global experience. Clinics and courses act as portals for new ideas, too. At Peking University, home to one of China's top law schools, several hundred students took a course on the American public interest law tradition between 2006 and 2011. The course, taught by a visiting American lawyer, looks at the past, present, and future of American public interest law and its applicability to China. Under the heading "New Words," the syllabus explicitly takes on the issue of translation:

In the globalizing world, people in public life (lawyers, officials, managers) increasingly use the same words (for example, rule of law,

NGOs, governance), but the words may mean different things in different places. An important purpose of the course is to help students and professor learn the ways in which basic words and concepts used in American law (for example, "class action," "reasonable man," "discovery," "precedent") "translate" into Chinese concepts, and vice versa. Students will be expected to keep a list of American law terms and concepts that they find interesting and possibly useful.[26]

Although students are expected to be thoughtful about difference ("words may mean different things in different places"), the assumption is that at least some American concepts are "interesting and possibly useful." The syllabus lends itself to a nuanced discussion of different strands of the American experience while also steering students away from the possibility that public interest law is a foreign import ill-suited to China. Translation is meant to mete out a local understanding of public interest law after which course graduates will join a legal elite well-versed in indigenization, or the use of local language to gain legitimacy for ideas that originate elsewhere (Stern 2005, 422).

International actors have also directly funded some of China's legal advocacy organizations. Just as private money made civil rights litigation possible in twentieth–century America, international organizations provided critical early funding for China's first legal aid centers and public interest law firms. Perhaps due to its history supporting rights litigation in the United States, the Ford Foundation was one of the first to support China's emerging legal community.[27] Ford started work in China in 1979, and its first law-related programs were academic

---

26 Syllabus and information about the course provided by the instructor. The course has grown into part of a larger public interest law program that includes a clinic and a law journal.

27 As Charles Epp recounts: "The Ford Foundation gave $7.4 million to the National Legal Aid and Defender Association from 1953 to 1972; $15 million to create the pro-civil liberties fund for the American Republic in 1953–1972; $8.6 million to the Southern Regional Council from 1953 to 1977; $3.3 million to the NAACP-LDF from 1967 to 1976; and $13 million for the development of public interest law centers from 1970 to 1977" (1998, 58).

exchanges. By 1992, however, program officers were fiscally and strategically ready to directly fund China's first legal aid center: the Wuhan
University Center for the Protection of the Rights of Disadvantaged Citizens (Liebman 1999, 233). Following Ford's lead, other international
organizations, including the Asia Foundation, the Canadian International Development Agency, and the United Nations Development Pro-
gramme (UNDP), funded legal services in the late 1990s and early 2000s.
Although there is no tally of total international funding for litigation, an
examination of Ford's annual reports shows that it gave at least US$2.9
million to Chinese legal aid organizations between 2000 and 2008.[28] This
is not a huge amount in absolute terms, but the landscape of legal advocacy would clearly look quite different without international support.

As others have noted, Chinese legal reformers are divided between
those want to bring law in line with international practice and adherents
to a local socialist legal tradition (Liebman 2008; Liu 2011). Both camps
can find something to like about Chinese cause lawyers. Legal activism
can be interpreted as grassroots populist enthusiasm for socialist values
or as a new form of international professionalism. For every Pu Zhiqiang,
a Chinese lawyer who deployed freedom-of-speech arguments inspired
by the 1964 *New York Times Co. v. Sullivan* decision, there is a lawyer
inspired by China's socialist and revolutionary past.[29] This means that
adroit lawyers can also switch rhetoric as the situation demands, winning
support (or at least grudging acceptance) from both Western-oriented
reformers and socialist conservatives.

---

28 Calculations by the author. The Ford Foundation Web site (http://www.fordfound.org)
   includes a grant database for the years 2005–2008 and annual reports for 2000–2004.
   I searched both the grant database and annual reports for the keyword "China" and
   used discretion to sort out grants that 1) directly supported legal aid organizations,
   2) supported networking between public interest lawyers, and 3) supported the development of clinical legal education in China. Other legal aid organizations that have
   received significant financial support from Ford include the Research Center on Juve-
   nile Legal Aid, the Beijing University Center for Women's Law Studies and Legal
   Research, and the Yunnan Xishuangbanna Prefecture Women and Children Psychological and Legal Consultation Service Center. All dollar totals are approximate
   because single grants could cover multiple types of activities.
29 For more on Pu, see Pan (2008, chapter 10).

Tensions and Divisions

It is hard to forge solidarity across such different motivations and, as of the late 2000s, China's environmental lawyers were still trying to team up and stand together.[30] One reason that environmental lawyers are not more unified is disagreement over goals and tactics, sometimes exacerbated by jealousy and competition. Sometimes naming names and sometimes keeping silent, nearly everyone in China's environmental law community can think of someone who is out for publicity, and grumbling about "fishing for fame and compliments" (*guming diaoyu*) is widespread.[31] "If a lawyer wants to be famous," one lawyer commented to me at a workshop in March 2007, "it's just too easy." However, as a few are willing to admit, the rewards of reputation are real (Interviews 12, 118, 121). Lawyers rely on "cheerleaders" (*lala dui*), especially the media, to build a reputation and bring in clients (Qiu 2006, 15–16; see also Liebman 1999, 238).[32] At times, caustic remarks about publicity seekers also indicate strategic disagreement. Some lawyers pursue a self-consciously "low profile" (*didiao*) strategy where they "just do stuff, but don't talk about it" (Interview 85; see also Interviews 70, 92). From their perspective, lawyers in the headlines only attract unwanted state attention. Others see the media as a critical ally in the vital business of attracting clients, capturing public opinion, and pressuring judges. Coverage from official state media, in particular, stamps lawsuits with an official imprimatur that increases the likelihood of a sympathetic hearing.

---

30 Although many environmental lawyers are loosely affiliated with either the Center for Legal Assistance to Pollution Victims (CLAPV) in Beijing or the environmental law committee of ACLA, these networks are not particularly tight-knit.

31 See Interviews, 6, 12, 30, 118, 119, 129, and 151 as well as dozens of other comments in more informal exchanges.

32 For well-known lawyers, on the other hand, controversial cases can be more risky than rewarding. Self-proclaimed public interest lawyer Yan Yiming, for example, told *Southern Weekend* in 2009 that he lost foreign clients over his public interest work (Meng 2009).

Across these fissures, the pleasure of moral action moves many. Acting on conviction expresses personal alligences and deepens self-respect. Law, like protest, offers a satisfying opportunity to "plumb our moral sensibilities and convictions and to articulate and elaborate them" (Jasper 1997, 5). Better yet, heightened societal respect frequently accompanies the self-contained pleasure of taking a stance. Idealism begets status, visible in newspaper coverage, awards, and the admiration that permeates everyday social encounters. All but the humblest lawyers would enjoy being introduced to a conference as "our rights-upholding hero," as I once observed, or like Chinese academic and lawyer Wang Canfa, being selected as an international "hero of the environment" by *Time* magazine (Ramzy 2007). As one lawyer explained, "There's so much to do in China, it's easy to be a hero" (Interview 92). Or it is at least easy to be a hero to someone. Heroic sensations of power, righteousness, and gratitude can arise from even one pro bono case. Grateful clients, the kind who thank lawyers with a commemorative banner or perhaps mark the end of a lawsuit with a group photo, can be deeply fulfilling. As one environmental lawyer recalled the mood during his final client meeting, "Although we faced opposition from the local government, we felt at that moment like it was worth it" (Interview 116).

Serving justice and rights can also be fun. As one Zhejiang lawyer told me, suing the government "fits my personality because I like being a tiger" (Interview 121). Some lawyers even appreciate the long odds of environmental cases. As one lawyer put it, "A case has to be challenging before it's interesting" (*you weidao*) (Interview 101).[33] For those who like performing, the spectacle of litigation is especially enjoyable. At an environmental hearing I attended in December 2008, the legal team (which included the plaintiff) seized every opportunity for drama. Here is a typical exchange:

---

33 Criminal defense lawyers likewise report that they enjoy the professional challenge and sense of achievement in their work (Liu and Halliday 2011, 846).

Plaintiff: Did you visit the neighboring fruit farms to assess damages there? What were they like?

Representative from the appraisal team: [long pause] I believe we went several times.

Plaintiff: Hah! You went! [Snort] No way! You saw them across the way! [Snort]

Regardless of the outcome, this was first-rate theater. As one of the lawyers commented afterward, it was like watching a play or starring in a Hollywood movie.

Signals, Self-Censorship, and Control Parables

Part of the daily experience of legal activism is managing political risk to successfully navigate the grey zone between what is tolerated and what is forbidden. Once a case is underway, lawyers can suss out political sensitivities through signs such as whether local courts take the case and the presence (or absence) of warnings from government contacts.[34] Ahead of time, however, information is less reliable. The state's bottom line is unclear rather than a "socially shared rule," and lawyers must make judgment calls about risk (Helmke and Levitsky 2006, 4). Typically, uncertainty exacerbates self-censorship.[35] Would-be environmental lawyers wrestle with "attitudes, fears and uncertainties" that counsel against risk-taking and toward safer choices, such as turning down a case or quitting later on (Fernandez 2008, 34).

Especially among those with imperfect information, interpreting state signals is a common way to assess risk and cope with uncertainty.

---

34 Thanks to John Givens for drawing my attention to this point.

35 There are strong parallels between lawyers and journalists. Chinese journalists also "self-censor to a critical degree" because the Central Propaganda Department "demarcates the boundaries of the acceptable in such a deliberately fuzzy way" (Hassid 2008, 415). On the link between uncertainty and self-censorship, also see Link (2002).

Sometimes, encouraging signals serve as a green light. In 2007, for example, one Shanghai lawyer discussed his decision to start taking environmental cases:

> My goal has always been to protect citizens (*weihu gongmin*) and I've slowly moved from less sensitive cases to more sensitive ones (*cong bu mingan dao mingan*)...I thought about this strategy for a long time and I plan to file my first environmental lawsuit in May 2008, just after the open information regulations take effect. Access to information will make this kind of lawsuit much easier (Interview 72).

At other times, signals serve as a warning. A Beijing lawyer saw the 2011 detention of activist lawyer Teng Biao as "a reminder to be cautious. I look to see which way the wind is blowing. It's like Japan [after the Fukushima nuclear meltdown] where they are looking to see which way the wind is coming from" (Interview 152).

In addition to individual efforts to tally confusing and sometimes contradictory signs of state preferences, the unwritten rules of political conduct are also shaped by the collective retelling of control parables. Control parables are stories about transgression that counsel caution and restrict political possibilities (Stern and Hassid 2012).[36] Often told informally during conference breaks or over meals, control parables are *a type of didactic story* that invent or recapitulate shared understandings about how to manage the risks of uncertainty.

Typically, control parables begin with news of how a colleague ran into political trouble. Then, rather than uncritically accepting the state's explanation (when there is one), storytellers and listeners speculate about the hidden reasons for retribution. In the ensuing back-and-forth of conversation, what starts as a nugget of gossip turns into a parable as listeners and storytellers suggest and refine lessons about when

---

36 I call them parables because they are less detailed than a story (often there is no true beginning, middle, or end) but more open-ended than an adage (which summarizes a moral in a pithy proverb).

and why tolerance thins. Sometimes, listeners and storytellers converge on a single understanding of which political tripwires triggered official displeasure. Other times, the conversation ends without the participants reaching consensus. Over time, however, proffered explanations start to take on authority by dint of repetition. As a control parable circulates through a community, speculation surrounding a warning or punishment begins to coalesce into a set of imagined rules designed to prevent future clashes with authority. Without state involvement or necessarily even knowledge, this kind of gossip influences behavior by making some "courses of action seem reasonable, fitting, even possible and others seem ineffectual, ill-considered, or impossible" (Polletta 2006, 4). Control parables, in other words, are the flip side of stirring resistance stories.[37] Instead of inspiring action, they dissipate possibilities.

One good place to hear control parables is inside the legal community. When a lawyer or organization runs into political trouble, gossip nearly always follows to explain why. One example came on the heels of a training program for public interest lawyers that I attended in 2007. Over the following six months, I heard (and overheard) at least a half-dozen conversations about political blowback from this meeting.[38] The consistent kernel of the rumor was that local officials reported the conference (*huibao*) up the Party chain of command to President Hu Jintao on the grounds that some participants vilified (*chouhua*) the government. Given routine reports of surveillance, harassment, and detention of outspoken attorneys around the same time, this account was both credible and scary. (It was not until 2011 that I was able to confirm with

---

37 See Ganz (2001), Polletta (2006), and Khalili (2007) on resistance stories. Interestingly, I did not hear many resistance stories while working on this project. The few heroic references, discussed in Chapter 7, were to international heroes rather than domestic ones.

38 I was an active participant in some of these conversations. Overhearing several similar conversations, however, convinced me that my presence did not change the basic script.

the organizer that the Beijing Bureau of Justice did, in fact, launch an investigation into the conference).[39]

For a time, this rumor about how the conference attracted hostile official attention was eagerly discussed among the community of Beijing lawyers, academics, and international NGO representatives involved in public interest law. Aside from the fun of passing on insider information, these conversations marked an attempt to decipher how the conference differed from dozens of similar meetings and, in particular, what the organizer did wrong. Storytellers, as Polletta observes, "rarely say explicitly to their audience, 'and the moral of the story is...'" (2006, 10). Instead, each conversation organically unearthed lessons about how to avoid political fallout.

Theories about why the conference ran into trouble included: 1) the location (a small town where it was hard to avoid notice); 2) the conservative attitude of the local government; 3) the source of financing (the politically sensitive Open Society Institute), and 4) the sponsors (there was no "protective umbrella" (*baohu san*) of university involvement).[40] These are all plausible explanations, but the more interesting point is how people draw meaning from seemingly random sanctions. Finding fault with an inexperienced conference organizer helps moderate the anxiety of uncertainty when government actions are inscrutable. Like all stories, the call-and-response of control parables fills a human impulse to "understand character and motive" (Khalili 2007, 226). Across retellings, storytellers and listeners refine a set of imagined rules designed to prevent future clashes with authority. Without state involvement or even knowledge, these parables weave uncertainty into socially shared understandings about the limits of tolerance.

39 After reviewing the list of attendees, conference materials, and a video recording of the proceedings, officials decided there had been a "misunderstanding" (*wujue*). Following the investigation, the lawyer self-consciously spent several years cautiously keeping a low profile.

40 The lawyer believed that the investigation was triggered by a separate case that angered a powerful real estate company. This explanation did not surface in the control parables told in 2007, likely because the lawyer kept silent during the investigation.

Drawing meaning out of seeming randomness is clearly not unique to Chinese lawyers. We tell ourselves stories to explain uncertainty all the time, coming up with theories about when highway police are most likely to be ticketing or who will be fired in upcoming layoffs. Control parables are a subset of these larger attempts to interpret and manage uncertainty. The difference is that control parables deal exclusively with one particular type of uncertainty: ambiguity about which actions authorities consider off limits.[41] Democracies, too, are capable of unpredictable crackdowns, at times harassing some groups that challenge the prevailing political orthodoxy and not others.[42] Still, democratic leaders are usually limited in ways that authoritarian leaders are not. Pressure to maintain the appearance of clear laws and consequences constrains discretion and, by extension, uncertainty.

The availability of information matters, too. People with first-rate connections inside the Chinese state may know exactly what went wrong, such that they feel less of a need to listen to control parables or recount them. Control parables thrive among those less well-connected, who experience the state as something of a black box.[43] Anxiety is the emotion that drives people to tell control parables, and, particularly when media reports are incomplete or disingenuous, people turn to their social network to interpret rumors. When these conversations turn to repression inside the legal community, lawyers can be heard telling parables that depict – and create – the limits of tolerance.

One of the most notable political consequences of control parables in contemporary China is the degree to which they shift blame away from the political system. Instead of criticizing top leaders or the CCP, control parables usually attribute repression to obstructionist officials or

---

41 Note that this is different from ambiguity surrounding whether citizens will be punished. Drivers frequently get away with speeding, for example, but everyone is clear that it is illegal.

42 For examples of surveillance and harassment in the United States, see Davenport (2005) and Starr, Fernandez, Amster, Wood, and Caro (2008).

43 I'm grateful to Alex Wang for helping me see this point.

hold participants responsible for the consequence of their own actions.[44] Political scientist Tim Hildebrant's book on Chinese NGOs, for example, points out that those who have never run into problems with authorities tend to see clashes as activists' fault, perhaps prompted by their excessive radicalism or ignorance of the rules. Hildebrant writes, "Leaders are quick to point to the 'poor choices' of others, while drawing attention to their own 'smart decisions'"(2013, 56). In deflecting blame from the politically powerful, control parables serve elite interests. Listening to what is not said underscores the extent to which the powerful have "successfully inserted themselves and their interests into the processes by which the weak understand themselves, their goals, their possibilities, and their constraints" (Stokes 1991, 270). Insofar as lawyers share a common understanding of the limits of the permissible, it is an understanding partly created by their own actions and interpretation.

The Weak and the Few

In the end, environmental lawyers in China are a minority. A back-of-the-envelope estimate, based on the roughly four percent of lawyers who reported an environmental case in the survey cited above, is that 7,800 of China's 195,170 lawyers are currently involved in some environmental work. Most of these environmental lawyers are occasional dabblers rather than expert "repeat players" (Galanter 1974). Without career fairs or summer scholarships, younger lawyers interested in environmental litigation say they are unsure how to break into the field (Interviews 3, 4, 170), and experienced environmental lawyers are as one complained, "too weak and too few" (Interview 110). For now, environmental lawyer remains an "unstable professional type" that shifts with the political winds and economic possibilities (Shamir and Chinksi 1998, 232). Experience tends to fade ideals, especially the day-to-day grind

---

44 See Li (2004) on Chinese citizens' "bifurcated" view of the state and how blame accrues to local mismanagement without denting the integrity of the central government.

of being underpaid and underappreciated. It is tiring to earn as little as an administrative assistant (Interview 37) or to get stiffed by clients on litigation fees (Interview 110), particularly when success is rare. It is discouraging to sink time into an environmental case, perhaps making multiple trips to far-off pollution sites, only to find plaintiffs suddenly unwilling to sue or the court unwilling to accept the case. Disillusionment and burnout are as common as recruitment and radicalization, especially among those just starting out (Interviews 53, 90, 108, 152, 161).

Still, the existence of anyone who could plausibly be called a Chinese cause lawyer marks a noteworthy shift from the early 2000s when lawyers were seen as "producers, peddlers and consumers of connections" (Michelson 2003, 6). Discussions about moral motivation and values-driven litigation also show how conflicting political cues can open up possibilities for activism. For many, even a hint of political sensitivity is enough to counsel a retreat to less controversial work. At the same time, however, uncertainty can be interpreted as inspired opportunity, especially when lawyers have a larger cause in mind.[45] For all the wariness the state displays toward activist lawyers, there is room to maneuver in the no man's land between the uncontroversial and the forbidden.

45 On how activists tend to be overly optimistic, see O'Brien and Li (2006, 47).

7 Soft Support

The International NGOs

OVER TEA IN INDUSTRIAL NORTHEASTERN CHINA, A GROUP of Chinese lawyers discuss O.J. Simpson as a symbol of America's commitment to human rights. For them, O.J.'s 1995 murder trial does not illustrate racism or the perils of celebrity justice, but a well-functioning legal system operating at its best. Sixteen hundred miles to the south, in Shenzhen, a group of lawyers hires a foreign tutor to convene weekly two-hour classes on American law. In their free time, they want both to practice English and learn about the US justice system. And in Washington DC, a Chinese environmental lawyer on an American-sponsored exchange program calls me to talk about his internship. Energized by new possibilities, he shares his plan to establish a Chinese environmental foundation when he returns home.

In a moment when nearly every culture has access to every other, it was impossible to observe China's legal landscape without noticing this kind of transnational influence. The global reach of the Internet, CNN, and Hollywood has increasingly brought the American experience into everyday Chinese lives. For those with an international bent, especially in big cities, it has become difficult not to know something about law elsewhere. Some, such as the environmental-lawyer-turned-Washington, DC-intern, are even more deeply integrated into a steady current of transnational activity. These lawyers are active participants in international networks: they attend and co-organize workshops funded by international non-governmental organizations (INGOs) and take advantage of American-sponsored opportunities to go abroad.[1]

Environmental litigation is not a purely domestic story, and turning our attention abroad, this chapter examines the influence of a final new actor: international NGOs. In particular, how (if at all) do international programs designed to support environmental litigation affect legal professionals' day-to-day practice and core commitments? Empirically, this is an important question because there has been little public evaluation of the programs designed to help lawyers leverage the law for social change.[2] China-based rule-of-law programs are a steady presence on the legal landscape, and INGOs looking to the next project are surely interested in how their money matters. For students of Chinese politics, this chapter also fits into a new wave of work on how international funding (Bentley 2003; Spires 2011) and networks (Shelley 2005; Wu 2005; Morton 2008) affect domestic NGOs.[3] Instead of focusing on organizations, however, I look at another potential sphere of activism: litigation.

Theoretically, links between INGOs and Chinese lawyers brings into focus a particular strain of transnational activism, which – extending Charles Epp's concept of a litigation support structure (1998) – I call soft support. Rather than lobbying for policy change or directly funding litigation, international organizers of soft support programs invest in human capital by enhancing activists' legal skills, knowledge, and experience. The hallmark of soft support, training programs backed by international expertise and funding is a common part of efforts to build civil society and promote democracy. My work explores this

---

1 By network, I mean the collection of overlapping, voluntary, personal, and professional connections that knit together individuals and organizations.

2 For a critique of US-sponsored rule-of-law programs, see Stephenson (2006). Alford also discusses the ethics of promoting democracy and rule of law in China (2000, 1707–1708).

3 On lack of attention to international influences, see O'Brien and Stern (2008, 22–23) and Morton (2008, 195).

broader trend by zeroing in on American-funded efforts to support Chinese environmental lawyers.[4]

This chapter traces soft support from conception to implementation and from the United States to China. The payoff is a new perspective on one specific way in which regions can be "linked and bounded" (Cooper 2001, 213). As researchers have noted, there are "different types of foreign connectedness" as well as "multiple Chinas, connected to the outside world in many ways" (Stark, Vedres and Bruszt 2006, 326; O'Brien and Stern 2008, 23). Soft support gives us another angle on globalization, particularly how middlemen translate goals into programs and the reasons why both Americans and Chinese seek out connections across borders.

Overall, American-funded soft support for environmental lawyers has met mixed results. To date, there is little evidence that soft support has recruited a substantial new corps of activist lawyers or improved the success of litigation. Instead, soft support is most effective in introducing ideas, inculcating hope, and encouraging new identities. While this kind of intangible outcome may leave hard-nosed grant makers uneasy, soft support programs offer a welcome reminder that environmental lawyers' efforts are appreciated abroad if not at home. At the same time, the American legal system – often distorted in the retelling – serves as an aspirational ideal for the future.

The Turn Toward Soft Support

Many of the classic accounts of transnational activism revolve around the state (Keck and Sikkink 1998; True and Minstrom 2001; Khagram 2004; Tarrow 2005). Building on the insight that transnational

---

4 This is not to say that the United States is the only game in town. European, Japanese, and Korean organizations run similar soft support programs in China that target lawyers, plaintiffs, activists, students, judges, and government officials. Although future research may want to examine variation, a first look suggests a striking similarity of values, curriculum, and approach across of the nationality of the organizers and the groups involved.

ties affect political outcomes, researchers have chronicled how coalitions "bound by a common agenda" influence government policy (Price 1998, 620). Activists promoting a different definition of development (Khagram 2004), for example, or an anti-land mine ban (Price 1998) lobby decision makers to accept their definition of a problem and its solution. Activist groups knock on the doors of power, leveraging moral suasion and social pressure to change minds (Price 1998, 616). Sometimes, the state also invites outsiders in, to pick their brains for a new "cheap means" to solve a problem (Dolowitz and Marsh 2000, 14; see also Kelemen and Sibbitt 2004; Weyland 2005). Uncertainty and complexity stimulate openness to outside ideas, and policymakers frequently turn to knowledgeable experts or epistemic communities to deal with tough issues (Haas 1992).[5]

Both transnational advocacy networks and epistemic communities are alive and well in China. Government officials scour the world for solutions to China's social problems even as international networks lobby top leaders on issues ranging from trade to Tibet. Indeed, INGOs frequently collaborate with government-backed organizations to cultivate allies inside government. In a strong, illiberal state, officials are impossible to ignore. But in a world "crisscrossed by an increasingly dense web of networks," not all activism is state-focused (Slaughter 2004, 6).[6] NGOs often bypass the state, for example, by directly pressuring polluters or staging events to shock an apathetic public into action (Wapner 1996; Wu 2005, 66).[7] Reaching around the state can be an

---

5 "An epistemic community is a network of professionals with recognized expertise and competence in a particular domain and an authoritative claim to policy-relevant knowledge within that domain or issue-area" (Haas 1992, 3).

6 In sociology and anthropology, much of the literature on diffusion looks at transnational ties outside the state. On the diffusion of social problems, see Best (2001). On the diffusion of ideas, see McAdam and Rucht (1993) and Dezalay and Garth (1996). On the diffusion of protest repertoires, see Soule and Tarrow (1991), Chabot (2000), and Chabot and Duyvendak (2002).

7 In China, there are also other examples of activism that reaches around the state. In 2004, *The Epoch Times* (a newspaper with close links to the banned sect Falun Gong)

effective strategy, particularly in non-democracies when lobbying offers uncertain results (Khagram 2004, 20–25).

One way of reaching out to "critical communities" is training Chinese lawyers in environmental law and advocacy (Chabot and Duyvendak 2002, 706). Steeped in the conviction that litigation can bring social change, American donors have taken seriously political scientist Charles Epp's charge that "proponents of expanded judicial protection for rights should... provide support to rights-advocacy lawyers and organizations" (Epp 1998, 6). This support can take many forms. In Epp's work, a "support structure" of organizations and lawyers backed by private and public money brought enough litigation to spark the 1960s American rights revolution (1998, 19). In contemporary China, in contrast, American organizational, legal, and financial resources seldom support the cost of litigation.[8] Although some Chinese lawyers say they would gladly accept cash to pay salaries and litigation fees, organizations generally opt for soft support: investing instead in skills to make future litigation and advocacy possible. This investment in human capital leaves a visible wake of flyers and e-mails announcing training workshops, conferences, and exchange programs.[9] During my fieldwork in the mid-2000s, international money often translated into an international perspective on environmental law. Foreign-financed opportunities to reflect and learn frequently included some discussion of what China can learn from abroad.

orchestrated a mass resignation from the Chinese Communist Party (Thornton 2008, 179).

8 For environmental litigation, one exception is the Ford Foundation. Between 2000 and 2008, the Ford Foundation gave over US$880,000 to the Center for Legal Assistance to Pollution Victims (CLAPV), China's leading environmental legal aid center. Some of this money was used by CLAPV for litigation, although it is important to note that Ford played no role in decisions regarding lawsuits (calculation by the author, data from Ford Foundation annual reports, and the online grants database). Among labor NGOs, direct foreign funding for litigation is somewhat more common. China Labour Bulletin, a Hong Kong-based NGO, also started a labor rights litigation project in 2003, which directly pays Chinese lawyers to take on labor cases. As of June 2008, China Labour Bulletin had taken on 274 cases and provided US$87,000 in lawyer fees (Han 2008, 4–5; see also Gallagher 2007, 209).

9 For more on investing in human capital, see Mendelson and Glenn (2002, 9).

Of course, this is not the first time China has encountered foreign money, ideas, or experts. Between the end of the Qing Dynasty in 1911 and the Chinese Communist Revolution in 1949, China was deeply internationalized (Kirby 1997). Foreigners translated international law textbooks (Svarverud 2007, 91–106), founded law schools (Conner 2003), financed railways, and worked as missionaries (Kirby 1997, 447 and 452–453). In 1947, the Rockefeller Foundation alone invested US$45 million in Chinese medical programs (Wu 2005, 7). In part, contemporary soft support reflects a resurgence of international involvement after the isolation of the Mao era.

On the American side, the Clinton and Bush administrations' support for rule-of-law programs in China evoke memories of earlier efforts to bring American legal assistance to Latin America, Africa, and parts of Southeast Asia during the 1960s law and development movement (Alford 2000; Stephenson 2006). The mid-1960s saw a zenith of belief in the transformative potential of law; experts spent the better part of a decade teaching the American experience in the hopes of inspiring imitation.[10] Legal scholars involved in this period of international outreach recall that law meant more than efficient, impartial justice; it was a "rational and effective method to protect individual freedom, expand citizen participation in decision making [and] enhance social equity" (Trubek and Galanter 1974, 1063). More than forty years later, the associate director of the Asia Law Initiative at the American Bar Association (ABA) made the same connection between values and soft support. In his words, "The environment is the wedge issue, the Trojan Horse, by which the ABA is working with the legal reform community in China to advance cutting edge concepts of rule of law, governance, and transparency" (Rohan 2003). Now, as before, the transmission of expertise is accompanied by the "indirect transfer of

---

10 For more on the 1960s law and development movement, see Trubek and Galanter (1974), Gardener (1980), and Widner (2001, 200–205).

underlying legal models, concepts, values and ideas" (Gardener 1980, 14). But whose morals anchor environmental law programs, and are they effectively transmitted? Following program development from the United States to China shows how aspirations shift between rhetoric and practice.

The American Side

By the early 2000s, American foundations, NGOs, and government offices were deeply interested in China. As a staff member at an US environmental NGO explained, "The single biggest issue right now is China and what China is going to do ... China holds the fate of the planet in its hands, so whatever we can do is worth it" (Interview 141). Even Chinese lawyers across the Pacific noticed that "China is unignorable," and, by 2007, it was clear to employees at some US government agencies that "people [in Washington] are realizing that China is a major player" (Interview 109).

In the first decade of the century, interest in China translated into funding for outreach. American foundations made just less than $443 million in grants to China between 2003 and 2009, placing China third among 195 countries in terms of number of grants received (Spires 2011, 316). In public money, the US government devoted $257 million between 2001 and 2011 for programs designed to support human rights, democracy, Tibetan communities, the environment, and rule of law (Lum 2012, 1). Soft support programs for environmental lawyers were usually part of this last category, rule of law. Often, legal reform is linked to proto-democratic values such as transparency, accountability, and public participation.[11] During the Bush administration, legal assistance ranked particularly high on what the president called his freedom agenda. The

---

11 On American efforts to promote democracy, see Carothers (1999), Azimi (2007), and Bush (2011).

Table 7.1. *Human Rights and Democracy Fund Support for China*

	2002	2003	2004	2005	2006	2007	2008	2009	2010	2011
Total budget (in millions)	13	26.7	32.9	34.2	69.8	69.8	64	70	79	66.9
$ for China (in millions)	4.7	8.6	13	11	–	–	15	17	17	17
China as % of total budget	36.5	32.3	40	34.8	–	–	23.4	24.2	21.5	25.4

Sources: Data from the US Department of State, Bureau of Democracy, Human Rights, and Labor Web site, accessed May 13, 2008, and supplemented by personal communication with State Department staff, October 22, 2010, and April 16, 2012. (Data on money allocated to China in 2006 and 2007 not available).

State Department's Human Rights and Democracy Fund earmarked $17 million for China-based programs in fiscal year 2011, nearly a four-fold increase over 2002 (Table 7.1).

Although there is no comprehensive list of environmental law programs, the ABA, the Rockefeller Brothers Fund, the Global Greengrants Fund, the Natural Resources Defense Council, the Ford Foundation, EcoLinx, the Environmental Defense Fund, and Vermont Law School ran programs between 2001 and 2008 on environmental information, legal aid, and public participation in environmental decision making in China.[12] Most of these programs were small-scale, ranging from several thousand dollars to several hundred thousand dollars.[13] There were also a few larger initiatives alongside small grants. In 2006, for example,

12 This chapter lumps together private and public money on the grounds that goals and programming tend to be similar. The boundaries between the two worlds can also blur. The National Endowment for Democracy and the Asia Foundation, to take two prominent examples of private foundations, receive a significant percentage of their budget from the US government. Further research might want to consider how the source of funding affects pressures on program organizers. Sometimes, moderation may not play well among donors. Representatives of one State Department-supported organization told me they have to work hard to persuade China critics on Capitol Hill that a good relationship to the CCP does not obviate an individual's "integrity as [an] advocate" (Interview 95).

13 There can be advantages to small budgets as well. As one NGO representative remarked, "It is harder for the [Chinese] government to keep tabs on all of us" (Interview 83).

US Senator Patrick Leahy was instrumental in helping Vermont Law School and Sun Yat-sen University win a three-year, $1.8 million grant from the US Agency for International Development (USAID) to focus on environmental law. In 2009, USAID renewed the grant for another $3 million over three years (Vermont Law School 2009).[14]

Some environmental law programs are designed to promote democratic values, and, at times, political change surfaces as an acknowledged part of the agenda. In 2003, a representative from the ABA told the Congressional-Executive Commission on China that "using environmental law as a means to promote broader rule of law … is the right approach at the right time … [T]he reform community with whom we are working sees this project as a well-timed, viable approach to political reform" (Rohan 2003). Depending on the donor, couching programs in terms of democracy and human rights can also help win grants. Tackling big issues can be part of an appealing application, especially in the years directly after former President Bush made "ending tyranny" and "the growth of democratic movements and institutions in every nation and culture" key parts of his second inaugural address and American foreign policy (Bush 2005). Law-focused INGOs say they find it "relatively easy to make the argument that any one of our programs contributes to democracy and human rights" because litigation "forces the government to respond and that's very democratic" (Interview 95). Even the low-key training and exchange of soft support can be linked to political change. One academic involved with rule-of-law programs argued that training Chinese lawyers in critical thinking is "the most subversive thing we can get to happen. That starts to create subterranean fissures by changing the way people think, understand, and process issues. That's ultimately more effective than standing in Tiananmen Square" (quoted in Stephenson 2006, 201).

---

14 Between 2006 and 2011, Congress earmarked funds specifically for USAID to run environment, governance, and rule-of-law programs in China (Lum 2012). Leahy helped secure a portion of these funds for his home state.

Difficulties on the Ground

Would-be philanthropists looking to work in China quickly find themselves in need of local contacts and expertise. Those starting out often first look to China's most internationalized enclaves for local partners: charismatic, English-speaking Chinese activists or Beijing-based INGOs. There are not many well-established Chinese NGOs, and grant makers sometimes find themselves in competition to work with the same "four and a half [Chinese] people" (Interview 102; see also Interviews 21, 23, 112; Spires 2011). Out of both necessity and convenience, much money is also allocated to INGOs with an office in China. These middlemen play a pivotal role in turning grant applications into workable projects. These are the people on "the outposts of intercultural collision" who, at times, find themselves responsible for promoting democratic values in a state committed to one-party rule (Cohen 1974, 214).

This is no easy task in a difficult, high-pressure environment. One problem is that some INGOs are not legally registered with the government because of difficulties finding a Chinese government agency willing to officially sponsor and supervise them.[15] Operating in a legal gray zone raises practical problems, such as the lack of an organizational bank account. In the mid-2000s, one program head could only secure enough local currency for daily operations by recruiting visiting Americans to change dollars into Chinese *renminbi*. Although she found it "totally unprofessional" to drag visitors to the bank, there was no other way to operate considering that each individual could only convert $50,000 a year (Interview 83). Being unregistered also intensifies awareness that continued operation depends on the Chinese government's forbearance. American program officers worry constantly about being shut

---

15 Other INGOs and foundations are officially registered with a Chinese supervisory agency, including the Clinton Foundation, the Gates Foundation, and the Ford Foundation.

down and the safety of their Chinese staff. The 2007 closing of English-language operations at China Development Brief, a newsletter on Chinese social development and civil society, reminded many that these concerns were real.[16] Even when the risk of closure feels remote, psychological pressure remains, especially if a staff member has been recently invited for a chat with the Public Security Bureau. At his most high-stress moments, one Beijing-based expert involved in environmental law-related soft support said "I felt like I was on the bottom of Niagara Falls" (Interview 102).

The toll of state surveillance (both real and imagined) helps explain enthusiasm for soft support programs. Although local training and skill building is a common component of aid work everywhere – capacity building is an industry buzzword – soft support is central to efforts to support environmental lawyers because the desire to stay engaged moderates possible courses of action. A few Chinese NGO leaders complain international donors have "no appetite for risk" (Interview 162; see also Interview 70), and many Beijing-based representatives of American NGOs and foundations agree that direct financial support for an environmental lawsuit falls beyond their comfort zone (Interviews 71, 83, 86, 95, 111, 112). Their goal is to support local reformers, not to get expelled from China or draw attention to themselves. One foundation representative avoids "radical, radical reformers" because support for them would mean getting "shut down quickly" (Interview 111). Or, as another funder put it, "[Our foundation] has been very conservative in China ... because we have a long-term view [and] we want to be able to work there for a long time ... I've been a social activist all my life. This is the most conservative institution I've ever worked for" (quoted in Spires 2011, 321).

---

16 The closure of the English-language section of China Development Brief sent ripples through the INGO community as organizations wondered if they would be next. The Chinese language version of the newsletter suspended operation for a month or two, but was able to start up again after obtaining an official publication number (*kanhao*).

Unlike their 1960s counterparts, who were criticized for "a rather awkward mixture of goodwill, optimism, self-interest, arrogance, ethno-centricity and simple lack of understanding" (Gardner 1980, 4), today's American program heads living in China are largely bilingual and self-reflective. These graduates of top American universities and law schools are well aware that legal aid runs the danger of being labeled neo-imperialism and that America is not the only model for the world. They frequently say things such as "You have to be careful because we don't have a monopoly on wisdom" (Interview 109) or "We are not import-ing a US vision...We want to try and learn what has worked and what hasn't" Interview 16. A consensus on the need for cross-cultural sensitiv-ity also means that INGOs are keen to follow local activists' lead. "If it is not homegrown," one China-based representative of an American NGO told me, "it is not going to happen" (Interview 83).

In private, some China-based American program officers express concerns about the assumptions and effectiveness of their work. "One isn't sure that one is proceeding in the right direction" (Interview 111) especially when "you have no idea if these things take" (Interview 102; see also Interviews 86, 95). Qualms that the American way of doing things is "certainly not something that's going to be transported into a place like China" (Interview 111) generate fears that "we are [just] cre-ating English-speaking foundation hustlers" (Interview 102). At the very least, they say, "This work is so long-term [that] it is not often you see concrete change" (Interview 95). Still, despite doubts, many INGOs end up "providing the US experience because that's what we have access to" (Interview 83). As insiders, there are also limits on self-criticism. A near-constant conversation among these professionals about how to improve current programs rarely touches on the validity of the enterprise.[17]

---

17 Such earnest conversations should not obscure the fact that this work can be a lot of fun. Contemporary China is a dynamic place, and many American program offi-cers enjoy the opportunity to stand between two cultures and work with inspira-tional, visionary people. It is satisfying as well as "aesthetically interesting," as one American expert put it, to forge Sino-American partnerships and watch the results unfold (Interview 102).

In the end, on-the-ground program organizers typically define success in small steps rather than in terms of democratization or human rights. One American NGO representative feels successful if her group "first, identif[ies] a topic that has practical use for [its] Chinese partners. Second, that real dialogue takes place at the event and people make connections that didn't exist before. Third, that there's potential for ongoing work, ideally with concrete next steps" (Interview 95). China-based staff members are well aware that soft support is "three giant steps back" from the objectives policymakers and foundations espouse, and that large-scale change might take years (Interview 111).

The Chinese Side: The Demand for Soft Support

Any kind of conversion is a give-and-take process of persuasion. Seeding conviction is a "long conversation" that, over time, alters both the individuals and ideology involved (Comaroff and Comaroff 1991, 17–18). However, as many have pointed out, this is seldom a conversation between equals (Thayer 2004; Bob 2005). American NGOs' financial resources introduce power inequalities that underlie even the most collaborative programs. Regardless of organizers' intentions, deference to power makes it impossible for international sponsors to blend in "as just another participant" (Roelofs 2007, 479). Still, Chinese lawyers have choices. Lawyers volunteer to attend conferences, workshops, and training programs when they could be handling cases and making money. Indeed, soft support programs are only possible because international initiatives have a domestic constituency.

In large part, Chinese participation reflects a homegrown hunger to hear about law elsewhere. Transmission of the American experience with environmental law occurs not only because American organizations publicize the US experience, but because Chinese audiences genuinely want to hear what they have to say.[18] As in Meiji Japan

---

18 Elsewhere, other legal communities have been similarly interested in international ties. Tanzanian judges actively sought out opportunities for international exchange

or turn-of-the-century China, slogans like "learn from abroad" (*jiejian guowai*) and "link up with the international track" (*yu guoji jiegui*) are commonplace. The end of Chinese isolation after Mao's death also meant the beginning of government-sponsored international exchange programs for everyone ranging from legal scholars at the Chinese Academy of Social Sciences (CASS) to Shanghai judges (Interview 3, 74). There is a widespread belief that "contemporary environmental law comes from the West," as one Chinese academic put it at a roundtable I attended, and foreign experts are occasionally invited to give feedback on changes to domestic environmental law (Ferris and Zhang 2002, 601–602).[19] The idea is that best practices from abroad should guide legal development at home and, rather than imitating any one country, China should pick and choose elements that best fit the national situation (*guo-qing*).

Many Chinese lawyers are similarly swept up in the national rush toward an "advanced" legal system.[20] One lawyer compared the American legal system to Lei Feng, a well-known model soldier from a 1960s propaganda campaign, and suggested that China should learn from the American example (Interview 106; see also Interviews 79, 90). International exchange is helpful in "mastering new thinking" (*zhangwo xin de sixiang*) and figuring out where China should be heading (Interview 28). On a personal level, lawyers report that learning about international experience broadens their outlook and improves their "legal reasoning" (*falü luoji*) capacity (Interview 37). It can also be enjoyable, especially for intellectually inclined Chinese lawyers who are curious about environmental law elsewhere.

(Widner 2001), and even during the 1960s law and development movement, there were "relatively few unsolicited requests for American legal assistance" (Gardner 1980, 242).

19 Foreign experts gave feedback, for example, on the Noise Pollution Control Law and amendments to the Land Administration Law (Ferris and Zhang 2002, 601).

20 The word "advanced" (*xianjin*) frequently came up in interviews with lawyers (Interviews 73, 113, 123, 125, 127, 132).

Others turn up for soft support programs because they think that international exchange will offer them a competitive edge. In a tough market, Chinese lawyers continually review how to enhance their symbolic capital, or "the social class, education, career, and expertise that is contained within a person" (Dezalay and Garth 1996, 18). A significant number of Chinese lawyers are self-taught, and symbolic capital is particularly important when there are no degrees to connote authority. As one lawyer explained, "You have to develop yourself" to attract business, and an international gloss helps project urbane professionalism (Interview 131). Sometimes, soft support is seen as a professional enrichment opportunity that will help locally trained lawyers attract lucrative, international clients. One lawyer, for example, was willing to give up three months of salary to go on a US exchange program because he thought he could improve his English enough to work with foreigners when he returned (Interview 82).[21]

Uncovering motivation is always difficult. Just as Chinese converts to Christianity were attracted by "dreams of adventure, social advancement, influence, and the promise of salvation," Chinese conference attendees are moved by a blend of curiosity and self-interest (Barker 2005, 95). Sometimes, the appeal of the exotic is enough to pique interest. The Chinese organizer of a 2007 roundtable for Chinese environmental lawyers in Harbin, for example, insisted on including an American speaker because foreign participation would spur local attendance. As one American expert complained, "You are put on stage as a trained dog...the vapidity of the substance doesn't matter" (Interview 102).

---

21 Symbolic capital is an idea borrowed from sociologist Pierre Bourdieu. In Bourdieu's work, symbolic capital can be leveraged to make money (monetary capital). One of the interesting things about this example is that the link between symbolic capital and monetary capital is stronger in the lawyer's mind than in reality. Given the number of foreign-trained Chinese lawyers, it is hard to see how participants in soft support programs could cash in on the experience. It seems unlikely that, as the lawyer discussed in this paragraph suggests, someone's English could improve enough in three months to take on clients in that language. For the most part, the foreign niche is dominated by lawyers with LLMs or JDs from top foreign law schools.

Backlash

Some Chinese lawyers, of course, are not interested in international exchange or learning from abroad. In fact, an undercurrent of dissatisfaction is often present during discussions of the American experience, occasionally audible in back-of-the-room exclamations such as, in one whisper that I overheard, "This isn't America, this is China!" (see also Interviews 61, 121). At times, backbench displays indicate not only a few bored participants, but a broader backlash. For every admirer of the American legal system, there is someone concerned about the negative influence of Western rule of law. Many, like Peking University dean Zhu Suli, think that China should rely on "native resources" to solve its legal problems (Upham 2005). Lawyers also worry about excessive Westernization. As one lawyer wrote online in 2006, "If we blindly magnify the importance of law, thus using rights consciousness to blindly expand, this is an expansion of selfishness and not taking responsibility."[22]

Strategically, many of China's lawyers also became wary of foreign funding after the Eastern European color revolutions and the Arab Spring placed international grant givers under scrutiny. Some lawyers will not take money from organizations with open political goals, such as the National Endowment for Democracy or the Open Society Institute (Interview 27), and others refuse foreign money altogether (Interviews 72, 151, 152). Those in the latter group agree with Iranian democracy activist Fariba Davoudi Mohajer's belief that "besides ourselves, our independence from foreign funding is our only strength" (quoted in Azimi 2007, 55). Staying impoverished and independent makes more sense than taking on perceived political risk. In 2005, for example, the Chinese government audited all domestic NGOs receiving foreign funding in an attempt to ensure that none harbored anti-state goals (Wilson 2009, 376). Concern about foreign funding meant that INGOs sometimes found it hard to find Chinese partners to co-sponsor domestic workshops

---

22 Lawyer Tiankun's thoughts about the law (*Tiankun Lüshi de falü sixiang*), October 17, 2006. Blog post on file with the author.

on public interest law in the mid- and late-2000s. One INGO representative routinely heard: "We think you are a good partner, but we don't want to put your name on the [conference] banner" (Interview 95). Even with the advantages of solid funding and local interest, pulling together international conferences and workshops was still a daily struggle.

The Limits of Conversion

Global philanthropy involves significant sums – likely $55 trillion in the US alone over the next forty years (Edwards 2008, 9) – and even impeccable intentions are no guarantee of good results. There is a need to unravel some of the intended and unintended consequences of INGO choices, even if assessing the impact of soft support is notoriously difficult. As one program organizer explained, when you are "dealing with values" and "an incremental influence," it is "as impressionistic as any aid can be" (Interview 111). As a starting point, one obvious gold standard of success is conversion. Are soft support programs recruiting a new corps of active, environmental lawyers? Or do graduates return to business as usual? Program heads are understandably wary of external attempts to assess their work, and these are not easy questions for them to answer internally. Reports to donors are generally due three to six months after a program ends, which is too soon to observe long-term influence. As measureable outcomes are increasingly prioritized (Merry 2009; Natsios 2010; Bush 2011), these self-evaluations often rely on numbers, indicating impact through the number of trainings held or the number of participants. Time is short, and there are also good reasons to move on quickly. By the time evaluation deadlines arrive, even the most introspective organizers are caught up in the next project or writing the next grant. There are strong incentives to claim success and move on.

To gain an outside perspective, I looked at potential conversion in a case where it seemed reasonably likely: China's largest, longest-running environmental litigation soft support program, the Beijing-based Center for Legal Assistance to Pollution Victims' (CLAPV) annual training for environmental lawyers and judges.[23] The training, which I attended in 2007, features a week of lectures on Chinese and international environmental law, interspersed with case studies and small-group discussion. CLAPV covers participant expenses, including transportation, lodging, and food. In exchange, lawyers are expected to accept at least one pro bono environmental case when they return home.

In addition to its annual training program, CLAPV runs an environmental law clinic that handles about fifteen cases per year. The cases are mostly referrals from CLAPV's legal assistance hotline and come from all over the country.[24] The center often recruits a local lawyer who has completed the training program to handle the day-to-day work of filing documents, collecting evidence, and managing clients. Indeed, annual training has been quite successful in helping a small organization with no full-time staff develop a national network of volunteer lawyers. From 2001 to 2006, CLAPV staff told me that they cooperated on cases with 36 of the 289 lawyers they trained.

Although this is an impressive amount of outreach for a small legal aid center, what happened to the remaining 253 lawyers? Did commitment fade, despite initial interest, or are CLAPV graduates taking environmental cases at home? To start to answer this question, my research assistants and I contacted thirty-four lawyers from CLAPV's class of 2004 in 2007.[25] We asked them to compare the number of times they gave advice in environmental disputes and handled

---

23 In 2007, some Environmental Protection Bureau officials also attended. Since its inception in 2001, a number of international donors have funded this weeklong workshop, including the Ford Foundation, the Natural Resources Defense Council, the ABA, and the Canadian, Dutch, and Norwegian governments.

24 For more on CLAPV, in English, see Xu and Wang (2006).

25 A random sample across the six years of the training program was not feasible because we had complete contact information for only the class of 2004. We were able to reach thirty-four of the forty lawyers present in 2004 by phone. Of the six remaining lawyers, we were unable to contact five, and one lawyer opted not to talk to us. The advantage of talking to lawyers three years after the training program is that it offers some insight onto the longer-term effects of soft support. It was possible to ask them about numbers of cases because environmental disputes are fairly rare, and lawyers can generally remember how many they've handled without reference to records. CLAPV staff later

environmental lawsuits before and after the CLAPV training. We found that the 2004 training program did not lead to a spike in environmental litigation. A Shanxi lawyer saw the most dramatic rise in number of cases, ten after the training compared to one before it, thanks to a run of complaints about restaurant smells. After excluding this one lawyer from the sample, however, lawyers' behavior between 2004 and 2007 showed no statistically significant change from the far longer preceding period.[26] CLAPV's class of 2004 handled roughly the same number of environmental lawsuits before and after the training. Requests for legal advice held relatively steady or declined slightly, despite increased environmental complaints nationwide.[27] In addition, the five converts in the class of 2004 – lawyers who took their first environmental case after the training – were counterbalanced by six lawyers who handled an environmental case before the training, but failed to take another afterward. Nor did our phone conversations suggest a future jump in caseload. Most lawyers seemed focused on new ventures as the training faded in memory.

A great many caveats are in order. Clearly, this small-scale survey is far from the last word in assessing impact. A larger survey across different issue areas and target groups would be an obvious next step, as it is certainly possible that some groups respond better to soft support or that new habits more easily take root outside environmental law. Examining multiple years of a training program would also be helpful. Organizational learning may well be taking place, as program organizers adjust curriculum, and training becomes more effective over time. With all this in mind, however, the results from this preliminary survey suggest that soft support has a marginal effect on most lawyers' daily practice.

told me that the class of 2004 was fairly typical – neither especially inspired nor uninterested. Like other classes, they came from around the country, although Beijing was somewhat overrepresented with a quarter of participants.

26 Note that the pre-training period includes significantly more time than the post-training period because most lawyers practiced law for more than three years before 2004.

27 Between 2001 and 2009, the number of environmental complaints rose from 369,127 to 696,134 (China Environment Yearbook 2002; China Environment Yearbook 2010).

Judging by the class of 2004, conversion is more wishful thinking than on-the-ground reality.

Cross-Cultural Missteps

In many ways, it is not surprising that environmental law training programs might only rarely forge newly committed lawyer-activists. The long process of conversion takes time, and all but the most compelling experiences stimulate new awareness more than they change routines. Even over the course of several weeks, new information flows by as fast as, in the words of one Chinese study tour participant, "glimpsing flowers from horseback" (*zou ma kan hua*) (Interview 99). In addition to time limitations, it is also challenging to effectively transfer skills and knowledge in what is typically a bilingual and bicultural setting.

Visiting experts are a frequent feature of soft support, and it is an ongoing struggle to make American expertise relevant. As one Chinese lawyer complained, "It is always the same people ... We come, talk about America and go home" (Interview 127). At times, international exchange fails because visiting experts are tone deaf to the local situation. During a one-day training program on alternative dispute resolution in 2007, for example, the group spent several hours discussing a toxic spill by the fictitious Acme Chemical Company. The case study, written in English and translated into Chinese, made a number of assumptions, including: 1) a quick and effective response by a concerned government, 2) effective representation of community concerns by a group called the Chinese Society for the Protection of People from Toxic Clouds, and 3) polluters willing to negotiate. In China, it is difficult to imagine any of these things happening, let alone all three. Missteps like this are not uncommon, even when local organizers carefully cue visiting experts.[28]

Even when experts get the basics about China right, it is hard to find the right level of detail about international experiences. At one extreme,

---

28 This happens outside China, too. In Bahrain, one international exchange veteran recalled launching into a discussion of river water quality before a local participant reminded him that there aren't any rivers in Bahrain (Interview 109).

lecturers "talk as if the students are going to wake up screaming in the middle of the night because they can't remember what section 103.c is" (Interview 102). At the other extreme, complicated history is reduced to simplistic parables. This is especially common when experts, relying on a translator, want to make sure a Chinese audience is following them. In explaining a landmark toxic waste case, an American lawyer told one group that "the judge agreed because he was a brave and wise judge and told the government to clean up." If a brave and wise judge sounds like a character from a children's story, so do other protagonists from retellings of American legal history, such as the "very bad chemical company that makes children sick" introduced by an American expert at a different workshop. Pared down to archetypes, these stories are distilled Americana: tales about "the little guy against the big system, the right to a day in court, principle's triumph over expediency, the taming of corporate power, the disciplining of rogue or heartless bureaucracies, and the possibility of fundamental and structural social change" (Schuck 2000, 35).[29] Although these themes make for effective storytelling, they frustrate Chinese lawyers who have read a great deal about the American system. Behind the scenes, they complain that these introductory, law-for-the-layman lectures are superficial. "If [American law] is that simple," one Chinese lawyer sarcastically commented, "Why haven't you solved all your societal problems?" (Interview 79).

Many savvy program organizers try to find experts who are knowledgeable about China and can find a useful middle ground for exchange. They know that you "can't take a lawyer, drop him into a country and expect him to speak the same language as local lawyers" even if "funders think that it's a good idea" (Interview 111; see also Interview 35). In fact, one INGO stopped inviting international experts altogether because "you could see the Chinese eyes glaze over" (Interview 111). As laudable as these efforts to fine-tune existing practices are, it is also as important to

---

29 Creating strong, simplified story lines, of course, is not unique to US-China international collaborations. For many NGOs, strong stories are critical to transmitting a message, raising money, and recruiting participants.

look beyond quantifiable results to see the overlooked, quieter influence of soft support: cultivated hope.

Cultivated Hope

Talking about hope brings us to a terrain more familiar to preachers and politicians than social scientists. Despite calls for more attention to emotions (Finnemore and Sikkink 1998, 916; Aminzade and McAdam 2001), academic accounts of activism usually steer clear of feelings. Yet emotions, especially hope, can enable and even compel action. Hope, as St. Thomas Aquinas put it, "aims at a future good that is arduous and difficult but nevertheless possible to obtain" (quoted in Abrams and Keren 2006, 8). The key point here is possibility. Unlike dreaming, hope is based on concrete, achievable goals (Abrams and Keren 2006, 9). Sometimes, hope grows out of optimism and a belief that almost anything is possible. At other times, especially in difficult circumstances, hope can be a decision with political consequences (Wallis 2005, 346).

When hope does not organically well up from within, it can sometimes be induced. Cultivated hope, "an active external effort to cultivate emotions in others," helps people envision new possibilities and brainstorm strategies (Abrams and Keren 2006, 6). Despite the fact that it is seldom discussed, constructing hope is a critical element of soft support. Explicitly (or more often implicitly), program organizers encourage lawyers to take on new identities and imagine a better future. The goal, in the words of one INGO representative, is to instill "the courage to take action" (Interview 21; see also Interview 23).

The first challenge in building new identities is that Chinese lawyers are socialized into a profession that tends to measure success in terms of salary.[30] Social pressure is very real, especially when many others are speculating on the stock market and hustling to get ahead. The few lawyers who prioritize a cause over money often feel like "outcasts" (*hen*

30 On how professions serve as inculcators of norms, see Finnemore and Sikkink (1998, 905).

linglei) because their work "isn't popular at home" (Interview 110). In an increasingly acquisitive culture, soft support helps plant the idea of the public interest. Lawyers are left with the message that it is both possible and admirable to "work on behalf of the public interest to help other people" (Interview 113). "Public interest lawyer" (*gongyi lüshi*) is now a familiar Chinese term, thanks in part to local efforts to popularize it by Chinese visiting scholars and exchange program graduates. After spending time abroad, one lawyer wrote that "Chinese lawyers need to vigorously develop their profession...[and] win societal respect. It is not only a question of salary, or the size of law offices, but of taking social responsibility" (Wu 2006).

Reordering priorities is easier when foreign recognition serves as tangible indications of encouragement (*guli de zuoyong*). In a money-centered profession, trips abroad, trophies, and even invitations to conferences offer alternative signs of status. One activist told me he would have dropped out of the environmental movement were it not for international support. His wife used to nag him about his low salary, but his home life improved after he started traveling abroad. He did not make more money, but his wife could at least tell friends and neighbors "look how many times [my husband] has been out of the country!" (Interview 30). Other plaintiffs and lawyers proudly display prizes and awards from both national and international NGOs (Interviews 33, 58), reminders that their efforts are appreciated elsewhere if not at home. As the chairman of the Pesticide Eco-Alternative Center (PEAC) explained, "With the support of INGOs we feel that our work here at PEAC is very valuable" (quoted in Morton 2008, 210). External validation generates prestige or, to use Bourdieu's term, symbolic capital that is both personally satisfying and locally legible. At the very least, as one lawyer told me, "No one is going to laugh at you" (Interview 125).

International support bolsters not only Chinese lawyers, but anyone working in an unfriendly or indifferent place. Just before he was executed by the Nigerian government in 1995, activist Ken Saro-Wiwa wrote that "the exhilarating thing is near total support of the Ogoni people and the support I find in the national and international community. It makes my suffering worthwhile" (quoted in Wiwa 2001, 114). Even simple gestures matter. Tanzanian judges recall being "amazed and delighted" by former Irish president Mary Robinson's visit to the court of appeal. The event "helped forge solidarity, an important resource in times of stress and change" (Widner 2001, 213). In uncertain times, international recognition can also catalyze hope about the future. China's leading environmental lawyer might one day win the Nobel Peace Prize, one lawyer speculated. After all, "why not think that way?" (Interview 110). Even as they worked to overthrow Slobodan Milosevic, Serbian activists were similarly aware that they "would like to be in the encyclopedia of nonviolent resistance with Gandhi and Martin Luther King [and] have a right to dream about that" (Cohen 2000, 148).

These hopes cast local activists as members of an international heroic pantheon. Flattering comparisons to international heroes often resonate, especially when stories about successful local stars are scarce. For Chinese environmental lawyers, the most common reference point during my fieldwork was the 2000 movie *Erin Brockovich* (*Yong Bu Tuoxie*) starring Julia Roberts as a legal assistant who wins $333 million in damages for California residents exposed to toxic chromium.[31] For at least some Chinese lawyers, Brockovich is a source of inspiration. When one lawyer posed as a journalist to obtain information from reluctant employees at an Environmental Protection Bureau (EPB), for example, she was reminded of Brockovich's subterfuge and bravery when collecting evidence (Interview 31). Another lawyer thinks about Brockovich's courage when he feels disappointed, and this helps him "conquer that feeling" (Interview 125). Even plaintiffs are inspired by Brockovich's story. One asked rhetorically, "Have you seen the movie *Erin Brockovich?* ... One small lawyer won over a million dollars in corporate compensation: our victory can't be far away" (quoted in He 2004).

---

31 Unprompted, the following people brought up the movie: Interviews 53, 58, 70, 75, 96, 106, 125, 130, and 131. Although small talk about an American movie was undoubtedly a way to make polite conversation with me, the frequency and specificity of these references suggested that the movie was locally important, too.

In part, Erin Brockovich's ubiquity in the mid- and late-2000s reflects the power of Hollywood. The movie illustrates the potential of environmental law and Chinese lawyers sometimes tap into the magic of film and show the film to motivate one another. A Beijing academic, for example, screened the film at a meeting of the environment committee of the All China Lawyers Association (ACLA) (Interview 39). Others report recommending *Erin Brockovich* to clients to encourage them (Interview 53, 70). Brockovich's popularity also indicates that lawyers are reaching out for role models. As they reconsider priorities, lawyers find solace in a larger-than-life exemplar of moral conviction.

Mixing social values and the law is a big step for most Chinese lawyers. It requires, if not a wholesale identity shift, a "reordering of the priorities that guide individual action," sometimes called a transvaluation of values (Wickham 2005, 240). Insofar as soft support offers status, imported heroes, and encouragement, international ties can nudge along this process of personal change. However, there is nothing magical about the international part of the equation. External validation can, and often does, come from domestic visitors. Big-city journalists and domestic NGO representatives, for example, can encourage claims and boost status just by appearing in isolated villages (Interviews 80, 81). One Chinese NGO staff member felt obligated to maintain communication even after he returned to Beijing because "without good support and hope, what can [the plaintiff] do?" (Interview 69). When work is risky and poorly paid, an appreciative audience helps. In January 2008, I accompanied a Beijing lawyer to an environmental hearing in Hebei province. At lunch afterward, the local lawyer told us that having outside observers made him "feel like a big man."

Of course, values change only when personal commitment accompanies external prodding. As our survey of the CLAPV class of 2004 suggests, most soft support participants go home to the same daily grind. However, soft support can be extremely important for minority of lawyers for whom international exposure accelerates transformation. Some come back from the United States with a heightened sense of responsibility and commitment. "If it wasn't for that trip to America," one commented, "I wouldn't be doing public interest work full-time" (Interview 110). For this group, soft support is a bridge to an alternative path. As one staff member at an INGO explained, "These big meetings are useful because they pull people in [and] validate fields like public interest law that have no validation" (Interview 145).

The City on the Hill

New paths, however, are appealing only insofar as they lead to a desired destination. In addition to promoting the idea of the socially committed lawyer, soft support also cultivates hope by offering a vision of the future. In trainings and workshops, America often comes across as a city on a hill where citizens have well-respected legal rights and polluters are held to task. In part, US presenters feel pressure to talk up America even when, as one commented to me over lunch, "It is weird to be talking about the American model because we complain about [our system] all the time." Of course, visiting experts are not just cheerleaders. Many, especially in question-and-answer sessions, offer a nuanced critique of US environmentalism. And Chinese lawyers, especially in big cities like Beijing and Shanghai, often know about America's environmental problems. They know that Europe devotes more resources to environmental protection and that the United States consumes one-third of the world's oil (Interview 82).

Still, an understanding of American shortcomings does not obviate the appeal of the American legal system. The taken-for-granted reality of an independent, respected judiciary deeply impresses many Chinese listeners. At a training for public interest lawyers sponsored by an American foundation, for example, a Beijing academic recently returned from a trip to the United States talked about how amazing it is that American courts respond in writing to each case filed. American environmental lawyers may face challenges, but as one lawyer put it, at least "the results are very good" (Interview 79). Sometimes, caveats about the American experience also go unheard. A lawyer told a workshop that "Situ Lei [my Chinese name] says that American environmental lawyers make a lot of money" when in fact I had said the opposite.

Persistent belief in the American experience, even given an awareness of the setbacks that accompany real-life struggles, shows the importance of a real-life model rather than a far-off utopia. It helps that the broad-brush story of American environmental law prominently features heroic lawyers, an appealing self-image for an often denigrated profession. The city on the hill, even with its blemishes, offers an attractive alternative future where lawyers are activists working on behalf of society. If anything, the American ideal is even stronger in small and mid-sized cities where relatively isolated lawyers are often more sanguine about the US system than their internationalized, somewhat more cynical big-city counterparts. American lawyers have it easy, one such lawyer from a small town in Fujian province explained to me: if they want to sue someone, they just go ahead and sue (Interview 34). Another lawyer in a mid-sized city in Jiangsu province told me he had read an article online about an American environmental lawyer who got rich thanks to a million-dollar contingency fee (Interview 46). American law, even dimly perceived, can also suggest new possibilities. As one Chinese activist put it, "We've seen a lot of Hollywood movies – they feature weddings, funerals and going to court. So now we think it is only natural to go to court a few times in your life" (quoted in Nye 2002, 72).

Sometimes, misrepresentations of American law can help envelope-pushing activism look less radical. As discussed in Chapter 3, six Peking University professors and graduate students tried to file a lawsuit following the 2005 benzene spill in the Songhua River on behalf of the Chinese sturgeon, Taiyang Island, and the Songhua River itself. Some members of the group were working on a translation of American environmental law decisions at the time, and their lyrical brief draws inspiration from US precedent. In keeping with Justice Douglas's minority view in *Sierra Club v. Morton* (1972), the brief argues that "woodpeckers, coyotes and bears, lemmings, and river salmon should all be able to stand in court."[32] Furthermore, "Foreign countries with an advanced conception of environmental protection have already started to put this new legal idea into practice ... In America, for example, it is firmly established that endangered species and environmental NGOs can act as co-plaintiffs in litigation."

These two statements, both of which are repeated throughout the brief, jumble some complicated issues in American environmental law. Although the 1973 Endangered Species Act protects endangered species and their habitats, non-endangered bears, lemmings, and river salmon enjoy no such protection. Furthermore, standing in civil environmental cases is limited to people who have suffered economic, physical, psychological, or aesthetic harm. If a species is listed on a brief as a co-plaintiff, perhaps to boost the emotional appeal of a case, a plaintiff with clear standing typically accompanies it.[33] The Songhua brief glosses over these details and leaves the mistaken impression that even a river can serve as a plaintiff in America. In reality, such a case would be thrown out of an American court.

It is not clear whether the authors of the brief misunderstood American environmental law or took their inspiration from a minority view that "the voice of the inanimate object ... should not be stilled" (quoted in Percival, Schroeder, Miller, and Leape 2006, 981). In either case, the legitimacy of international precedent – even fudged around the edges – simultaneously justified and de-radicalized their argument. Misconstruing American law helped the plaintiffs argue, as they wrote in their legal brief, that "What we are advocating does not clash seriously with existing law [and] there's no need for the court to feel uneasy about this."

To some extent, the existence of misunderstanding needs no explanation. Urban legends are proof enough that good stories are repeated regardless of truth. It is worth noting, however that academics act as a portal for misinformation as well as new ideas. The rise of

---

32 Unpublished document on file with the author.
33 This may explain why why three of the Peking University representatives listed themselves as co-plaintiffs on the brief. Under Chinese law, however, their claim to standing was equally tenuous.

comparative legal research has generated a pile of new books about foreign law, and while some are scrupulously accurate, small mistakes occur, too.[34] Once made, mistakes are easily replicated by others who work from Chinese secondary sources or books translated into Chinese.[35]

For those interested in how ideas change as they move across borders, this chapter illustrates how much misunderstanding and misrepresentation matter. Like the children's game "telephone," stories mutate during transmission, and both intentional and inadvertent alterations have consequences for activism. At times, as in the Songhua River lawsuit, misrepresentation helps activists cast themselves as reasonable moderates rather than dangerous radicals. And across languages and retellings, the complicated history of American environmental law is smoothed into a myth capable of cultivating hope by invoking an alluring, feasible future.

Implications

International organizations deal daily with multiple layers of uncertainty. First, there are the uncertainties of "altruism at long distance" and the need to hire middlemen to manage faraway programs (Watkins, Cotts, Swindler, and Hannan forthcoming, 4). Then, there is the political sensitivity of international funding in China. The limits of official tolerance are rarely clear and shift in response to recent events (like the color revolutions) as well as in anticipation of future ones (like the 2012 leadership turnover). For groups running law-related programs, uncertainty is further intensified by mixed signals about the desirability of

---

34 To take one example, Zhang writes that environmental rights first entered legislation in the US 1969 National Environmental Policy Act (NEPA), an odd claim considering that the word "rights" never appears in NEPA (2006, 63). Zhang is almost certainly thinking about the section of NEPA that reads: "The Congress recognizes that each person should enjoy a healthful environment and that each person has a responsibility to contribute to the preservation and enhancement of the environment." However, NEPA stops short of recognizing environmental rights in law.

35 For a Chinese scholar researching environmental law, key texts might include Boyle and Bernie (2007) or Wang (2006).

empowering courts, lawyers, or citizens even in the service of a government-approved cause. And on top of these concerns, there is also pressure to secure enough funding to keep going. By the end of the first decade of the 2000s, there were signs that American government money might start to taper off. Inside the Beltway, some were asking alongside Representative Donald Manzullo why, "given the state of the US economy.... any US government entity would spend a single dollar trying to encourage China to do the right thing" (quoted in Pennington 2011).

Excavating multiple levels of uncertainty helps explain why so many international organizations converge on soft support as a form of action. In the end, however, how much impact do these programs have? To start, this chapter suggests that soft support programs are better suited to modest goals tempered by humility than to lofty rhetoric about democracy and freedom. No American program will change China – surely a near impossible task – but participation can inspire lawyers and feed a "heady feeling of belonging... to one another and to some promise, however dim, of changing the world" (Cohen 2000, 144). Jointly run US-China programs also serve as a form of intercultural exchange that boost understanding of America and perhaps even more important, help build American knowledge about China. China-based program officers, in particular, often have the kind of valuable, firsthand insight into a country that comes only from living and working there. At the same time, however, there are a fair share of painful blunders and wasted money, especially among newcomers who lack Chinese language skills and a local network.

One critical issue is evaluation and measurement. With a few exceptions, American donors are increasingly concerned with quantifiable outcomes as evidence of effectiveness (Carothers 2009; Natsios 2010; Bush 2011; Merry 2011; Watkins et al. forthcoming). The trouble is that impressive numbers may not reflect impact. Andrew Natsios, the head of USAID from 2001 to 2005, fears "those development programs that are most precisely and easily measured are the least transformational, and those programs that are the most transformational are the least measurable" (2010, 2). The survey results from the 2004 CLAPV class, to take one example, suggest training programs should focus on group cohesion rather than the number of lawyers trained. A smaller class seems more likely to nurture social bonds strong enough to encourage and support lawyers after the training ends. A number of lawyers contacted for the survey also mentioned a desire for post-training follow-up and reunions. Without this kind of community, it is easy to see how initial interest in environmental law might quickly fade.

Smaller grants might also help. One of the first attempts to track American philanthropy in China found that Beijing-based organizations received nearly 70 percent of the grant money spent by private foundations and public charities between 2002 and 2009. Furthermore, nine of the top ten grantees were either universities for government-controlled institutions (Spires 2011, 317).[36] These numbers point to a need to reach out to a deeper pool of grantees. A more extensive grassroots effort would likely require giving grants to people who may not speak English for smaller sums of money. Although small grants multiply paperwork – one reason at least some donors subscribe to the "more money means more impact" school of thought – small amounts can make a big difference. A grant of US$10,000, for example, would be enough to pay a competitive lawyer fee for three environmental cases.[37] Less money also means less waste, insofar as smaller budgets reduce the amount available for dinners or to fly university deans overseas for study tours.

Finally, there are tools available to identify the most successful components of soft support programs. Randomized trials could help answer questions like whether legal professionals learn more in smaller groups

---

36 Spires' data comes from the Foundation Center's online database. The database provides information on grants from 100,000 US-based foundations and public charities.
37 This is an estimate based on a fee of 20,000 RMB (US$3,175) per case. In poorer areas of China, lawyers might be willing to take a case for less.

or whether reunions encourage lawyers to take environmental cases.[38] Still] incentives to declare success make this kind of experimentation rare. Program evaluation is usually limited to counting participants, collecting testimonials, or hiring a consultant to sum up lessons learned (Watkins et al. forthcoming, 17). There is room for much more creativity, especially if accompanied by patience for failure and evaluations that are taken as seriously as program activities themselves.

[38] Social science tools that can help answer this type of question include randomized control trials, pre-and-post intervention surveys, or surveys in intervention and control populations (Watkins et al. forthcoming, 16). For more on how these tools are transforming development economics, see Banerjee and Duflo (2011).

8 Thinking about Outcomes

THIS FINAL CHAPTER TURNS TO OUTCOMES OF LEGAL ACTION. Can this kind of litigation reduce pollution and change long-term practices? And theoretically, what can environmental lawsuits tell us about the relationship between law and social change in one-party states? More than a bit of curiosity lurks behind these questions. Environmentalists want to know if lawsuits can help solve China's environmental problems while those concerned with political liberalization hope that courts can slowly expand citizens' rights. Both groups are likely to be disappointed. As this chapter discusses, environmental lawsuits are unlikely to dramatically improve environmental quality, let alone spark a rights revolution in China.

There is a danger, however, in letting a moral agenda dictate desired outcomes. No matter how well intentioned, concern about political reform and environmental improvement diverts attention from quieter shifts more indicative of how law seeds itself in tough terrain. Before turning to a broader discussion of law and social change, this chapter examines an example of one slow-moving shift: the emergence of an elite conversation over public interest law. Some of the lawyers, academics, officials, and international NGOs encountered in the last three chapters have become vocal advocates for the idea of public interest litigation, and, in a country where the marketplace of ideas is closely monitored (if not absolutely controlled), public promotion of this concept is a development worth noting. In combination with the

211

bottom-up experimentation detailed in Chapters 4–7, this suggests a pathway between law and social change in an extraordinarily unlikely place: under a Party-controlled legal system in a resilient authoritarian state. Without official intent or even awareness, political ambivalence can crack open space for subtle yet significant changes in ideas and identities.

Toward a Rights Revolution?

To begin, it is worth pausing to consider why environmental litigation is neither a harbinger of a rights revolution nor a panacea for China's all-too-immediate environmental problems. One route to judicial protection of rights is through a corps of charismatic, risk-taking judges who are politically savvy enough to win allies and avoid retribution (Shapiro 2008, 332). Right now, few (if any) Chinese judges fit this description. Incentives for evaluation and promotion, outlined in Chapter 5, leave most judges reluctant to test the limits of their authority. In addition, a few crackdowns on innovative judges in the 2000s increased caution among the risk-averse majority. In 2003, two judges were fired in Luoyang, Henan province, for example, over a decision that invalidated a provincial regulation on the grounds that it contradicted national law (Yu 2009, 37–38). The case made national news and signaled that judicial review remains unwelcome, even if judges faithfully reinforce central policy.

What about lawyers? A 2009 survey showed that lawyers held more liberal political values than any other legal group except law school faculty and ranked political rights as more important than economic rights to a similar degree as people in Sweden, Australia, and the United States (Michelson and Liu 2010). But despite their political opinions, a lawyer-led rights revolution seems unlikely for two reasons. First, as Chapter 6 makes clear, few lawyers act on their beliefs. Second, China's most political lawyers lack national organization. Elsewhere, bar associations have eased political coordination when leading lawyers agree on the need for action.[1] In 2007, for example, the Pakistani bar association decided that lawyers would boycott court appearances as a form of protest against the Musharraf regime. Although the ban was a financial burden, a combination of social pressure and the threat of losing licenses issued by provincial bar councils compelled widespread compliance with the boycott (Ghias 2010, 1008). By virtue of national profile and social standing, bar associations can also broadcast and validate politically iconoclastic ideas. The Egyptian Lawyers' Syndicate, for example, was an important political force in the 1980s before infighting between liberals and Islamists split the organization (Moustafa 2007). Even in failed states, bar associations can retain a critical gloss of moral authority. As a Sudanese lawyer explained, "The bar association has real weight...If any statement of all these lawyers that [Sudan's] laws [or government actions] go against the Constitution, the statement would make all the difference" (quoted in Massoud 2008, 138).

The All China Lawyers Association (ACLA), in contrast, enjoys much less credibility among either activist lawyers or its rank-and-file members. Membership is compulsory, and when mainstream lawyers mention ACLA at all, it is usually to grouse about membership fees that range from a few hundred RMB to a few thousand RMB per year (Liu 2009, 107). This can be a significant burden, especially considering how little the organization delivers in return. "The bar association is also a weak party in China," one Shanghai lawyer explained (quoted in Liu and Halliday 2011, 856). More activist lawyers usually dismiss ACLA leaders as wealthy conservatives with close ties to the government.

Indeed, many of the legal crackdowns of the 2000s were designed to disband or discourage networks that might become capable of sustained, national mobilization. In 2009, for example, the authorities closed the Beijing-based Open Constitution Initiative (OCI) for alleged tax evasion

---

1 For more on how lawyers are most politically effective when the profession is ideologically cohesive, see Moustafa (2007, 213).

and arrested its director. The OCI had taken a number of controversial rights cases, and observers – without knowing what triggered retribution – agreed that the organization must have overstepped the limits of tolerance. Some of OCI's volunteer lawyers were also involved in a 2008 petition for direct elections in the Beijing Lawyers Association (BLA) aimed at reducing annual fees and securing new leaders (Clarke 2009). The BLA declared such "rabble rousing" illegal, a response that clearly demonstrated the association's opposition to reform. Later, several of the lawyers involved also lost their license to practice law.

Considering the regular repression of legal activists, it hardly seems likely that lawyers, judges, legal academics, and their supporters will usher in dramatic political change anytime soon. China's lawyers have yet to network themselves, let alone develop alliances with judges (as in Pakistan in 2007) or prosecutors (as in Franco's Spain). And in contrast to the halcyon years of US rights litigation in the 1950s and 1960s, there is no Chinese Justice Earl Warren willing to push the law to embrace wider issues or even a Chinese Thurgood Marshall, a respected lawyer with financial support from a prominent civil rights group. Perhaps even more importantly, Chinese courts lack two of the lynchpins of judicial influence: judicial review and binding precedent. It is no wonder that many Chinese domestic environmental NGOs felt in the mid- and late-2000s that "the time isn't yet ripe" to use the law for environmental protection (Interview 138) and NGOs "shouldn't push too hard for things that aren't possible" (Interview 61; see also Interviews 22, 32, 80). As one NGO staff member asked rhetorically, "Is there any way that [Chinese] courts can solve problems that the government can't?" (Interview 171).[2]

---

2 This started to change somewhat in the late 2000s. The opening of environmental courts prompted newfound interest in legal advocacy tools, including administrative review (*xingzheng fuyi*), access to information requests for environmental data, and public interest litigation (Interviews 162, 170). Still, most environmental NGOs are proceeding cautiously. As one former head of an environmental group explained, "Environmental litigation is the new baby in the bathtub and we all want to be careful for different reasons that we do not ruin the water" (Interview 169).

Courts and Environmental Protection

China is a strong, state-led system accustomed to enforcing policy priorities through bureaucratic targets. As the national rush to meet environmental goals in the eleventh Five-Year Plan shows, holding officials accountable to quantifiable targets remains the most effective way to change incentives, beat local protectionism, and improve environmental protection.[3] Environmental litigation is a weak tool by comparison, especially considering the obstacles detailed in Chapter 2.[4] For example, despite the establishment of an environmental court in nearby Wuxi, as well as millions of *renminbi* spent on cleanup, 85 percent of Tai Lake remains unsuitable for drinking, irrigation, or even recreation (Wan 2010).

In Brazil, another developing country with tightening environmental standards and largely ineffectual regulatory agencies, active public prosecutors used litigation to enforce environmental law and make it matter (McAllister 2008). For now, though, it is difficult to imagine Chinese public prosecutors playing a similar role, despite experiments with public interest litigation. And, as discussed in the previous section, judges are not poised to step into the breach. Unlike activist courts in democratic developing countries such as India, Chinese judicial decisions are far more likely to tinker with standard operating procedure than suddenly hold the government accountable for policy implementation or expound on sustainable development principles (Narain and Bell 2005; Preston 2006, 47–48).

Sometimes, however, administrative environmental lawsuits can reinforce environmental protection efforts by changing Environmental Protection Bureau (EPB) protocol and boosting agency status. At least for EPB heads willing to admit mistakes, being sued reinforces commitment to scrupulously follow the law (Jahiel 1994, 386; Zhang 2008, 116–117). EPB officials also find that lawsuits offer a justification

---

3 For more on the importance of bureaucratic evaluation, see Guttman (2008), van Rooij (2006a, 310), and Wang (2013).

4 For a pessimist's view on China's environmental law, see Wang (2010a).

for pressuring polluters. EPB officials can say, "We have to do our job [collecting fines]. Otherwise, we will be sued and even lose in court like XX lawsuit" (quoted in Zhang 2008, 157). Finally, courts can help EPBs collect outstanding pollution levies. Polluters are more likely to pay up when the court detains top managers, which is legally permissible for up to fifteen days, or confiscates company cars. Repeat cases involving the same polluter are also rare (Zhang 2008, 193–195). Of course, EPBs are also capable of ignoring court decisions or averting courts altogether. Much depends on the relationship between courts and regulatory agencies, which can be symbiotic, indifferent, or suspicious (McAllister 2008; Zhang 2008).

In civil environmental cases, difficulty enforcing court decisions limits the impact of even successful cases. Respect for court decisions is not a well-embedded norm, and even after a case is over, bargaining over compensation frequently continues. Plaintiffs routinely settle for less than court-mandated compensation for a range of reasons, including expediency and bankruptcy. Sometimes polluters legitimately go bankrupt, and sometimes they successfully feign poverty by stashing cash in bank accounts in another province or under a family member's name (Interviews 6, 93). In addition, reliance on after-the-fact monetary compensation, rather than preventing harm or restoring the natural environment, suggests that civil lawsuits act more as a fire alarm to alert government to extreme abuses than as the centerpiece of serious bid to improve environmental quality.

Of course, countries rarely turn to litigation as a first response to industrial pollution. As Chinese leaders often remind the world, China is a developing country and balancing economic growth with environmental protection is not easy. Indeed, contemporary Chinese environmental disputes bear more than a passing resemblance to the late nineteenth-century Ashio copper mine incident that marked Japan's first experience with industrial pollution (Upham 1987, 69–72). Japanese government officials viewed the technologically advanced Ashio copper mine as critical to economic development. Even though copper runoff was poisoning the rice paddies of entire prefectures, it took a string of petitions from local peasants, a massive protest march, a lawsuit, and an outpouring of public support to trigger government intervention. Like early industrial Japan, China is still a place where local environmental activists are frequently called disorderly, crazy, or retarded (van Rooij 2010, 67), and closing down a factory often means just moving it to a poorer part of the province.

Still, Japan's twentieth-century path to environmental protection is instructive. The "Big Four Pollution Suits" of the 1960s called national attention to the health effects of industrial waste and forced officials to take action (Upham 1987). The Minamata lawsuit, the most famous of the four, came to "symbolize the dark side of economic growth," particularly after iconic photographs of locals suffering from mercury poisoning firmly fixed the event in public memory (George 2001, 283–284). Could a Minamata-like lawsuit rock China today? It seems possible, especially if journalists, photographers, and bloggers join the cause.

Policy Entrepreneurs and Public Interest Law

Given the scale and importance of China's environmental problems, it is disappointing that litigation remains a relatively weak tool for environmental protection. However, pessimism obscures a more contingent process of slow-moving social change. This quiet story is not one of big, landmark cases, or a groundswell of roiling environmental activism, but rather an accretion of "the seemingly small changes in state-society relations" that indicate how law is slowly remaking China (O'Brien and Li 2006, 114). Although China has been an "authoritarian state" from Mao Zedong through Hu Jintao, the consistency of this label masks dramatic changes to the content and practice of law. Tracing China's legalization requires attention to what political scientist Paul Pierson calls a "moving picture of important social processes" (2004, 2). These processes include such long-term trends as rising incomes, urbanization, and as this book explores, conflicting cues over the importance of courts and litigation. With this in mind, this section zooms out from the focus on individual actors that sustained the last four chapters and pans wider, looking at national experimentation with new policy proposals, labels, and institutions as one marker of legal change.

In March 2009, a source inside the Supreme People's Court (SPC) told *Legal Daily* that "establishing a system for public interest environmental litigation is just a matter of time. It's a matter of vital urgency for some of China's developed areas" (Yuan 2009). At first blush, this is an odd remark. Why would a Chinese government insider publicly insist on the inevitability of an approach so strongly associated with citizen activism? After all, there are many ways to strengthen environmental protection without allowing private parties such as citizens and NGOs to sue on behalf of the public interest. In 1970s West Germany, for example, courts and legislatures considered and rejected the idea of environmental litigation based on grounds other than the violation of private rights (Greve 1989).[5]

In contemporary China, however, this comment fits easily into an emerging civic conversation over public interest litigation. In the 2000s, the term "public interest litigation" (*gongyi susong*) – likely translated from English – entered elite parlance as legal academics and journalists began writing about the possibility of allowing a wider range of groups and individuals to sue. A search of 738 newspapers shows that the phrase "public interest litigation" appeared in 2,700 articles in 2009–2010, compared to just 345 articles in 2000–2001.[6] As early as 2007, researchers at the Zhongnan University of Economics and Law could claim a consensus among scholar that some combination of the public prosecutors, environmental bureaus, NGOs, and citizens should be allowed to initiate public interest environmental litigation.

---

5 This still left room for quite a bit of litigation. Most large-scale construction projects, for example, end up in court because they infringe on someone's private rights (Greve 1989, 202).
6 This search was performed through the China Core Newspapers Database (CKNI) in May 2012.

By the mid-2000s, there were visible supporters of public interest litigation inside government too. One high-profile advocate was SPC vice-president Wan E'xiang, whose articles outline the legal and political arguments for expanding standing, shifting fees, and even allowing injunctions in public interest cases (Wan 2010). At the 2012 annual meeting of the Chinese People's Political Consultative Conference (CPPCC), a government advisory body, one of China's minority political parties joined the debate with calls for public interest litigation to counter "sluggish enthusiasm" for environmental protection. Their plan envisioned empowering a new army of environmental public interest groups – each supervised by a Party cell inside it – to sue polluters (Caixin 2012). This brainstorm is not as far-fetched as it might seem. Amendments to the Civil Procedure Law made in 2012 allow lawful authorities (*falü guiding de jiguan*) and relevant organizations (*you guan zuzhi*) to initiate environmental public interest lawsuits (Standing Committee of the National People's Congress 2012). These changes, which go into effect at the start of 2013, mark the beginning of a remarkable national experiment with public interest litigation. Judicial authorities now must decide how to implement the law and, in particular, how liberally to interpret who qualifies as a "relevant organization." Already, some environmental NGOs fear they may be denied standing, as public interest litigation becomes the exclusive privilege of government-backed organizations (Interviews 169, 171; see also Shen 2012).[7]

In a country hardly known for political debate, the success of elite advocacy for public interest litigation is noteworthy. By publishing articles, speaking up at conferences, and lobbying for new legislation, promoters of public interest litigation cast themselves as visible policy

---

7 The main way that courts are likely to limit standing is through registration status. Many environmental NGOs are either unregistered or registered as companies, non-profit organizations (*minban fei qiye*), or foundations (*jijinhui*) rather than social organizations (*shehui tuanti*). Limiting standing to social organizations would effectively ban most groups without formal government ties from public interest litigation. For more on NGO difficulties with registration, see Hildebrandt (2011).

entrepreneurs or advocates for an idea.[8] At least in public, the debate continues to revolve around how fast and how much to expand standing rather than whether to expand it at all. It is a rather one-sided dialogue, as those opposed to the public interest enterprise rarely publish or speak publicly. Although articles with titles like "How public interest litigation can act as a shield for malicious accusations" exist, neither the mainstream media nor legal journals typically publish anything so vitriolic. In fact, the "malicious accusations" article was self-published online under the pen name "Dr. Water" (shui bo).[9]

Of course, the absence of robust public opposition does not mean public interest litigation is not controversial. It is likely that hardliners primarily express their concerns in closed-door meetings, and the few officials active in the public debate tend to support a more cautious, government-led approach. In the mid-2000s, one well-known champion of public interest litigation within the Ministry of Environmental Protection (MEP), for example, publicly stated his view that standing should be limited to government-approved NGOs (Bie 2007). There are visible fissures among government reformers, too. While parts of the procuratorate appreciate the responsibility that would accompany the newfound right to sue in the public interest, other officials are wary of expanding the agency's authority. As one judge put it, allowing the procuratorate to supervise the judicial system and initiate public interest litigation would be "like playing ball and umpiring at the same time" (Interview 104).

Across these divides, this group of policy entrepreneurs shares a willingness to look abroad for concepts like public interest litigation that might be useful at home. As explored in the previous chapter, academics are a critical "channel through which new ideas circulate"

---

8 For more on policy entrepreneurs in China, see Mertha (2008, 6–12).

9 Nor does the anonymous Dr. Water jettison the idea of public interest litigation entirely. Instead, he concludes that environmental public interest litigation should replace petitions (shangfang) because public participation should not be "monopolized by extreme environmental activists and international anti-China forces." See Dr. Water, "How public interest litigation can act as a shield for malicious accusations" (Gongyi susong qineng dangzuo eyi wugao de hushenfu). Blog post on file with the author.

(Haas 1992, 27), and importing ideas is a significant part of Chinese legal scholarship.[10] More than sixty percent of a group of sixty-two Chinese-language articles collected in 2007 explicitly discuss foreign approaches to environmental law.[11] Just over a third of the articles drew on multiple countries' experiences, as authors picked and chose the solutions best suited to China's situation (*guoqing*). America was the clear favorite for authors focused on one country, a reflection of both US importance and the fact that Chinese researchers have better access to such sources because many speak English.[12] A good number of Chinese academics are also aware that they serve as a portal for new ideas. As one Chinese law professor explained (in English), China "needs to learn something from US law...I want to write something to tell [the] Chinese people what is the American [way]" (Interview 45).[13]

10 The privileged place accorded to comparative research surfaces in many ways. On an August 2007 trip to Jilin Law School, I noticed that the hallways were decorated with cartoon cutouts of famous legal thinkers. The few Chinese scholars, notably Confucius and Han Feizi, were far outnumbered by Western luminaries, including Aristotle, Oscar Wendell Holmes, and legal scholar Roscoe Pound. The Chinese Academy of Social Sciences (CASS) law institute, a government-affiliated research institute, also told visitors to its Web site in 2006 that "a comparative method of legal research is always emphasized...[as well as] research co-operations with foreign universities."

11 In total, my research assistants and I collected sixty-two articles on legal reforms that would facilitate environmental litigation, particularly public interest environmental lawsuits. Fifty-seven of these articles were downloaded from the China Knowledge Infrastructure (CKNI) database. In December 2007, we searched CKNI's twenty-one legal core journals (*hexin qikan*) for articles published between 2000 and 2007 with the key words environmental lawsuit (*huanjing susong*), pollution lawsuit (*wuran susong*), and environmental public interest lawsuit (*huanjing gongyi susong*). Off-topic articles were discarded, and we did not review articles written by graduate students due to time limitations. In addition, we added relevant articles from volumes 1–6 of China's only environmental law journal, *Environmental and Resources Law Review (Huanjing Fa Luncong)*, published annually, and the edited volume *Environmental public interest litigation (Huanjing gongyi susong)* (Bie 2007).

12 Of the sixteen articles that discussed only one country's experiences, twelve focused on America, two on France, one on Japan, and one on Germany. Soft support programs run by US organizations tend to focus attention on the American experience, especially when long-term collaboration produces, as one program did, edited volumes like *Environmental public interest litigation: A China-US comparison* (Lü and Wang 2009).

13 Legal academics also often look abroad for practical reasons. The MEP is in the midst of revising China's environmental laws, and top domestic experts are often invited to

Tensions and Possibilities

Among practitioners, tensions over emerging labels such as rights protection lawyer (*weiquan lüshi*) and public interest lawyer (*gongyi lüshi*) indicate disagreement over how to translate the concept of public interest law into practice. There is particular friction between advocates for an inclusive, umbrella concept and those who insist that some work is more meaningful than others. For some, an expansive definition of public interest law is a necessity in a place with little tradition of high-profile litigation. Many lawyers and activists point out that litigation is only one facet of legal activism and spend much of their time petitioning, filing requests for administrative review, influencing legislation, educating decision-makers, and promoting legal awareness instead (Lü 2008, 21–22; see also Interviews 20, 162).[14] Frustration with current laws, particularly strict limits on standing, steers even active practitioners toward outreach and legislative reforms. Well-known lawyers and academics, the sort who might be invited to comment on draft regulations or join the local CPPCC, are particularly likely to seize behind-the-scenes lobbying opportunities. As one lawyer involved in local government said, "Different levels of people have to solve different levels of problems" (Interview 90).

At the same time, promoters of public interest law are also sometimes in the business of exclusion. Limiting membership, as in any social movement, is one way to protect the advantages of association – benefits like contacts, recognition, or even the thrill of feeling special. One divide in the mid-2000s separated lawyers who represent real-life clients from those who act as plaintiffs themselves. In one 2004 case described by the lawyer who brought it as a "successful environmental public

---

assist with drafting. In this context, policy-oriented research makes sense as academics are called on to consider China's options.

14 Cause lawyers in other developing countries also often deemphasize litigation in favor of other types of activism (Ellmann 1998, 359).

interest lawsuit," Beijing lawyer and homeowner Chen Yueqin con-
tested the lack of green space in her Haidian district apartment complex. Although the prospectus promised owners 41 percent green space
(*lüdi*), the final built complex delivered only 16.3 percent.[15] Chen sued
the developer for breach of contract as well as various city bureaus
for failing to enforce local regulations that mandate 30 percent green
space (Chen 2006a). Despite Chen's claim of success – the city promised
to start inspections to make sure developments meet green-space standards – the case was controversial in the legal community. Although
self-representation can lessen the political sensitivity of a case by keeping the most aggrieved, angriest plaintiffs out of the courtroom, lawyers
disagree over whether this constitutes an opportunity for activism
or turns public interest law into an elite activity that ignores real
injustice.

More tensions, audible in heated conference exchanges and back-
stabbing asides, emerge when audiences try to pin down what public
interest actually means. In practice, most lawyers and academics tend
to equate public interest with pro bono work (Interviews 33, 37, 49, 70;
see also Wu 2006; Bie 2007, 10). By so doing, public interest lawyers are
corralled into avoiding profitable cases, a constraint that sidesteps the
need for an exact definition of the public interest while also seizing the
moral high ground. This not-for-profit constraint, however, limits public
interest law to those who can afford it. Charging market-rate contingency
fees of 20 or 30 percent and suing clients for unpaid bills, as well-known
labor lawyer Zhou Litai has done courts controversy. Still, some lawyers
seethe over the impossibility of building a self-sustaining practice on pro
bono work. As Zhou explains it, "As an organization specializing in protecting other people's rights, my own rights were severely infringed ... I
have to live!" (2005, 203).

---

15 The definition of "green space" (*lüdi*) is not clear to me. Having visited the complex
   (called *huaqing jiayuan* in Chinese), as well as many similar complexes, most of the
   "green space" is occupied by playgrounds and concrete walkways.

A few advocates have become so associated with public interest lit-igation that they seem to have staked their careers on the adoption of the idea. It is not clear if they will be successful. Policy entrepreneurs spend years pushing change, and in these early days, it is imaginable that public interest litigation could still founder. However, it is also possible that this kind of litigation could become influential. After all, intellectual influence is often indirect as ideas that were once marginal slowly seep into the mainstream. The roots of the 1960s American rights revolution, for example, wind back to an earlier generation of legal realist schol-ars whose work justified re-shaping law to reflect social values (Kagan 2008, xx). Or the Federalist Society, to take another example, built an influential network of conservative legal elites in the United States by emphasizing ideas over lobbying or litigation (Teles 2008). As founding member Gary Lawson explained:

> The reason we've succeeded is that [the leaders] all have a very clear idea of what this organization should do, which is promote ideas. Bring debates into the law schools, bring debates into the legal com-munity, and everything else that happens... we'll take it (quoted in Teles 2008, 162).

For Chinese supporters of public interest litigation, winning support is likely to depend on selling the idea as patriotic. An anti-state conno-tation can be fatal, both among officials and with the public. Russian environmentalists, for example, have long struggled against the public perception that they are anti-Russian and beholden to foreign interests (Henry 2010, 214–215). Looking forward, much rests on the evolution of how "public interest litigation" is understood, especially as environmen-tal groups start to test the limits of standing and the authorities judge how wide to open it. For now, there seems to be an affinity between state-endorsed values, such as public safety and environmental protection, and public interest litigation. As the Party Secretary of the Panyu dis-trict procuratorate in Guangdong province explained his organization's role, "The main value of legal supervision is safeguarding the people. The masses look forward to blue sky and clear water and [we] must help achieve this" (quoted in Luo 2009).

Mixed Signals, Law, and Social Change

In democracies, law and social change are usually linked in two ways. First, laws reflect and promote certain social values. Second, social movements, NGOs, and interest groups strategically use litigation to call attention to a cause and compel judges to weigh in on social controversies. Even in Japan, a country known for strong business and bureaucratic interests rather than grassroots movements, lawsuits can underscore social discontent and spur politicians to take remedial action (Upham 1987).

The litigation-as-fire-alarm model holds true in China, too, especially because the CCP has an ongoing interest in co-opting pressing social problems. However, this book maps a different pathway between law and social change as well. In keeping with the understanding that law rarely "directly and simplistically" leads to social transformation, the last four chapters detail a less direct route by which mixed signals over environmental litigation contribute to changes in internal legal culture (Roach Anleau 2010, vi).[16] What is changing is not the legal consciousness of the general population – although media coverage of environmental lawsuits has undoubtedly drawn domestic attention to pollution problems – but how legal specialists see the scope of law and their role in it. The consequence of the political ambivalence discussed in Chapter 4 is bottom-up experimentation. Without official sanction or intent, there are activist lawyers, policy entrepreneurs talking about public-interest litigation, local officials opening environmental courts, and judges willing to stand behind limited, local innovation. My field-work in the 2000s, in short, coincided with a slow "enlargement of the

16 The term "internal legal culture" is borrowed from Friedman (1975, 223).

scope of legal inquiry" surrounding the idea that law should serve the public as well as the Party (Nonet and Selznick 2008, 97).

Inside the bar and the judiciary, contradictory cues have lent judges and lawyers political cover and even incentives to experiment, provided they do not overstep the limits of official tolerance. As in other accounts of slow-moving institutional change, these "change agents" are motivated by a range of concerns besides a conscious desire for transformation (Mahoney and Thelen 2011, 22). Some are opportunists hoping to advance their careers. For ambitious judges, handling challenging cases is one way to build a reputation and get promoted (Yu 2009, 73). Enterprising lawyers have incentives to handle high-profile litigation too. Sympathetic media coverage pays off, especially in a profession reliant on publicity and personal networks to find clients. At times, innovation can also be accidental. Pragmatic creativity in judicial decision making, for example, is often a logical ad hoc response to conflicting Party priorities. And, finally, some innovators are reformers trying to transform the legal system from within.[17] There are the cause lawyers profiled in Chapter 6, for example, interested in pushing forward personal values through law. For all the signs of a "crackdown on troublesome lawyers" at the end of the 2000s (Ford 2009), there was also space for a degree of legal activism throughout the decade, as long as lawyers appeared loyal to the regime.

In addition, mixed signals have provided openings for new actors to wedge themselves into the legal system. In contrast to Mao's China, and perhaps even Deng's China, it is impossible to study environmental litigation in the late 2000s and fail to notice the INGOs and policy entrepreneurs working to support lawsuits and change the law. As is also true elsewhere in China, "charismatic" and even "visionary" individuals are backing new ideas and experiments (Lee and Hsing 2010, 8). Significant changes include the growing popularity of "public interest" talk

---

17 James Mahoney and Kathleen Thelen use the term "subversives" to describe reformers working within the system (2011, 25).

and the appearance of environmental courts. These labels and institutions have symbolic value as cultural markers that help change minds and envision new possibilities (Jasper 1997, 11).

Of course, it is hard to prove that these kinds of grassroots changes are linked to high-flying ambivalence over courts and law. Absent a laboratory-like ability to manipulate history, a thought experiment is helpful: how would unequivocal signals change the landscape of activism? At one end of the spectrum, none of the experimentation or advocacy discussed in these pages would be possible if officials were as determined to stamp out environmental litigation as, say, they were willing to stamp out Falun Gong. On the other end of the spectrum, however, unambiguous state support would allow cases to move forward much more smoothly, possibly supported by a corps of government lawyers empowered to bring forth civil actions like the Ministério Público in Brazil (McAllister 2008). These alternatives are hard to imagine, if only because they diverge so dramatically from the current situation of neglect that is punctuated by reactive crackdowns and intermittent praise. At least when officials are looking in another direction, state incoherence seems to lend legal professionals limited freedom to act on values and commitments that might be Party-inspired, but are not Party-dictated.

At the same time, ambivalence is not a synonym for liberalization, and conflicting signals can encourage self-censorship as easily as experimentation. Every chapter in this book shows people backing away from risk, too, including judges who listen to political instructions (Chapter 5), lawyers who avoid risky cases (Chapter 6), and international supporters who prefer soft support over direct funding for litigation (Chapter 7). Even emerging labels like "public interest lawyer" are complicated concepts that repel as well as appeal. In public, lawyers frequently reject the label with statements like "I'm not a public interest lawyer, I'm just someone interested in public interest law," as I heard at one conference, or "I am a just a little bit of a public interest lawyer" (Interview 125). One lawyer whose entire practice revolves around serving the disadvantaged insists, "I am absolutely not a public interest lawyer. The government should be in charge of looking after the public interest [and] if you need people to sacrifice themselves, there are real problems in society" (Interview 121; see also Interview 163). Moreover, self-chosen labels do not necessarily compel action. Lawyers frequently complain about "so-called public interest lawyers" who excel at grandstanding and little else.

Legal scholars have long been aware that the law shows two faces. Law and courts reflect and protect existing power relations while also providing rules and a venue to challenge the status quo. In authoritarian states, the dual nature of the law is even more pronounced because courts are both useful and politically threatening. Extending this insight, the argument here is that mixed signals over one type of litigation prompt risk aversion for some, and crack open opportunities for grassroots legal change for others. As political scientists are starting to chronicle, ambiguity can be a source of "slow and piecemeal changes" that shape human behavior and political outcomes (Mahoney and Thelen 2010, 1). Over time, "ad hoc adjustments to standard operating procedures" can redefine political boundaries and create new understandings of what is politically permissible (Hall 2010, 218).[18] Political ambivalence, then, is a source of ambiguity that arises from the simultaneous existence of opposing preferences within the state.[19] In turn, ambivalence over law allows "creative leeway" for grassroots innovation (Scheingate 2010, 168). Law is not an ossified relic of political control, but an in-motion amalgam of rules and practices.

New Directions

How does China fit into the universe of modern authoritarian states? A starting observation is that China is not alone in striving toward "urbane

---

18 On redefining boundaries, see Scheingate (2010) and Stern and O'Brien (2012).

19 Individual signals may be ambiguous, or they also may be crystal clear and collectively point in different directions.

authoritarianism" (Halliday and Karpik 2012, 27). Around the world, plenty of regimes are determined to keep political control while projecting the image of a well-run modern state. Law is a major part of this image, even though courts and legal professionals can be tricky to control. The solution deployed in Singapore and Russia, as well as China, is a bifurcated legal system. Singapore scrupulously follows laws related to commerce and the economy while laws relating to civil and political rights remain repressive (Silverstein 2003; Rajah 2011). In Russia, too, occasional political interference co-exists with impartial adherence to law much of the time (Solomon 2008, 280; Hendley 2009, 258–259). And at the start of the 21st century, Chinese law seems deeply split. The same year civil rights activist Chen Guangcheng pointed to lawlessness as "the fundamental question" facing the government, one World Bank study ranked China the fifth easiest country in which to enforce a contract in court, just above France and United States (Chen 2012; World Bank 2012).[20]

For scholars studying authoritarian states and the bifurcated legal systems sometimes found inside them, it helps to separate two concepts that are often blurred: 1) judicial performance, or how well courts work in terms of cost, efficiency, fairness, and user satisfaction, and 2) judicial independence, or the extent of political interference and control (Michelson and Li 2012). Performance and independence may move in tandem, or they may diverge, such that courts accustomed to interference in high-profile politicized cases also perform reasonably well. For all the attention paid to the ways in which authoritarian courts are dysfunctional, they can also be effective. To be sure, a forum that fairly resolves run-of-the-mill disputes also boosts satisfaction with the government. As one well-known unlicensed lawyer in Shandong province summed up, "It is easy to handle small cases, but difficult to handle big ones" (quoted in Xing 2010, 76).

---

20 The World Bank rankings take into account the procedures, time, and cost of resolving a commercial dispute in court. The data is based on a survey given to local experts. Regardless of the truth of either claim, it remarkable that two such diametrically opposed views of the Chinese legal system could plausibly coexist.

The trouble with the word "bifurcate," or to divide in two, is that it implies too clear-cut a line between a commonplace case and a politically sensitive one. This boundary is often blurry, and when this is true, there is particular value in looking at the cases that fall between uncontroversial and forbidden. Boundary-pushing cases make visible charged interactions that define and test understandings of the politically permissible. Over time, important decisions can also sketch a map of how political boundaries have been patrolled, negotiated, or transformed. Cross-nationally, it is also worthwhile to compare which kinds of cases attract mixed signals. Differences in the authorities' zone of tolerance expose how history and culture shape threat perception and define what is considered politically sensitive. Future research will want to stack up different types of cases to see when authoritarian states send a mishmash of conflicting signals as well as the moments in which official priorities are lucidly clear. This book is far from the last word. It is an open question whether this account of political ambivalence and bottom-up experimentation holds true elsewhere and, where it does, how creeping social change unfolds over a longer time span. This kind of work calls for a textured approach that shies away from grand pronouncements and disassembles "rule of law" into more manageable pieces.

At several points in these pages, a discussion of incentives and pressures also gives way to a consideration of emotions. Although hope comes up in Chapter 7, the emotional theme that runs through these pages is anxiety. The unease of anxiety is less intense than fear, an emotion that receives much attention in accounts of politics, and less paralyzing than terror.[21] Anxiety is the emotion that gives rise to self-censorship and hastens the spread of control parables. Still, this observation only gestures in the direction of those who write about the history, psychology, and sociology of emotions. A conversation about emotions is well underway across the social sciences and political scientists should add their thoughts, particularly when political considerations

---

21 For work that examines the political implications of fear, see Makiya (1998), Robin (2004), and Laffen and Weiss (2012).

arise. For the emerging group interested in comparative authoritarianism, emotions also offer a fresh angle of comparison between countries (and within them) as new work develops a fuller emotional palette of everyday political life.

For scholars of Chinese politics, my hope is that drawing attention to the implications of mixed signals and political ambivalence in just one area – environmental litigation – will open up research possibilities. Rather than hunting for signs of political liberalization, or despairing when flare-ups of repression occur, attention can be focused on how conflicting signals are transmitted and understood. Even a quick glance through the newspaper, or through recent issues of *China Quarterly* or *China Journal*, shows conflicting official or quasi-official signals about a wide range of topics. From the Internet to free trade, the Chinese leadership is ambivalent about realizing the benefits of new institutions, ideas, and technologies if it means ceding political control.

In the end, it is perhaps unsurprising that political ambivalence is such a prominent theme in a state visibly committed to three core contradictions. In economics, China is a communist country pursuing capitalism, an irony rife with ideological tension. In politics, China is a one-party state running long-term experiments in village elections, intraparty democracy, and other types of public participation. And in law, China has spent thirty years of legal reforms working toward an efficient, predictable legal system despite certain knowledge that law can subvert those in power as well as support them. Even though unequivocal repression garners much news coverage, as during the 2008 Tibetan protests or the 2009 unrest in Xinjiang, future research will want to examine how groups as diverse as foreign law firms,[22] environmental NGOs,[23]

---

22 For more on how the Ministry of Justice's attitude toward foreign law firms is ambivalent, see Liu (2009, 158).

23 Liang Congjie, the founder of Friends of Nature, summed up political ambivalence in this way: "It is hard to generalize what the government thinks about us. The government is not a monolithic bloc in this regard. SEPA [the State Environmental Protection Agency] supports us and has called us their 'natural ally.' The MOWR [Ministry of Water Resources] probably likes us much less, and the provincial government in Yunnan undoubtedly hates us" (quoted in Mertha 2008, 27).

and documentary filmmakers[24] cope with mixed signals. Even at its most repressive, the Chinese state is not as single-minded as it is sometimes portrayed. The stable, high-capacity juggernaut familiar from the headlines is also a "hodgepodge of disparate actors," and divisions within the state make the experience of political ambivalence commonplace (O'Brien and Li 2006, 66).

A serious effort to look inside the state also obliges researchers to complicate a familiar narrative in Chinese politics: the idea that local officials subvert the central leadership's good intentions. As a starting point, the central-local divide of course captures an important dynamic. Local protectionism is real. Local officials often shelter pillar industries to protect the economy even if it means ignoring environmental rhetoric and policies from Beijing. Still, it is too simple to call the central government pro-environment and the local government pro-growth. The standard story of parochial locals and wise leaders conceals divisions and leaves too little room for variation. Reactions to environmental lawsuits are not uniform, especially when frontline judges juggle multiple priorities endorsed by Beijing (Chapter 5). Sometimes, local initiatives surpass anything happening on the national level, such as recent experiments with new types of plaintiffs in environmental courts (Chapter 4). Local officials are so frequently blamed inside China that it can be difficult not to join in. Expositions on the central-local divide are proffered freely both for the core of truth they contain and because they are politically safe. If anything, complaints about lousy local officials are welcomed insofar as they help the central leadership appear benevolent and unified. Rather than reinforcing this narrative, researchers need to search out the moments in which it breaks down – the moments in which simple dichotomies no longer hold, and a deeper understanding of divisions and pressures within the state is required.

For now, the best way to think about environmental litigation is as a topic on the "cutting edge of society's understanding of itself as it

---

24 Independent documentary filmmakers work in a "measured free space, the limits of which are constantly being tested by filmmakers and festivals alike" (Nornes 2009, 52).

changes" (Jasper 1997, 13). This book reflects China in the first decade of the 21st century, a moment in the midst of a massive experiment over how to exploit law and maintain political control at a time when outcomes are far from certain. Seen from this vantage point, multiple futures are possible. As occurred in Egypt or Singapore, it is easy to imagine repression of courts, judges, or lawyers who start to act like political challengers. Indeed, instances of violence, intimidation, and retribution already frequent the news. In 2009 alone, authorities suspended or shut down two prominent legal advocacy organizations, Yitong Law Firm and the Open Constitution Initiative.

Despite these high-profile crackdowns, it is also possible to imagine an extension of the status quo: a period of sustained ambivalence long enough to see how much new actors are able to accomplish and how much legal professionals' perceptions of their roles continue to shift.[25] Much will depend on the 2012 leadership turnover and how the next generation attempts to leave its mark on Chinese politics. Most of *Environmental Litigation in China: A Study in Political Ambivalence* deals with the years that Hu Jintao and Wen Jiabao led China. In retrospect, those years may come to look like a distinct era: a high tide of mixed signals that were allowed to persist because the duo at the helm lacked the interest, gumption, or capacity to steer a more definitive course.

Although China watchers typically default to cynicism (it is far safer to be pessimistic than to risk being called Pollyannaish), the decision about whether to be optimistic or discouraged about environmental litigation reflects nothing as much as prior expectations. Those expecting an inflexible communist court system bent on bending the law to protect polluters will be pleasantly surprised and those searching for stirrings of 1960s-style American judicial activism will be disappointed. The main

---

25 One potential change worth watching for is a shift from a top-down strategy calling for legislative change to bottom-up strategy designed to push the limits of the current system. Just as Richard Cloward and Frances Fox Piven called for a welfare enrollment drive in the 1960s to force a bureaucratic crisis and compel reform in the United States, Chinese policy entrepreneurs could push legal reforms by overwhelming courts with cases.

implication is simply to keep watching. Considering that the majority of lawyers were state employees as recently as 1995, it is early for an evaluation of long-term outcomes. Trends can take years to unfold, especially if it takes a distant tipping point to trigger a cascade of results.[26] Rather than hunting for signs of major transitions, such as revolution, liberalization, or democratization, research should remain attuned to changes that leave the top leadership largely untouched. Without official intent or even awareness, the steady pressure of litigation can rework the legal system from within, especially when laws are also changing fast. Change, now subtle and slow, may also rapidly accelerate. In Pakistan, a supreme court handpicked by the president developed distinct anti-regime sympathies in just two years (Ghias 2010, 1000). As China's leaders know, law requires vigilance precisely because change can be so unexpected.

---

26 Paul Pierson calls these cumulative causes (where change is slow-moving and gradual) and threshold effects (when major change happens at a critical level) (2004, 82–83).

Acknowledgments

Every page of this book bears traces of the intellectual and personal debt I owe to a host of people and institutions. First and foremost, I am grateful for the support and guidance of a group of mentors who modeled how to be both an outstanding scholar and an exceptional person. When I was an undergraduate at Wellesley College, Kathy Moon showed me that the best classes teach a way of thinking as well as new facts. Sally Merry taught me to take proper research notes and gently nudged me first toward teaching and, then, toward the study of law and society. Later, when I turned to environment, law, and China, I was fortunate to encounter Kate O'Neill, Bob Kagan, and Kevin O'Brien at Berkeley. Kate helped keep me grounded and offered important advice at key moments. Bob, a crystal-clear thinker, pointed the way out of more than one mashed-up chapter and intellectual dead end. He is also responsible for calling my attention to many of the most delightful (and useful) articles I read over the life of this project. And nearly ten years of interactions with Kevin, over e-mail, in person, and sometimes on the hiking trails of Contra Costa county, shaped my thinking about China, sharpened my writing, and taught me much about the ins and outs of the profession. Sharp-eyed readers may also notice that portions of the introduction were hammered out in our joint 2012 article, "Politics at the Boundary: Mixed Signals and the Chinese State," published in *Modern China* 38(2): 175–199.

Early on, as I shared thoughts and drafts around Berkeley, I benefited greatly from comments by Margaret Boittin, Jen Brass, Chen Zongshi, Jenny Chio, Mark Dallas, Jennifer Dixon, Eli Friedman, Tom Gold, Sam Handlin, Jonathan Hassid, Ron Hassner, Alison Kaufman, Mark Massoud, Dann Nassemullah, Carsten Vala, Leslie Wang, Steve Weber, Susanne Wengle, and Xiao Suowei. As my dissertation became a book manuscript, and I moved back to the East Coast, I developed new debts to Bill Alford, John Givens, Tim Hildebrandt, Tamir Moustafa, Anthony Spires, Stephanie Stern, and Alex Wang for finding the time to read parts or all of the manuscript and offer feedback. Ji Weidong at Shanghai Jiaotong University also deserves special thanks for granting me access to the data from his 2007 survey of lawyers, which augmented Chapter 6.

Before I started my fieldwork, I spent several months at the Center for Chinese Legal Studies at Columbia University Law School. Many thanks to Ben Liebman for his assistance during that period, as well as for his thoughtful feedback later on. In China, I am grateful to Wang Mingyuan for arranging a home for me in 2006 and 2007 at Qinghua University Law School's Center for Environmental, Natural Resources, and Energy Law. Research help from Shi Wenyu in China, and later Han Rongbin and Shao Heng in the United States, helped compensate for some of the difficulties of doing research in a second language. And above all, a score of conversations during my fieldwork helped me make sense of what I was seeing. I am particularly thankful to Cui Wei, Patrick Deegan, Chad Futrell, Dan Gutman, Karrie Koesel, Patrick Deegan, Jeremy Wallace, Jessica Weiss, Hyeon-Ju Rho, Glenn Tiffert, and Alex Wang as well as to Chinese friends and interviewees whose anonymity has been preserved.

In 2009, I left Berkeley to start a three-year fellowship at the Society of Fellows at Harvard University, and I am deeply appreciative of the time and financial freedom provided by my time there. During this critical pause, which gave me time to finish my dissertation, reflect, and write, I enjoyed first-rate conversation with the other fellows and, on more than one occasion, benefited from their spot-on advice. Thanks to Jason Aftosmis, Anthony Cheung, Matt Desmond, Jo Guldi, Sam Haselby, Maya Jasanoff, Kelly Katz, Rob Pringle, Giora Sternberg, Max Weiss, Glen Weyl, Winnie Wong, and Zeng Fanxu for their company in Cambridge.

At Cambridge University Press, I would like to thank John Berger for his early support and for recruiting the three anonymous reviewers whose comments helped improve the manuscript in ways that I never could have come up with on my own. Thanks also to Mary Bralove for her efforts to make my writing as accessible and as readable as possible, as well as to Stephen Voss for his permission to use the cover photograph.

Trips for fieldwork and research assistance were made possible by financial support from a Fulbright-Hays Doctoral Dissertation Abroad Fellowship, a Doctoral Dissertation Improvement Grant from the National Science Foundation, the Pacific Rim Research Program, the Abigail Reynolds Hodgen Publication Fund at UC Berkeley, the Center for Chinese Studies at UC Berkeley, the Center for International Studies at UC Berkeley, and the William F. Milton Fund at Harvard University. To these institutions and the staffers there who smoothed my way, deep thanks.

Interview List

1. American professor, New York City, September 11, 2006
2. Two Chinese lawyers, New York City, September 20, 2006
3. Chinese lawyer, New York City, September 28, 2006
4. Chinese LL.M. student, New York City, October 4, 2006
5. Chinese LL.M. student, New York City, October 18, 2006
6. Chinese former judge from Zhejiang province, New York City, October 26, 2006
7. Environmental Protection Bureau (EPB) official from Shanxi province, New York City, November 4, 2006
8. Chinese visiting scholar, New Haven, November 6, 2006
9. Chinese lawyer, phone interview, November 16, 2006
10. Chinese lawyer, Beijing, November 30, 2006
11. Chinese professor, Beijing, December 5, 2006
12. Chinese professor, December 6, 2006
13. Two staff members at an American NGO, Beijing, December 7, 2006
14. Chinese lawyer, Beijing, December 14, 2006
15. Chinese environmental NGO staff member, Beijing, December 15, 2006
16. American NGO staff member, Beijing, December 11, 2006
17. Chinese lawyer, Beijing, December 20, 2006
18. Chinese environmental NGO staff member, Beijing, December 11, 2006

19. State Environmental Protection Agency (SEPA) official, Beijing, December 21, 2006

20. Chinese professor, Guangdong province, January 5, 2007

21. Two staff members at an American NGO, Hong Kong, January 12, 2007

22. Chinese environmental NGO staff member working in Yunnan province, Beijing, January 19, 2007

23. Japanese professor and environmental activist, Beijing, January 21, 2007

24. Chinese environmental NGO staff member, Beijing, January 21, 2007

25. Chinese lawyer, Beijing, January 22, 2007

26. Chinese plaintiff in an environmental lawsuit, Beijing, January 24, 2007

27. Chinese lawyer, Beijing, January 25, 2007

28. Chinese lawyer, Beijing, January 26, 2007

29. Environmental reporter and activist, Beijing, January 30, 2007

30. Environmental reporter, Beijing, February 1, 2007

31. Chinese lawyer and environmental NGO staff member, Beijing, February 5, 2007

32. Chinese environmental NGO staff member, Fujian province, February 6, 2007

33. Chinese lawyer, Fujian province, February 7, 2007

34. Chinese lawyer, Fujian province, February 10–11, 2007

35. American NGO staff member, Beijing, February 12, 2007

36. Group of EPB officials and NGO staff members, Beijing, March 1, 2007

37. Chinese lawyer, Beijing, March 2, 2007

38. American NGO staff member, Beijing, March 4, 2007

39. Chinese professor, Beijing, March 5, 2007

40. Chinese lawyer, Hebei province, March 6, 2007

41. Group of Chinese lawyers and complainants in an environmental dispute, Beijing, March 8, 2007

42. Chinese lawyer, Beijing, March 14, 2007
43. American lawyer, Beijing, March 14, 2007
44. Plaintiff in an environmental lawsuit, Beijing, March 15, 2007
45. Chinese professor, Shanghai, March 19, 2007
46. Chinese lawyer, Jiangsu province, March 20, 2007
47. Chinese lawyer, Shanghai, March 21, 2007
48. American lawyer, Shanghai, March 21, 2007
49. Chinese lawyer and professor, Shanghai, March 22, 2007
50. Chinese lawyer, Shanghai, March 23, 2007
51. Group of plaintiffs in an environmental lawsuit, Hebei province, March 28, 2007
52. Chinese lawyer, Zhejiang province, March 31, 2007
53. Chinese lawyer, Zhejiang province, April 5, 2007
54. Chinese plaintiff in an environmental lawsuit, Beijing, April 10, 2007
55. Two Chinese lawyers, Beijing, April 12, 2007
56. Group of Chinese lawyers and professors, Beijing, April 16, 2007
57. Chinese environmental journalist, Beijing, April 19, 2007
58. Chinese plaintiff in an environmental lawsuit in Fujian province, Beijing, April 21, 2007
59. Chinese environmental journalist, Beijing, April 21, 2007
60. Chinese lawyer, Beijing, April 23, 2007
61. Chinese environmental NGO staff member, Beijing, April 26, 2007
62. Complainant in an environmental dispute, Beijing, April 27, 2007
63. Group of complainants in an environmental dispute, Shanghai, May 2, 2007
64. Group of complainants in an environmental dispute, Shanghai, May 3, 2007
65. Two complainants in an environmental dispute, Shanghai, May 4, 2007
66. Two complainants in an environmental dispute, Beijing, May 7, 2007
67. Chinese lawyer, Guangdong province, May 10, 2007

68. Two Chinese lawyers, Guangdong province, May 12, 2007
69. Chinese environmental NGO staff member, Beijing, May 17, 2007
70. Chinese lawyer, Beijing, May 17, 2007
71. American foundation representative, Beijing, May 22, 2007
72. Chinese lawyer, Shanghai, May 24, 2007
73. Chinese lawyer, Shanghai, May 24, 2007
74. Chinese judge, Shanghai, May 25, 2007
75. Chinese environmental activist and plaintiff, Zhejiang province, May 28, 2007
76. Chinese lawyer, Zhejiang province, May 29, 2007
77. Chinese lawyer, Hebei province, June 2, 2007
78. Group of staff members at a Chinese environmental NGO, Beijing, July 5, 2007
79. Chinese lawyer, Beijing, July 6, 2007
80. Chinese environmental NGO staff member, Beijing, July 10, 2007
81. Chinese environmental journalist, July 11, 2007
82. Chinese lawyer, Beijing, July 11, 2007
83. American NGO staff member, Beijing, July 15, 2007
84. Chinese lawyer, Beijing, July 17, 2007
85. Chinese lawyer, Beijing, July 20, 2007
86. American foundation representative, Berlin, July 25, 2007
87. EPB official, Jilin province, August 16, 2007
88. Chinese judge, Jilin province, August 16, 2007
89. Chinese lawyer, Jilin province, August 17, 2007
90. Chinese lawyer, Beijing, August 21, 2007
91. Chinese lawyer, Beijing, August 23, 2007
92. Two Chinese lawyers, Beijing, August 28, 2007
93. Chinese judge, Hebei province, August 28, 2007
94. Chinese environmental journalist, Beijing, August 30, 2007
95. American NGO staff member, Beijing, September 2, 2007
96. Chinese lawyer, Hubei province, September 4–5, 2007
97. Chinese lawyer, Hubei province, September 5, 2007

98. Chinese lawyer, Hubei province, September 6, 2007
99. Municipal EPB official, Hubei province, September 7, 2007
100. Chinese lawyer, Hubei province, September 10, 2007
101. Group of Chinese lawyers and complainants in an environmental dispute, Hubei province, September 11, 2007
102. American expert, Beijing, September 16, 2007
103. Chinese judge, Beijing, September 18, 2007
104. Chinese judge, Beijing, September 20, 2007
105. EPB official, Shanghai, September 24, 2007
106. Chinese lawyer, Shanghai, September 25, 2007
107. Complainant in an environmental dispute, Shanghai, September 27, 2007
108. Group of Chinese lawyers, Shanghai, September 27, 2007
109. American expert, phone interview, October 12, 2007
110. Chinese lawyer, Beijing, October 13, 2007
111. American NGO staff member, Hong Kong, October 18, 2007
112. American NGO staff member, Hong Kong, October 19, 2007
113. Chinese lawyer, Guangdong province, October 22, 2007
114. American lawyer, phone interview, October 24, 2007
115. Chinese lawyer, Beijing, October 25, 2007
116. Chinese lawyer, Beijing, October 25, 2007
117. Group of Chinese lawyers and professors, Beijing, October 26, 2007
118. Environmental lawyer from Inner Mongolia, Beijing, October 29, 2007
119. Group of staff members from Chinese environmental NGOs, Beijing, November 1, 2007
120. Chinese lawyer, Beijing, November 3, 2007
121. Chinese lawyer, Zhejiang province, November 5, 2007
122. Chinese lawyer, Jiangsu province, November 7, 2007
123. Chinese lawyer, Beijing, November 11, 2007
124. Group of Chinese lawyers and NGO staff members, Beijing, November 12, 2007
125. Chinese lawyer, Beijing, November 15, 2007

126. Chinese lawyer, Guangxi province, November 17, 2007
127. Chinese lawyer, Guangxi province, November 18, 2007
128. Chinese lawyer, Yunnan province, November 27, 2007
129. Chinese lawyer, Yunnan province, November 27, 2007
130. Chinese lawyer, Yunnan province, November 28, 2007
131. Chinese lawyer, Yunnan province, November 28, 2007
132. Chinese lawyer and professor, Yunnan province, November 29, 2007
133. Group of Chinese lawyers, Beijing, December 2, 2007
134. Group of Chinese lawyers, Heilongjiang province, December 7, 2007
135. Chinese professor, Beijing, December 18, 2007
136. European foundation representative, Beijing, December 21, 2007
137. Chinese lawyer, Shanghai, December 27, 2007
138. Chinese environmental NGO staff member, Yunnan province, January 4, 2008
139. Two Chinese lawyers, Hebei province, January 10, 2008
140. Two SEPA officials, Beijing, January 13, 2008
141. American NGO staff member, phone interview, May 14, 2008
142. Group of staff members at a Beijing-based legal database, Beijing, January 9, 2009
143. Chinese professor, Beijing, January 12, 2009
144. Group of staff members at a Beijing-based legal database, Beijing, January 13, 2009
145. American NGO staff member, Beijing, January 13, 2009
146. Chinese lawyer, Beijing, January 20, 2009
147. Chinese lawyer, Beijing, March 14, 2011
148. Chinese lawyer, Beijing, March 15, 2011
149. Chinese lawyer, Beijing, March 16, 2011
150. American foundation representative, Beijing, March 17, 2011
151. Chinese lawyer, Beijing, March 18, 2011
152. Chinese lawyer, Beijing, March 19, 2011
153. Chinese judge, Yunnan province, March 21, 2011

154. Chinese lawyer, Yunnan province, March 22, 2011
155. Chinese lawyer, Yunnan province, March 22, 2011
156. Chinese lawyer, Beijing, June 14, 2011
157. Chinese lawyer, Beijing, June 16, 2011
158. Chinese professor, Beijing, June 17, 2011
159. Chinese NGO staff member, Beijing, June 20, 2011
160. Chinese lawyer, Chongqing, June 22, 2011
161. Chinese lawyer, Chongqing, June 23, 2011
162. Chinese environmental NGO leader, Chongqing, June 24, 2011
163. Chinese lawyer, Chongqing, June 25, 2011
164. Chinese professor, Beijing, July 13, 2011
165. Complainant in an environmental dispute and his lawyer, Hebei province, July 14, 2011
166. Chinese judge, Hubei province, July 15, 2011
167. Chinese former judge, Hubei province, July 15, 2011
168. Chinese lawyer, Beijing, July 18, 2011
169. Chinese environmental NGO former staff member, Beijing, August 9, 2012
170. Chinese lawyer, Beijing, August 9, 2012
171. Chinese environmental NGO staff member, Beijing, August 9, 2012
172. Chinese judge, Yunnan province, August 13, 2012
173. Chinese judge from Guizhou province, Beijing, August 18, 2012
174. Chinese lawyer, Shanghai, August 28, 2012
175. Chinese lawyer, Jiangsu province, August 29, 2012

References[1]

ENGLISH LANGUAGE

Abrams, Kathryn R., and Hila Keren. 2006. Law in the cultivation of hope. Bpress Legal Series, Working Paper 1205. http://tinyurl.com/ykvznq5

Alford, William P. 2000. Exporting "the pursuit of happiness." *Harvard Law Review* 113(7): 1677–715.

Alford, William P., and Benjamin L. Liebman. 2002–2003. Clean air, clean processes? The struggle over air pollution law in the People's Republic of China. *Hastings Law Journal* 52: 703–748.

Alford, William P., Robert P. Weller, Leslyn Hall, Karen R. Polenske, Yuanyuan Shen and David Zweig. 2002. The human dimensions of pollution in policy implementation: Air quality in rural china. *Journal of Contemporary China* 11(32): 495–513.

Allison, Graham. 1969. Conceptual models and the Cuban missile crisis. *American Political Science Review* 63(3): 689–718.

Aminzade, Ronald R., and Doug McAdam. 2001. Emotions and contentious politics. In *Silence and voice in the study of contentious politics*, eds. Ronald R. Aminzade, Jack A. Goldstone, Doug McAdam and Elizabeth J. Perry, 14–50. Cambridge: Cambridge Univ. Press.

Amsterdam, Anthony G., and Jerome Bruner. 2000. *Minding the law*. Cambridge, MA: Harvard Univ. Press.

Associated Press. 2007. Paris Hilton visits Shanghai, November 22. http://tinyurl.com/yjnhoy7

---

1 All links active as of June 2012. Copies of all online materials also on file with the author.

Azimi, Negar. 2007. Hard realities of soft power. *New York Times Magazine*, June 24. http://tinyurl.com/cswwrqh

Balme, Stephanie. 2010. Local courts in Western China: The quest for independence and dignity. In *Judicial independence in China: Lessons for global rule of law promotion*, ed. Randall Peerenboom, 154–179. Cambridge: Cambridge Univ. Press.

Banerjee, Abhijit and Esther Duflo. 2011. *Poor economics: A radical rethinking of the way to fight global poverty*. New York: Public Affairs.

Barboza, David. 2007. In China, fish farming in toxic waters. *New York Times*, December 15. http://tinyurl.com/yhd878m

Barker, John. 2005. Where the missionary frontier ran ahead of empire. In *Missions and Empire*, ed. Norman Etherington, 86–106. Oxford: Oxford Univ. Press.

Baum, Richard. 1986. Modernization and legal reform in post-Mao China: The rebirth of socialist legality. *Studies in Comparative Communism* 19(2): 69–103.

BBC News. 2012. Lawyers in China to swear allegiance to Communist Party, March 12. http://tinyurl.com/7q6f3rm

Bentley, Julia Greenwood. 2003. The role of international support for civil society organizations in China. *Harvard Asia Quarterly* (Winter): 11–20.

Best, Joel. 2001. The diffusion of social problems. In *How claims spread: Cross-national diffusion of social problems*, ed. Joel Best, 1–18. New York: Aldine de Gruyter.

Bisharat, George. 1998. Attorneys for the people, attorneys for the land: The emergence of cause lawyering in the Israeli-occupied territories. In *Cause lawyering: Political commitments and professional responsibilities*, eds. Austin Sarat and Stuart Scheingold, 452–486. Oxford: Oxford Univ. Press.

Bob, Clifford. 2005. *The marketing of rebellion: Insurgents, media, and international activism*. Cambridge: Cambridge Univ. Press.

Bourdieu, Pierre. 1986. The force of the law: Toward a sociology of the juridical field. *Hastings Law Journal* 38: 805–53.

Burningham, Kate. 2000. Using the language of NIMBY: A topic for research, not an activity for researchers. *Local Environment* 5(1): 5–67.

Bush, George W. 2005. Second inaugural address, January 20. http://tinyurl.com/8etxlx

Bush, Sarah. 2011. The taming of democracy assistance. Working paper on file with the author.

Cai, Yongshun. 2004. Managed participation in China. *Political Science Quarterly* 119: 425–451.

Cai, Yongshun. 2005. China's moderate middle class: The case of homeowners' resistance. *Asian Survey* 45(5): 777–799.

Cai, Yongshun, and Songcai Yang. 2005. State power and unbalanced legal development in China. *Journal of Contemporary China* 14(42): 117–34.

Cai, Yongshun. 2008. Disruptive collective action in the reform era. In *Popular Protest in China*, ed. Kevin J. O'Brien, 163–178. Cambridge, MA: Harvard Univ. Press.

Cai, Yongshun. 2010. *Collective resistance in China: Why popular protests succeed or fail.* Stanford: Stanford Univ. Press.

Carothers, Thomas. 1999. *Aiding democracy abroad.* Washington DC: Carnegie Endowment for International Peace.

Cary, Eve. 2011. China's policy impasse: The case of the "Green GDP" initiative. *The China Brief*, May 6. http://tinyurl.com/6hpq5vp

Chabot, Sean. 2000. The African American reinvention of the Ghandian repertoire. *Mobilization* 5(2): 201–216.

Chabot, Sean, and Jan Willem Duyvendak. 2002. Globalization and transnational diffusion between social movements: Reconceptualizing the dissemination of the Gandhian repertoire and the "coming out" routine. *Theory and Society* 31: 697–740.

Chaskalson, Arthur. 2003. From wickedness to equality: The moral transformation of South African law. *International Journal of Constitutional Law* 1(3): 590–609.

Cheeseman, Nick. 2011. How an authoritarian regime in Burma used special courts to defeat judicial independence. *Law & Society Review* 45(4): 801–830.

Chen, Gang. 2009. *Politics of China's environmental protection: Problems and progress.* Singapore: World Scientific Publishing.

Chen, Guangcheng. 2012. How China flouts its laws. *New York Times*, May 29. http://tinyurl.com/d6qhfx9

Chen, Jianfu. 2008. *Chinese law: Context and transformation.* Leiden: Martinus Nijhoff Publishers.

Chen, Titus C. 2012. Recalibrating the measure of justice: Beijing's effort to recentralize the judiciary and its mixed results. *Journal of Contemporary China* 21(75): 499–518.

Cheng, Xiang. 2011. The work load dilemma for Chinese street-level environmental regulators: Better work vs. more work. Paper presented at the annual meeting of the Law and Society Association, San Francisco, California.

Chenzhong, Xiaolu. 2009. Shanghai suspends maglev project. *Caijing*, March 10. http://tinyurl.com/bsu553

China Environmental Awareness Program. 2008. 2007 China general public environmental survey: Report abstract, April 3.

China Dialogue. 2011. Eight cases that mattered. July 26. http://tinyurl.com/3pt6ujl

China Labour Bulletin. 2007. Public interest litigation in China: A new force for social justice, October 10. http://tinyurl.com/yzoakns

Clarke, Donald. 2009. Lawyers and the state in China: Recent developments. Testimony before the Congressional-Executive Commission on China, October 7. http://tinyurl.com/78gh8eg

Coates, Austin. 1987 [1968]. *Myself a mandarin: Memoirs of a special magistrate*. Hong Kong, China: Oxford Univ. Press.

Cohen, Jerome. 1997. Reforming China's civil procedure: Judging the courts. *American Journal of Comparative Law* 45(4): 793–804.

Cohen, Jerome. 2008. Body blow for the judiciary. *South China Morning Post*, October 18, A-13.

Cohen, Paul A. 1974. Littoral and hinterland in nineteenth century China: The "Christian" reformers. In *The Missionary Enterprise in China and America*, ed. John K. Fairbank, 197–225. Cambridge, MA: Harvard Univ. Press.

Cohen, Roger. 2000. Who really brought down Milosevic? *New York Times Magazine*, November 26. http://tinyurl.com/c8jgvrt

Comaroff, Jean, and John Comaroff. 1991. *Of revelation and revolution, volume 1: Christianity, colonialism, and consciousness in South Africa*. Chicago: Univ. of Chicago Press.

Conner, Alison W. 2003. The comparative law school of China. In *Understanding China's legal system*, ed. C.S. Hsu, 210–273. New York: New York Univ. Press.

Conner, Alison W. 2007. Chinese lawyers on the silver screen. In *Cinema, law, and the state in Asia*, eds. Corey K. Creekmur and Mark Sidel, 195–211. New York: Palgrave Macmillan.

Cooper, Fredrick. 2001. What Is the concept of globalization good for? An African historian's perspective. *African Affairs* 100: 189–213.

Davenport, Christian. 2005. Understanding covert repressive action: The case of the U.S. government against the republic of new Africa. *Journal of Conflict Resolution* 49(1): 120–140.

Dawson, Jane I. 1996. *Eco-Nationalism: Anti-nuclear activism and national identity in Russia, Lithuania and Ukraine.* Durham: Duke Univ. Press

Dezalay, Yves, and Bryant G. Garth. 1996. *Dealing in virtue: International commercial arbitration and the construction of a transnational legal order.* Chicago: Univ. of Chicago Press.

Dimitrov, Martin. 2006. The rise of the rule of law in China. Conference paper presented at *China's rise: Domestic and external Issues*, Tuck School of Business, Hanover, NH.

Dolowitz, David P., and David Marsh. 2000. Learning from abroad: The role of policy transfer in contemporary policy-making. *Governance* 13(1): 5–24.

Economy, Elizabeth. 2004. *The river runs black: The environmental challenge to China's future.* 1st Edition. Ithaca: Cornell Univ. Press.

Economy, Elizabeth. 2010. *The river runs black: The environmental challenge to China's future.* 2nd Edition. Ithaca: Cornell Univ. Press.

Edin, Maria. 2003. State capacity and local agent control in China. *The China Quarterly* 173: 35–52.

Edwards, Michael. 2008. *Just another emperor? The myths and realities of philanthrocapitalism.* Demos: A Network for Ideas and Action: The Young Foundation.

Einhorn, Bruce. 2010. From China, the future of fish. *Businessweek*, October 21. http://tinyurl.com/26r9bpb

Ellmann, Stephen. 1986–1987. Lawyers and clients. *UCLA Law Review* 34: 717–779.

Ellmann, Stephen. 1998. Cause lawyering in the third world. In *Cause lawyering: political commitments and professional responsibilities*, eds. Austin Sarat and Stuart Scheingold, 349–430. Oxford: Oxford Univ. Press.

Elvin, Mark. 2004. The retreat of the elephants: An environmental history of China. New Haven: Yale Univ. Press.

Epp, Charles. 1998. *The rights revolution: lawyers, activists and courts in comparative perspective.* Chicago: Univ. of Chicago Press.

Epstein, Lee, Jack Knight, and Olga Shvetsova. 2001. The role of constitutional courts in the establishment and maintenance of democratic systems of government. *Law & Society Review* 35: 117–164.

Fernandez, Luis. 2008. *Policing dissent: Social control and the anti-globalization movement.* New Brunswick: Rutgers Univ. Press.

Ferris, Richard J., and Hongjun Zhang. 2002. Reaching out to the rule of law: China's continuing efforts to develop an effective environmental law regime. *William and Mary Bill of Rights Journal* 11: 569–602.

Feynman, Richard P. 2007 [1988]. *What do you care what other people think? Further adventures of a curious character.* New York: Penguin Books.

Finnemore, Martha, and Kathryn Sikkink. 1998. International norm dynamics and political change. *International Organization* 52(4): 887–917.

Ford, Peter. 2009. China cracks down on human rights lawyers. *Christian Science Monitor*, February 25.

Freeman, Charles W., and Xiaoqing Lu. 2008. Assessing Chinese government response to the challenge of environment and health. Washington DC: Center for Strategic and International Studies.

Freeman, David J., and Lynn Feng. 2010. China's revised tort law significantly increases environmental liability risks. *Paul Hastings Newsletter for Investing and Operating in the People's Republic of China*, August 19.

Friedman, Lawrence M. 1975. *The legal system: A social science perspective.* New York: Russell Sage Foundation.

Fu, Hualing. 2006. When lawyers are prosecuted: The struggle of a profession in transition. Social Science Research Network working paper. http://tinyurl.com/yglvxad

Fu, Hualing, and Richard Cullen. 2008. Weiquan (rights protection) lawyering in an authoritarian state: Toward critical lawyering. *China Journal* 59: 111–27.

Fu, Yulin, and Randall Peerenboom. 2010. A new analytical framework for judicial independence. In *Judicial independence in China: Lessons for global rule of law promotion,* ed. Randall Peerenboom, 95–133. Cambridge: Cambridge Univ. Press.

Fürst, Kathinka. 2008. Access to justice in environmental disputes: Opportunities and obstacles for Chinese pollution victims. M.A. dissertation, University of Oslo.

Galanter, Marc. 1974. Why the "haves" come out ahead: Speculations on the limits of legal change. *Law & Society Review* 9(1): 95–160.

Gale, Fred, and Jean C. Buzby. 2009. Imports from China and food safety issues. Washington DC: United States Department of Agriculture Economic Research Service.

Gallagher, Mary E. 2006. Mobilizing the law in China: "Informed disenchantment" and the development of legal consciousness. *Law & Society Review* 40(4): 783–816.

Gallagher, Mary E. 2007. "Hope for protection and hopeless choices:" Labor legal aid in the PRC. In *Grassroots political reform in contemporary China*, eds. Elizabeth J. Perry and Merle Goldman, 196–227. Cambridge, MA: Harvard Univ. Press.

Gao, Jie. 2010. Environmental public interest litigation and the vitality of environmental courts: The development and future of environmental courts in China. *People's Court Daily*, January 29. http://tinyurl.com/ydn77g8

Ganz, Marshall. 2001. The power of story in social movements. Conference paper presented at the annual meeting of the American Sociological Association, Anaheim, California.

Gardner, James. A. 1980. *Legal imperialism: American lawyers and foreign aid in Latin America*. Madison: Univ. of Wisconsin Press.

Garton Ash, Timothy. 2009. Velvet revolution: The prospects. *New York Review of Books* 56(19), December 3. http://tinyurl.com/yjhwmtk

George, Timothy S. 2001. *Minamata: Pollution and the struggle for democracy in post-war Japan*. Cambridge, MA: Harvard Univ. Asia Center.

Ghias, Shoaib A. 2010. Miscarriage of chief justice: Lawyers, media and the struggle for judicial independence in Pakistan. *Law & Social Inquiry* 35(4): 985–1022.

Gilboy, George J., and Benjamin L. Read. 2008. Political and social reform in China: Alive and walking. *Washington Quarterly* 31(3): 143–164.

Ginsburg, Tom. 2003. *Judicial review in new democracies: Constitutional courts in Asian cases*. Cambridge: Cambridge Univ. Press.

Ginsburg, Tom. 2008. Administrative law and the judicial control of agents in authoritarian regimes. In *Rule by law: The politics of courts in authoritarian regimes*, eds. Tom Ginsburg and Tamir Moustafa, 58–72. Cambridge: Cambridge Univ. Press.

Ginsburg, Tom, and Tamir Moustafa. 2008. Introduction. In *Rule by law: The politics of courts in authoritarian regimes*, eds. Tom Ginsburg and Tamir Moustafa, 1–22. Cambridge: Cambridge Univ. Press.

Green, Nat. 2009. Positive spillover? Impact of the Songhua River benzene incident on China's environmental policy. Environmental Health Research Brief. http://tinyurl.com/82rzoal

Greve, Michael S. 1989. The non-reformation of administrative law: Standing to sue and public interest litigation in West German environmental law. *Cornell International Law Journal* 22: 197–211.

Gu, Peidong. 2008. On the settlement mechanism of irregular disputes in China. *Frontiers of Law in China* 3(2): 256–293.

Guiyang Municipal Government. 2009. Guiyang municipal regulations on promoting the construction of an ecological civilization. Reprinted in *Chinese Law and Government* 43(6): 43–52.

Guttman, Dan. 2007. Different operating systems. *The Environmental Forum* (November/December): 27.

Haas, Peter M. 1992. Introduction: Epistemic communities and international policy coordination. *International Organization* 46(1): 1–35.

Hall, Peter A. 2010. Historical institutionalism in rationalist and sociological perspective. In *Explaining institutional change: Ambiguity, agency and power*, eds. James Mahoney and Kathleen Thelen, 204–223. Cambridge: Cambridge Univ. Press.

Halliday, Terence C., and Lucien Karpik. 1997. Politics matter: A comparative theory of lawyers in the making of political liberalism. In *Lawyers and the rise of political liberalism*, eds. Terence C. Halliday and Lucien Karpik, 15–64. Oxford: Clarendon Press.

Halliday, Terence C., and Lucien Karpik. 2012. Political liberalism in the British post-colony: A theme with three variations. In *Fates of political liberalism in the British post-colony: The politics of the legal complex*, eds. Terence C. Halliday, Lucien Karpik and Malcolm M. Feeley, 3–58. Cambridge: Cambridge Univ. Press.

Halliday, Terence C., Lucien Karpik, and Malcolm Feeley. 2007. The legal complex in struggles for political liberalism. In *Fighting for political freedom: comparative studies of the legal complex and political liberalism*, eds. Terence C. Halliday, Lucien Karpik and Malcolm M. Feeley, 1–40. Oxford: Hart Publishing.

Halliday, Terence C., and Sida Liu. 2007. Birth of a liberal movement? Looking through a one-way mirror at lawyers' defence of criminal defendants in China. In *Fighting for political freedom: comparative studies of the legal complex and political liberalism*, eds. Terence C. Halliday, Lucien Karpik and Malcolm M. Feeley, 65–107. Oxford: Hart Publishing

Halliday, Terence C., and Sida Liu. 2008. Dancing handcuffed in a minefield: Survival strategies of defense lawyers in China's criminal justice system.

Conference paper presented at the annual meeting of the Law and Society Association, Montreal, Canada.

Hamilton, Mark S. 2002. Sailing in a sea of obscurity: The growing importance of China's martime arbitration commission. *Asian-Pacific Law & Policy Journal* 3: 477–527.

Hand, Keith J. 2006. Using the law for a righteous purpose: Sun Zhigang and evolving forms of citizen action in the People's Republic of China. *Columbia Journal of Transnational Law* 45: 114–195.

Hassid, Jonathan H. 2008. Controlling the Chinese media: An uncertain business. *Asian Survey* 48(3): 414–430.

Hassid, Jonathan H. 2011. Four models of the fourth estate: A typology of contemporary Chinese journalists. *China Quarterly* 208: 813–832.

Hazard, Geoffrey C. 1969. Social justice through civil justice. *University of Chicago Law Review* 36: 699–712.

He, Xin. 2009. Routinization of divorce law practice in China: Institutional constraints' influence on judicial behavior. *International Journal of Law, Policy and the Family* 23: 83–109.

He, Xin. 2011. Debt collection in the less developed regions of China: An empirical study from a basic-level court in Shaanxi province. *China Quarterly* 206: 257–275.

He, Xin. (forthcoming). Black hole of responsibility: The adjudication committee's role in the Chinese court. *Law & Society Review*.

Helmke, Gretchen, and Steven Levitsky. 2006. *Introduction*. In *Informal Institutions and democracy: Lessons from Latin America*, eds Gretchen Helmke and Steven Levitsky, 1–30. Baltimore: Johns Hopkins Univ. Press.

Heilmann, Sebastian. 2008. From local experiments to national policy: the origins of China's distinctive policy process. *China Journal* 59: 1–30.

Heilmann, Sebastian and Elizabeth J. Perry. 2011. Embracing uncertainty: Guerilla policy style and adaptive governance in China. In *Mao's invisible hand: The political foundations of adaptive governance in China*, eds. Sebastian Heilmann and Elizabeth J. Perry, 1–29. Cambridge, MA: Harvard Univ. Press.

Hendley, Kathryn. 1996. *Trying to make law matter: Legal reform and labor law in the Soviet Union*. Ann Arbor: University of Michigan Press.

Hendley, Kathryn. 2009. 'Telephone law' and the 'rule of law:' The Russian case." *Hague Journal on the Rule of Law* 1(2): 241–264.

Henry, Laura. 2010. *Red to green: Environmental activism in post-soviet Russia*. Ithaca: Cornell Univ. Press.

Hertsgaard, Mark. 1997. Our real China problem. *The Atlantic*, November. http://tinyurl.com/6gpzhky

Hilbink, Lisa. 2007. *Judges beyond politics in democracy and dictatorship*. Cambridge: Cambridge Univ. Press.

Hildebrandt, Timothy. 2011. The political economy of social organization registration in China. *China Quarterly* 208: 970–989.

Hildebrandt, Timothy. 2013. Social organizations and the authoritarian state in China. Cambridge: Cambridge Univ. Press.

Hirschl, Ran. 2008. The judicialization of mega-politics and the rise of political courts. *Annual Review of Political Science* 11: 93–118.

Hirschman, Albert O. 1978. Beyond asymmetry: Critical notes on myself as a young man and on some other old friends. *International Organization* 32(1): 45–50.

Ho, Peter, and Eduard B. Vermeer, eds. 2006. *China's limits to growth: prospects for greening state and society*. Oxford: Blackwell Publishers.

Hook, Leslie. 2010. China feels the strain in rush to save energy. *Financial Times*, October 19. http://tinyurl.com/25o4qzm

Hu, Meidong, and Yining Peng. 2010. Protesters dump on E China landfill site. *China Daily*, November 20. http://tinyurl.com/2w3opar

Human Rights Watch. 2008. Walking on thin ice: Control, intimidation and harassment of lawyers in China. New York: Human Rights Watch. http://tinyurl.com/yl657qq

Jacobsohn, Gary. 2003. *The wheel of law: India's secularism in comparative constitutional perspective*. Princeton: Princeton Univ. Press.

Jahiel, Abigail R. 1998. The organization of environmental protection in China. *China Quarterly* 156: 757–787.

Jancar-Webster, Barbara. 1998. Environmental movement and social change in the transition countries. *Environmental Politics* 7(1): 69–90.

Jasper, James M. 1997. *The art of moral protest: Culture, biography and creativity in social movements*. Chicago: Univ. of Chicago Press.

Ji, Xiangde. 2010. Legal education. In *The China legal development yearbook*, Volume 4, ed. Lin Li, 299–306. Leiden: Brill Press.

Jiang, Ping. 2006. Give law greater clout in battle against pollution. *China Daily*, July 31. http://tinyurl.com/yz9foaf

Jiang, Ping. 2010. China's rule of law is in full retreat. Speech given February 21. http://tinyurl.com/yj8z249

Jing, Jun. 2000. Environmental protests in rural China. In *Chinese Society, change, conflict and resistance*, eds. Elizabeth J. Perry and Mark Selden, 204–222. London: Routledge.

Kagan, Robert A. 2008 [1978]. *Introduction*. In *Law & society in transition*, Philippe Nonet and Philip Selznick, vii–xxvi. New Brunswick: Transaction Publishers.

Kagan, Robert A. 2001. *Adversarial legalism: The American way of law*. Cambridge, MA: Harvard Univ. Press.

Kahn, Joseph. 2007. Chinese official warns against independence of courts. *New York Times*, February 3. http://tinyurl.com/ya9lw6d

Kahn, Joseph. 2007a. Rule by law. *New York Times*, February 25, A-1.

Kahn, Joseph, and Jim Yardley. 2007. As China roars, pollution reaches deadly extremes. *New York Times*, August 26. http://tinyurl.com/ys3j2y

Kapiszewski, Diana, and Mathew M. Taylor. 2008. Doing courts justice? Studying judicial politics in Latin America. *Perspectives on Politics* 6(4): 741–767.

Karpik, Lucien. 2007. Political lawyers. In *Fighting for political freedom: Comparative studies of the legal complex and political liberalism*, eds. Terence C. Halliday, Lucien Karpik and Malcolm M. Feeley, 463–494. Oxford: Hart Publishing.

Keck, Margaret E., and Kathryn Sikkink. 1998. *Activists beyond borders: Advocacy networks in international politics*. Ithaca: Cornell Univ. Press.

Kelemen, Daniel R., and Eric C. Sibbitt. 2004. The globalization of American law. *International Organization* 58: 103–136.

Kellogg, Thomas E. 2007. Courageous explorers? Education litigation and judicial innovation in China. *Harvard Human Rights Journal* 20: 141–184.

Kennedy, Scott. 2005. *The business of lobbying in China*. Cambridge, MA: Harvard Univ. Press.

Khagram, Sanjeev. 2004. *Dams and development: Transnational struggles for water and power*. Ithaca: Cornell Univ. Press.

Khalili, Laleh L. 2007. *Heroes and martyrs of Palestine: The politics of national commemoration*. Cambridge: Cambridge Univ. Press.

Kirby, David. 2011. Made in China: Our toxic, imported air pollution. *Discover*, March 18. http://tinyurl.com/6b6u6fw

Kirby, William C. 1997. The internationalization of China: Foreign relations at home and abroad in the Republican era. *China Quarterly* 150: 433–458.

Klug, Heinz. 2000. *Constituting democracy: Law, globalism and South Africa's political reconstruction.* Cambridge: Cambridge Univ. Press.

Kostka, Genia and William Hobbs. 2012. Local energy efficiency policy implementation in China: bridging the gap between national priorities and local interests. *China Quarterly* 211: 765–785.

Kostka, Genia. Forthcoming. Environmental Protection Bureau leadership at the provincial level in China: Examining diverging career backgrounds and appointment patterns. *Journal of Environmental Policy and Planning.*

Kritzer, Herbert M. 2002. Lawyer fees and lawyer behavior in litigation: What does the empirical literature really say? *Texas Law Review* 80: 1943–1983.

Kunming Intermediate Court et al. 2008. Implementation opinions on the establishment of mechanisms for coordinating the enforcement of environmental laws. Reprinted in *Chinese Law and Government* 43(6): 69–75.

Laffen, Michael and Max Weiss. 2012. Facing fear: The history of an emotion in global perspective. Princeton: Princeton Univ. Press.

Lam, Willy. 2008. The CCP strengthens control over the judiciary. *China Brief* 8(14), July 3. http://tinyurl.com/bjswpn3.

Lam, Willy. 2011. Beijing's "wei-wen" imperative steals the thunder at NPC. *China Brief* 11(4), March 10. http://tinyurl.com/7lh6qaf

Landry, Pierre F. 2008. *Decentralized authoritarianism in China: The Communist Party's control of local elites in the post-Mao era.* Cambridge: Cambrige Univ. Press.

Landry, Pierre. 2008a. The institutional diffusion of courts in China: Evidence from survey data. In *Rule by law: The politics of courts in authoritarian regimes*, eds. Tom Ginsburg and Tamir Moustafa, 207–234. Cambridge: Cambridge Univ. Press.

Lee, Ching Kwan. 2007. *Against the law: Labor protests in China's rustbelt and sunbelt.* Berkeley: Univ. of California Press.

Lee, Ching Kwan, and You-Tien Hsing. 2010. Social activism in China. In *Reclaiming Chinese society: The new social activism*, eds. Ching Kwan Lee and You-Tien Hsing, 1–13. New York: Routledge.

Leonard, Mark. 2008. *What does China think?* New York: Perseus Books.

Li, Jing. 2008. Group wants more polluters in court. *China Daily*, January 16. http://tinyurl.com/ye87odp

Li, Ling. 2010. Corruption in China's courts. In *Judicial independence in China: Lessons for global rule of law promotion*, ed. Randall Peerenboom, 196–220. Cambridge: Cambridge Univ. Press.

Li, Ling. 2012. The "production" of corruption in China's courts: Judicial politics and decision-making in a one-party state. *Law & Social Inquiry*. 37(4): 848–877.

Li, Lianjiang. 2004. Political trust in rural China. *Modern China* 30(2): 228–258.

Li, Victor H. 1978. *Law without lawyers: A comparative view of law in China and the United States*. Boulder: Westview Press.

Liang, Wendra. 2006. From protesters to plaintiffs: Pollution lawsuits and the tradition of protest in the People's Republic of China. M.A. dissertation, Stanford University.

Lieberthal, Kenneth G., and David M. Lampton. 1992. *Bureaucracy, politics and decision making in post-Mao China*. Berkeley: Univ. of California Press.

Lieberthal, Kenneth G., and Michel Oksenberg. 1990. *Policy making in China: Leaders, structures and processes*. Princeton: Princeton Univ. Press.

Liebman, Benjamin L. 1997–1998. Class action litigation in China. *Harvard Law Review*: 1523–1541.

Liebman, Benjamin L. 1999. Legal aid and public interest law in China. *Texas International Law Journal* 34: 211–286.

Liebman, Benjamin L. 2005. Watchdog or demagogue? The media in the Chinese legal system. *Columbia Law Review* 105(1): 1–157.

Liebman, Benjamin L. 2007. China's courts: Restricted reform. *China Quarterly* 191: 620–638.

Liebman, Benjamin L., and Timothy Wu. 2007. China's network justice. *Chicago Journal of International Law* 8(1): 257–322.

Liebman, Benjamin L. 2011. A return to populist legality? Historical legacies and legal reform. In *Mao's invisible hand: The political foundations of adaptive governance in China*, eds. Sebastian Heilmann and Elizabeth J. Perry, 165–200. Cambridge, MA: Harvard Univ. Press.

Liebman, Benjamin L. 2013. Malpractice mobs: Medical dispute resolution in China. *Columbia Law Review* (forthcoming January).

Lim, Lousia. 2009. Rights lawyers in China face growing threats. *National Public Radio*, May 3. http://tinyurl.com/dd7bbw

Link, Perry. 2002. China: The anaconda in the chandelier. *New York Review of Books*, April 11. http://tinyurl.com/7h6p526

Lipsky, Michael. 1968. Protest as a political resource. *American Political Science Review* 62: 1144–1158.

Liu, Jianguo, and Jared Diamond. 2005. China's environment in a globalizing world. *Nature*, June 30: 1179–1186.

Liu, Lee. 2010. Made in China: Cancer villages. *Environment* (March/April). http://tinyurl.com/2bpw8qo

Liu, Sida. 2006. Beyond global convergence: Conflicts of legitimacy in a Chinese lower court. *Law & Social Inquiry* 31(1): 75–106.

Liu, Sida. 2009. The logic of fragmentation: An ecological analysis of the Chinese legal services market. Ph.D. dissertation, University of Chicago.

Liu Sida, and Terence C. Halliday. 2011. Political liberalism and political embeddedness: Understanding politics in the work of Chinese criminal defense lawyers. *Law & Society Review* 45(4): 831–865

Lo, Carlos Wing-Hung, and Ed Snape. 2005. Lawyers in the People's Republic of China: A study of commitment and professionalization. *American Journal of Comparative Law* 53(2): 433–455.

Lo, Carlos Wing-Hung, and Shui-Yan Tam. 2007. Institutional reform, economic changes, and local environmental management in China: The case of Guangdong province. In *Environmental governance in China*, eds. Neil T. Carter and Arthur P.J. Mol, 42–62. New York: Routledge.

Lora-Wainwright, Anna. 2009. Of farming chemicals and cancer deaths: The politics of health in contemporary rural china. *Social Anthropology* 17(1): 56–73.

Lora-Wainwright, Anna. 2010. An anthropology of 'cancer villages:' Villagers' perspectives and the politics of responsibility. *Journal of Contemporary China* 19(63): 79–99.

Lorentzen, Peter L. 2006. Regularized rioting: Permitting public protest in an authoritarian regime. Social Science Research Network working paper. http://tinyurl.com/yghkcsu

Lubman, Stanley B. 1999. *Bird in a cage: Legal reform in China after Mao.* Stanford: Stanford Univ. Press.

Lum, Thomas. 2012. U.S. assistance programs in China. Congressional Research Service Report for Congress, January 6.

Lü, Yiyi. 2008. *Public interest litigation and political activism in China.* Montreal: International Centre for Human Rights and Democratic Development. http://tinyurl.com/yct89u3

Ma, Michael. 2003. Sue you sue me blues. *China Environment Series* 6: 81–83.

Ma, Jun. 2010. Minding the enforcement gap. *China Dialogue*, August 5. http://tinyurl.com/36x4gnm

Ma, Xiaoying, and Leonard Ortolano. 2000. *Environmental regulation in China*. Lanham, MD: Rowman & Littlefield Publishing Group.

Mackey, Robert. 2007. Expert roundtable: China – choking on growth. *New York Times*, August 29. http://tinyurl.com/ydexp8v

Mahoney, James, and Kathleen Thelen, eds. 2010. *Explaining institutional change: Ambiguity, agency and power*. Cambridge: Cambridge Univ. Press.

Makiya, Kanan. 1998. Republic of fear: The politics of modern Iraq. Berkeley: Univ. of California Press.

Markovits, Inga. 1996. Children of a lesser god: GDR lawyers in post-socialist Germany. *Michigan Law Review* 94: 2270–2308.

Markovits, Inga. 2010. *Justice in Lüritz: Experiencing socialist law in East Germany*. Princeton: Princeton Univ. Press.

Massoud, Mark F. 2008. Who rules the law? How government, civil society and aid agencies manipulate law in Sudan. Ph.D. dissertation, University of California, Berkeley.

Massoud, Mark. F. Forthcoming. *Law's Fragile State: Colonial, Authoritarian, and Humanitarian Legacies in Sudan*. Cambridge: Cambridge Univ. Press.

McAdam, Doug. 1989. The biographical consequences of activism. *American Sociological Review* 54(5): 744–760.

McAdam, Doug, and Dieter Rucht. 1993. The cross-national diffusion of movement ideas. *Annals of the American Academy of Political and Social Science* 528: 56–74.

McAllister, Lesley K. 2008. *Making law matter: Environmental protection and legal institutions in Brazil*. Stanford: Stanford Univ. Press.

McCann, Michael W. 1992. Reform litigation on trial. *Law & Social Inquiry* 17: 715–743.

McCubbins, Mathew D., and Thomas Schwartz. 1984. Congressional oversight overlooked: Police patrols versus fire alarms. *American Journal of Political Science* 28(1): 165–179.

McElwee, Charles R. 2011. *Environmental law in China: Mitigating risk and ensuring compliance*. Oxford: Oxford Univ. Press.

McMullin, Joseph. 2008–2009. Do Chinese environmental laws work? A study of litigation as response to fishery pollution. *UCLA Pacific Basin Law Journal* 26: 142–183.

Meisner, Maurice. 1999. *Mao's China and after: A history of the People's Republic*. Third edition. New York: The Free Press.

Mendelson Sarah E., and John K. Glenn. 2002. *The power and limits of NGOs*. New York: Columbia Univ. Press.

Merry, Sally. 2009. Measuring the world: Indicators, human rights and governance. *Current Anthropology* 52: S83–S95.

Merryman, John. 1985. *The civil law tradition: An introduction to the legal systems of Western Europe and Latin America*. Stanford: Stanford Univ. Press.

Mertha, Andrew C. 2008. *China's water warriors: Citizen action and policy change*. Ithaca: Cornell Univ. Press.

Merton, Robert K., with Elinor Barber. (1976 [1963]). *Sociological ambivalence and other essays*. New York: Free Press.

Michalowski, Raymond. 1998. All or nothing: An inquiry into the (im)possibilty of cause lawyering under Cuban socialism. In *Cause lawerying: political commitments and professional responsibilities*, eds. Austin Sarat and Stuart Scheingold, 523–545. Oxford: Oxford Univ. Press.

Michelson, Ethan. 2003. Unhooking from the state: Chinese lawyers in transition. Ph.D. dissertation, University of Chicago.

Michelson, Ethan. 2005. Global institutions, indigenous meaning: Lessons from Chinese law for the new institutionalism. *Legal Studies Research Paper Series*. Buffalo: Baldy Center for Law & Social Policy. http://tinyurl .com/y9r5576

Michelson, Ethan. 2006. The practice of law as an obstacle to justice: Chinese lawyers at work. *Law & Society Review* 40(1): 1–38.

Michelson, Ethan. 2007. Climbing the dispute pagoda: Grievances and appeals to the official justice system in rural China. *American Sociological Review* 72: 459–485.

Michelson, Ethan. 2007a. Lawyers, political embeddedness, and institutional continuity in China's transition from socialism. *American Journal of Sociology* 113 (2): 352–414.

Michelson, Ethan. 2008. Dear lawyer Bao: Everyday problems, legal advice and state power in China. *Social Problems* 55(1): 43–71.

Michelson, Ethan and Sida Liu. 2010. What do Chinese lawyers want? Political values and legal practice. In *China's Emerging middle class: Beyond economic transformation*, ed. Cheng Li, 310–333. Washington DC: Brookings Institution Press.

Michelson, Ethan, and Ke Li. 2012. Judicial performance without independence: The delivery of justice and political legitimacy in China. Paper presented at Columbia Law School, May 9.

Migdal, Joel S. 2001. *State in society*. Cambridge: Cambridge Univ. Press.

Miller, Richard E., and Austin Sarat. 1980. Grievances, claims and disputes: Assessing the adversary culture. *Law & Society Review* 15(3): 525–566.

Minow, Martha. 1990. Breaking the law: Lawyers and clients in struggles for social change. *University of Pittsburgh Law Review* 52: 723–751.

Minzner, Carl F. 2011. China's turn against law. *American Journal of Comparative Law* 59: 935–984.

Mol, Arthur P. J. 2009. Urban environmental governance innovations in China. *Current Opinion in Environmental Sustainability* 1: 96–100.

Morton, Katherine. 2008. Transnational advocacy at the grassroots: Benefits and risks of cooperation. In *China's embedded activism*, eds. Peter Ho and Richard Louis Edmonds, 195–215. New York: Routledge.

Moser, Adam, and Benjamin K. Sovacool. 2011. Public participation in China's environmental governance: The non-case of Chongqing Green Volunteers v. Guodian Yangzhonghai power company. National University of Singapore: Lee Kuan Yew School of Public Policy, Energy Governance Case Study 13.

Moustafa, Tamir. 2003. Law versus the state: The judicialization of politics in Egypt. *Law & Social Inquiry* 28(4): 883–930.

Moustafa, Tamir. 2007. Mobilizing the law in an authoritarian state: The legal complex in contemporary Egypt. In *Fighting for political freedom: Comparative studies of the legal complex and political liberalism*, eds. Terence C. Halliday, Lucien Karpik, and Malcolm M. Feeley, 193–217. Oxford: Hart Publishing.

Moustafa, Tamir. 2007a. *The struggle for constitutional power: Law, politics and economic development in Egypt*. Cambridge: Cambridge Univ. Press.

Muir, William Ker. 1973. *Law and attitude change*. Chicago: Univ. of Chicago Press.

Nader, Laura. 1990. *Harmony ideology: Justice and control in a Zapotec mountain village*. Stanford: Stanford Univ. Press.

Narain, Urvashi, and Ruth Greenspan Bell. 2005. *Who changed Delhi's air? The roles of the court and the executive in environmental policymaking*. Washington DC: Resources for the Future Discussion Paper. http://tinyurl.com/yhdw5xo

Natsios, Andrew. 2010. The clash of the counter-bureaucracy and development. Washington DC: Center for Global Development. http://tinyurl.com/6j4jfld

Natural Resources Defense Council. 2011. Reducing the health risks from industrial lead pollution: Case study-based recommendations. Draft on file with the author.

Nonet, Philippe, and Philip Selznick. 2008 [1978]. *Toward responsive law: Law & society in transition.* New Brunswick: Transaction Publishers.

Nornes, Abe Mark. 2009. Bulldozers, bibles and very sharp knives: The Chinese independent documentary scene. *Film Quarterly* 63(1): 50–55.

Nye, Joseph S. 2002. The information revolution and American soft power. *Asia-Pacific Review* 9(1): 60–76.

O'Brien, Kevin J. 1990. *Reform without liberalization: China's National People's Congress and the politics of institutional change.* Cambridge: Cambridge Univ. Press.

O'Brien, Kevin J., and Lianjiang Li. 1999. Selective policy implementation in rural China. *Comparative Politics* 31(2): 167–186.

O'Brien, Kevin J. 2003. Neither transgressive nor contained: Boundary-spanning contention in China. *Mobilization* 8(1): 51–64.

O'Brien, Kevin J., and Lianjiang Li. 2004. Suing the local state: Administrative litigation in rural China. *China Quarterly* 51: 75–96.

O'Brien, Kevin J., and Lianjiang Li. 2006. *Rightful resistance in rural China.* Cambridge: Cambridge Univ. Press.

O'Brien, Kevin J., and Rachel E. Stern. 2008. Studying contention in contemporary China. In *Popular protest in China*, ed. Kevin O'Brien, 11–25. Cambridge, MA: Harvard Univ. Press.

O'Brien, Kevin J. 2009. Local people's congresses and governing China. *China Journal* 61: 131–141.

Oi, Jean. 1999. *Rural China takes off: Institutional foundations of economic reform.* Berkeley: Univ. of California Press.

Oi, Jean, and Shukai Zhao. 2007. Fiscal crisis in China's townships: Causes and consequences. In *Grassroots political reform in contemporary China*, eds. Elizabeth J. Perry and Merle Goldman, 75–96. Cambridge, MA: Harvard Univ. Press.

Oster, Shai, and Mei Fong. 2006. In booming China, a doctor battles a polluting factory. *Wall Street Journal*, July 19. http://tinyurl.com/yd3yfbg

Palmer, Michael, and Chao Xi. 2009. *China. The Annals of the American Academy of Political and Social Science* 622: 270–279.

Pan, Philip P. 2008. *Out of Mao's shadow*. New York: Simon and Schuster.

Peerenboom, Randall. 2002. *China's long march toward rule of law*. Cambridge: Cambridge Univ. Press.

Peerenboom, Randall, and Xin He. 2008. *Dispute resolution in China: Patterns, causes, and prognosis*. Oxford: The Foundation for Law, Justice and Society.

Peerenboom, Randall. 2009. Economic development and the development of the legal profession in China. Social Science Research Network working paper. http://tinyurl.com/y98u372

Peerenboom, Randall. 2010. Judicial independence in China: Common myths and unfounded assumptions. In *Judicial independence in China: Lessons for global rule of law promotion*, ed. Randall Peerenboom, 69–94. Cambridge: Cambridge Univ. Press.

Pennington, Mathew. 2011. Lawmakers take aim at millions in US aid to China. Associated Press, November 15.

Percival, Robert V., Christopher H. Schroeder, Alan S. Miller, and James P. Leape. 2006. *Environmental regulation: Law, science and policy*. Fifth Edition. New York: Aspen Publishers.

Perry, Elizabeth J. 1994. Trends in the study of Chinese politics: State-society relations. *China Quarterly* 139: 704–713.

Pierson, Paul. 2004. *Politics in time: History, institutions, and social analysis*. Princeton: Princeton Univ. Press.

Pils, Eva. 2007. Asking the tiger for his skin: Rights activism in China. *Fordham International Law Journal* 30: 1209–1287.

Plumer, Bradford. 2008. Cultural devolution: Solving China's environmental catastrophe. *The New Republic*, July 9. http://tinyurl.com/yhvnboh

Polletta, Francesca. 2006. *It was like a fever: Storytelling in protest and politics*. Chicago: Univ. of Chicago Press.

Popova, Maria. 2006. Watchdogs or attack dogs? The role of Russian courts and the central election commission in the resolution of electoral disputes. *Europe-Asia Studies* 58(3): 391–414.

Posner, Richard A. 1993. What do judges and justices maximize? *Supreme Court Economic Review* 3: 1–41.

Preston, Brian J. 2006. The role of the judiciary in promoting sustainable development: The experience of Asia and the Pacific. *Asian Pacific Journal of Environmental Law* 9(2 &3): 109–211.

Price, Richard. 1998. Reversing the gun sights: Transnational civil society targets land mines. *International Organization* 52(3): 613–644.

Rajah, Jothie. 2011. Punishing bodies, securing the nation: How rule of law can legitimate the urban authoritarian state. *Law & Social Inquiry* 36(4): 945–970.

Rajah, Jothie. 2012. *Authoritarian rule of law: Legislation, Discourse and Legitimacy in Singapore.* Cambridge: Cambridge Univ. Press.

Ramzy, Austin. 2007. Heroes of the Environment. *Time*, October 17. http://tinyurl.com/yfgoqnj

Robin, Corey. 2004. *Fear: The history of a political idea.* Oxford: Oxford Univ. Press.

Roach Anleu, Sharyn L., and Kathy Mack. 2007. Magistrates, magistrate courts and social change. *Law & Policy* 29(2): 183–209.

Roach Anleu, Sharyn L. 2010. *Law and social change.* Second Edition. Los Angeles: Sage Publications.

Roelofs, Joan. 2007. Foundations and collaboration. *Critical Sociology* 33: 479–504.

Rohan, Brian. 2003. Clearing the air: The human rights and legal dimensions of China's environmental dilemma. Statement at the Congressional/Executive Commission on China Issues Roundtable. http://tinyurl.com/yafqaff

Rosenberg, Gerald N. 1993. *The hollow hope: Can courts bring about social change?* Chicago: Univ. of Chicago Press.

Scheingate, Adam. 2010. Rethinking rules: Creativity and constraint in the U.S. House of Representatives. In *Explaining institutional change: Ambiguity, agency and power*, eds. James Mahoney and Kathleen Thelen, 168–203. Cambridge: Cambridge Univ. Press.

Scheingold, Stuart. 2001. Cause lawyering and democracy. In *Cause lawyering and the state in a global era*, eds. Austin Sarat and Stuart Scheingold, 382–405. Oxford: Oxford Univ. Press.

Scheingold, Stuart A., and Austin Sarat. 2004. *Something to believe in: Politics, professionalism and cause lawyering.* Stanford: Stanford Univ. Press.

Schatz, Edward. 2006. Access by accident: Legitimacy claims and democracy promotion in authoritarian central Asia. *International Political Science Review* 27(3): 263–284.

Schuck, Peter H. 2000. Benched: The pros and cons of having judges make the law. *Washington Monthly* (December): 35–41.

Scott, James C. 1990. *Domination and the arts of resistance: Hidden transcripts.* New Haven: Yale Univ. Press.

Shamir, Roncn, and Sara Chinski. 1998. Destruction of houses and construction of a cause: Lawyers and Bedouins in the Israeli courts. In *Cause lawyering: political commitments and professional responsibilities*, ed. Austin Sarat and Stuart Scheingold, 227–257. Oxford: Oxford Univ. Press.

Shanghai Daily. 2011. Maglev link plan is suspended. January 19. http://tinyurl.com/7kyq73e

Shapiro, Judith. 2001. Mao's war against nature: Politics and the environment in revolutionary China. Cambridge: Cambridge Univ. Press.

Shapiro, Martin. 1981. *Courts: A comparative and political analysis*. Chicago: Univ. of Chicago Press.

Shapiro, Martin. 2008. Courts in authoritarian regimes. In *Rule by law: The politics of courts in authoritarian regimes*, eds. Tom Ginsburg and Tamir Moustafa, 326–335, Cambridge: Cambridge Univ. Press.

Shelley, Becky. 2005. Political globalisation and the politics of international non-governmental organisations: The case of village democracy in China. *Australian Journal of Political Science* 35(2): 225–238.

Shen, Kui. 2003. Is it the beginning of the era of the rule of the constitution? Reinterpreting China's 'first constitutional case.' *Pacific Rim Law and Policy Journal* 12: 199–232.

Shieber, Jonathan. 2009. Courting change: Environmental groups in China now have the ability to sue polluters, but will they? *Wall Street Journal*, December 7. http://tinyurl.com/ybm7aus

Sidel, Mark. 2008. *Law and society in Vietnam: The transition from socialism in comparative perspective*. Cambridge: Cambridge Univ. Press.

Silverstein, Gordon. 2003. Globalization and the rule of law: 'A machine that runs of itself?' *International Journal of Constitutional Law* 1(3): 427–445.

Slaughter, Anne-Marie. 2004. *A new world order*. Princeton: Princeton Univ. Press.

Smelser, Neil J. 1998. The rational and the ambivalent in the social sciences. *American Sociological Review* 63: 1–16.

Snow, David A., Daniel M. Cress, Liam Downey, and Andrew W. Jones. 1998. Disrupting the quotidian: Reconceptualizing the relationship between breakdown and the emergence of collective action. *Mobilization* 3(1): 1–22.

Solomon, Peter H. 2007. Courts and judges in authoritarian regimes. *World Politics* 60(1): 122–145.

Solomon, Peter H. 2008. Judicial power in authoritarian states: The Russian experience. In *Rule by law: The politics of courts in authoritarian regimes*, eds. Tom Ginsburg and Tamir Moustafa, 261–282. Cambridge: Cambridge Univ. Press.

Solomon, Peter H. 2010. Authoritarian legality and informal practices: Judges, lawyers and the state in Russia and China. *Communist and Post-Communist Studies* 43: 351–362.

Soule, Sarah A. and Sidney Tarrow. 1991. Acting collectively, 1847–49: How the repertoire of collective action changed and where it happened. Paper presented at the annual conference of the Social Science History Association, New Orleans.

Spector, Regine A. and Andrej Krickovic. 2007. The anti-revolutionary toolkit. Paper presented at the annual meeting of the American Political Science Association, Chicago.

Spiegel Online. 2007. A direct appeal to Merkel: Shanghai residents protest transrapid extension. *Spiegel Online*, March 13. http://tinyurl.com/ykwy96n

Spires, Anthony. 2011. Organizational homophiliy in international grant-making: US-based foundations and their grantees in China. *Journal of Civil Society* 7(3): 305–331.

Stalley, Philip. 2010. *Foreign firms, investment and environmental regulation in the People's Republic of China*. Stanford: Stanford Univ. Press.

Stark, David, Balazs Vedres, and Laszlo Bruszt. 2006. Rooted transnational publics: Integrating foreign ties and civic activism. *Theory and Society* 35: 323–349.

Starr, Amory, Luis A. Fernandez, Randall Amster, Lesley J. Wood and Manuel J. Caro. 2008. The impacts of state surveillance on political assembly and association: A socio-legal analysis. *Qualitative Sociology* 31: 251–270.

State Council. 2008. White paper: China's efforts and achievements in promoting the rule of law. http://tinyurl.com/yh78kkj

Steinfeld, Edward S., Richard K. Lester and Edward A. Cunningham. 2008. *Greener plants, grayer skies? A report from the front lines of China's energy sector*. MIT Industrial Performance Center, China Energy Group. http://tinyurl.com/624wjgc

Stephenson, Matthew. 2006. A trojan horse in China? In *Promoting the rule of law abroad: In search of knowledge*, ed. Thomas Carothers,

191–215. Washington DC: Carnegie Endowment for International Peace.

Stern, Rachel E. 2003. Hong Kong haze: Air pollution as a social class issue. *Asian Survey* 43(5) (September/October): 780–800.

Stern, Rachel E. 2005. Unpacking adaptation: The female inheritance movement in Hong Kong. *Mobilization* 10(3): 421–439.

Stern, Rachel E. and Jonathan H. Hassid. 2012. Amplifying silence: Uncertainty and control parables in contemporary China. *Comparative Political Studies* 45(10): 1230–1254.

Stern, Rachel E. and Kevin J. O'Brien. 2012. Politics at the boundary: Mixed signals and the Chinese state. *Modern China* 38(2): 175–199

Stokes, Susan C. 1991. Hegemony, consciousness and political change in Peru. *Politics & Society* 19: 265–290.

Supreme People's Court. 2010. Provisions of the Supreme People's Court concerning work on guiding cases, November 26. http://tinyurl.com/c7z4rbr

Tam, Weikeung. 2010. Political transition and the rise of cause lawyering: The case of Hong Kong. *Law & Social Inquiry* 35(3): 663–87.

Tarrow, Sidney. 2005. *The new transnational activism*. Cambridge: Cambridge Univ. Press.

Tate, C. Neal. 1993. Courts and crisis regimes: A theory sketch with Asian case studies. *Political Research Quarterly* 46(2): 311–338.

Teles, Steven M. 2008. *The rise of the conservative legal movement*. Princeton: Princeton Univ. Press.

Thayer, Millie. 2004. *Negotiating the global: Northeast Brazilian women's movements and the transnational feminist public*. Ph.D. dissertation, University of California, Berkeley.

Thornton, Patricia M. 2008. Manufacturing dissent in transnational China: boomerang, backfire or spectacle? In *Popular protest in contemporary China*, ed. Kevin J. O'Brien, 179–204. Cambridge, MA: Harvard Univ. Press.

Tiffert, Glenn D. 2009. Epistrophy: Chinese constitutionalism and the 1950s. In *Building constitutionalism in China*, eds. Stephanie Balme and Michael W. Dowdle, 59–76. New York: Palgrave Macmillan.

Tilly, Charles. 2008. *Credit and blame*. Princeton: Princeton Univ. Press.

Tilt, Bryan. 2007. The political ecology of pollution enforcement in China: A case from Sichuan's rural industrial sector. *China Quarterly* 192: 915–932.

Tilt, Bryan. 2010. The struggle for sustainability in rural China: Environmental values and civil society. New York: Columbia Univ. Press.

Toharia, Jose J. 1975. Judicial independence in an authoritarian regime: The case of contemporary Spain. *Law & Society Review* 9(3): 475–496.

Trubek, David M., and Marc Galanter. 1974. Scholars in self-estrangement: Some reflections on the crisis in law and development studies in the United States. *Wisconsin Law Review*: 1062–1102.

True, Jacqui, and Michael Mintrom. 2001. Transnational networks and policy diffusion: The case of gender mainstreaming. *International Studies Quarterly* 45: 27–57.

Ulc, Otto. 1972. *The judge in a communist state: A view from within.* Athens, OH: Ohio Univ. Press.

Upham, Frank K. 1987. *Law and social change in postwar Japan.* Cambridge, MA: Harvard Univ. Press.

Upham, Frank K. 2005. Who will find the defendant if he stays with his sheep? Justice in rural China. *Yale Law Journal* 114: 1675–1718.

van Rooij, Benjamin. 2006. Implementation of Chinese environmental law: Regular enforcement and political campaigns. *Development and Change* 37(1): 57–74.

van Rooij, Benjamin. 2006a. *Regulating land and pollution in China: Lawmaking, compliance and enforcement; theory and cases.* Leiden: Leiden Univ. Press.

van Rooij, Benjamin. 2010. The people vs. pollution: Understanding citizen action against pollution in China. *Journal of Contemporary China* 19(63): 55–77.

van Rooij, Benjamin, and Carlos Wing-Hung Lo. 2010. Fragile convergence: Understanding variation in the enforcement of China's industrial pollution law. *Law & Policy* 32(1): 14–37.

Vermont Law School. 2009. *US-China partnership develops next generation of environmental advocates.* Press Release, October 2. http://tinyurl.com/87zyoww

Vogel, Ezra F. 2011. *Deng Xiaoping and the transformation of China.* Cambridge, MA: Harvard Univ. Press.

Wald, Patricia. 1992–1993. Some real-life observations about judging. *Indiana Law Review* 26(1): 173–186.

Wallis, Jim. 2005. *God's politics.* San Francisco: Harper Collins.

Wan E'xiang. 2011. Establishing an environmental public interest litigation system and promoting the building of an ecological civilization. *Chinese Law and Government* 43(6): 30–40.

Wan, William. 2010. Pollution in China's Tai Lake worse despite national push for environmentalism. *Washington Post*, October 29. http://tinyurl.com/35cvqg2

Wang, Alex L. 2007. The role of law in environmental protection in China: Recent developments. *Vermont Journal of Environmental Law* 8: 195–223.

Wang, Alex L. 2010. The rivers run red: What can we learn from the recent spate of environmental accidents in China? http://tinyurl.com/26gqc36

Wang, Alex L. 2013. In search of a sustainable legitimacy: Environmental law and bureaucracy in China. *Harvard Environmental Law Review* 37.

Wang, Canfa. 2006–2007. Chinese environmental law enforcement: Current deficiencies and suggested reforms. *Vermont Journal of Environmental Law* 8. http://tinyurl.com/7mh7l9y

Wang, Jin. 2010a. China's green laws are useless. *China Dialogue*, September 23. http://tinyurl.com/364j7m2

Wang, Hongying. 2007a. Linking up with the international track: What's in a slogan? *China Quarterly* 189: 1–23.

Wapner, Paul. 1996. *Environmental activism and world civic politics*. Albany: State Univ. of New York Press.

Warwick, Mara, and Leonard Ortolano. 2007. Benefits and costs of Shanghai's environmental citizens complaints system. *China Information* 21(2): 237–268.

Watkins, Susan Cotts, Ann Swindler and Thomas Hannan (forthcoming). Outsourcing social transformation: Development NGOs as organizations. *Annual Review of Sociology* 38.

Watts, Jonathan. 2009. China's green champion sidelined. *Guardian*, March 12. http://tinyurl.com/b2a63z

Watts, Jonathan. 2010. Chinese farms cause more pollution than factories, says official survey. *Guardian*, February 9. http://tinyurl.com/ylrv4ru

Wedeen, Lisa. 1999. *Ambiguities of domination: Politics, rhetoric and symbols in contemporary Syria*. Chicago: Univ. of Chicago Press.

Wedeman, Andrew. 2001. Incompetence, noise and fear in central-local relations in China. *Studies in Comparative International Development* 35(5): 59–83.

Wee, Sui-Lee. 2012. China cancer village tests law against pollution. *Reuters*, January 16. http://tinyurl.com/6p9szmu

Weller, Robert P. 2006. *Discovering nature: Globalization and environmental culture in China and Taiwan*. Cambridge: Cambridge Univ. Press.

Weyland, Kurt. 2005. Theories of policy diffusion: Lessons from Latin American pension reform. *World Politics* 57: 262–95.

Wickham, Carrie Rosefsky. 2004. Interests, ideas and Islamist outreach in Egypt. In *Islamic activism: A social movement theory approach*, ed. Quintan Wiktorowicz, 231–49. Bloomington: Indiana Univ. Press.

Widner, Jennifer A. 2001. *Building the rule of law*. New York: WW Norton and Company.

Widner, Jennifer, and Daniel Scher. 2008. Building judicial independence in semi-democracies: Uganda and Zimbabwe. In *Rule by law: The politics of courts in authoritarian regimes*, eds. Tom Ginsburg and Tamir Moustafa, 235–260. Cambridge: Cambridge Univ. Press.

Wilson, Jeanne L. 2009. Coloured revolutions: The view from Moscow and Beijing. *Journal of Communist Studies and Transition Politics* 25(2): 369–395.

Wiwa, Ken. 2001. *In the shadow of a saint*. South Royalton, VT: Steerforth Press.

World Bank. 2012. Doing business 2012: Enforcing contracts. http://tinyurl.com/dxts952

Wright, Teresa. 2008. Student movements in China and Taiwan. In *Popular protest in China*, ed Kevin J. O'Brien, 26–53. Cambridge, MA: Harvard Univ. Press.

Wu, Fengshi. 2005. *Double-mobilization: Transnational advocacy networks for China's environment and public health*. Ph.D. dissertation, University of Maryland.

Wu, Peng. 2008. The good, the bad and the legal: Lawyering in China's wild West. *Columbia Journal of Asian Law* 183: 183–213.

Xia, Jun. 2012. China's courts fail the environment. *China Dialogue*, January 16. http://tinyurl.com/7t79x86

Xing, Ying. 2010. Barefoot lawyers and rural conflicts. In *Reclaiming Chinese society: The new social activism*, eds. You-Tien Hsing and Ching Kwan Lee, 64–82. New York: Routledge.

Xinhua News Agency. 2007. Shanghai maglev project suspended. May 26. http://tinyurl.com/cnsumrg

Xinhua News Agency. 2008. China to set up five new "super ministries." March 11. http://tinyurl.com/brdoow7

Xinhua News Agency. 2008a. Shanghai to solicit more opinion on maglev line. February 1. http://tinyurl.com/yg2rzvt

Xinhua News Agency. 2009. China acknowledges serious pollution, pledging tough measures. February 24.

Xinhua News Agency. 2011. China faces heavy task to cut pollution: Minister. April 23. http://tinyurl.com/3n9ptfj

Xinhua News Agency. 2011a. Number of cars in China hits 100 Mln due to rapid growth of private ownership: Ministry. September 16. http://tinyurl.com/3crgxp8

Xu, Kezhu, and Alex Wang. 2006. Recent developments at the Center for Legal Assistance to Pollution Victims (CLAPV). *China Environment Series* 8: 103–104.

Xu, Ming. 2010. Energy saving policy not a short-term goal. *Global Times*, September 20. http://tinyurl.com/2dgjcpe

Yardley, Jim. 2005. Spill in China brings danger, and cover up. *New York Times*, November 26. http://tinyurl.com/yhjwmhg

Yu, Xiaohong. 2009. Rise of local courts in China: Judicial hierarchy, institutional adaptation and regime resilience. Conference paper presented at *China's Changing Courts*, Columbia University Law School, New York.

Zemans, Frances Kahn. 1983. Legal mobilization: The neglected role of law in the political system. *American Political Science Review* 77(3): 690–703.

Zhan, Jiang. 2011. Environmental journalism in China. In *Changing media, changing China*, ed. Susan L. Shirk, 115–27. Oxford: Oxford Univ. Press.

Zhang, Jun. 2002. Environmental protection and legal system construction in China. Remarks at the United Nations Environment Program's Global Judges' Symposium on Sustainable Development and the Role of the Law. http://tinyurl.com/ygqfyhg

Zhang, Qianfan. 2003. The people's court in transition: The prospects of the Chinese judicial reform. *Journal of Contemporary China* 12(34): 69–101.

Zhang, Xuehua. 2008. Enforcing environmental regulations in Hubei Province, China: Agencies, courts, citizens. Ph.D. dissertation, Stanford University.

Zhang, Xuehua, Leonard Ortolano, and Zhongmei Lü. 2010. Agency empowerment through the administrative litigation law: Court enforcement of pollution levies in Hubei province. *China Quarterly* 202: 307–26.

Zhang, Fan. 2012. Sweeping pollution under the rug. *Caixin*, April 9. http://tinyurl.com/7mmkesl

Zhao, Yi. 2003. The expansion of judicial power in China. Ph.D. dissertation, Yale University.

Zhu, Suli. 2010. The party and the courts. In *Judicial independence in China: lessons for global rule of law promotion*, ed. Randall Peerenboom, 52–68. Cambridge: Cambridge Univ. Press.

Zou, Keyuan. 2006. *China's legal reform: Towards the rule of law*. Leiden: Martinus Nijhoff Publishers.

CHINESE LANGUAGE

Ai, Jiahui. 2008. *Managing court personnel amid social transition* (Shehui bianqian zhong de fayuan renshi guanli). Ph.D. dissertation, Beijing University Law School, China.

All-China Environment Federation (ACEF) and Natural Resources Defense Council (NRDC). 2011. Promoting environmental protection through the law (*Tongguo sifa shouduan tuijin huanjing baohu*), January. Working paper on file with the author.

All China Lawyers Association. 2004. Code of conduct for lawyers (for trial implementation) (*Lüshi zhiye xingwei guifan (shixing)*), effective March 20.

All China Lawyers Association. 2006. Guiding opinions on lawyers handling mass cases (*Zhonghua quanguo lüshi xiehui guanyu lüshi banli quntixing anjian zhidao yijian*), effective March 20.

Bie, Tao, ed. 2007. *Public interest environmental litigation* (Huanjing gongyi susong). Beijing: Law Press.

Boyle, Alan, and Patricia Birnie. 2007. *International law and the environment* (Guojifa yu huanjing). Beijing: Higher Education Press.

Caijing. 2006. The whole story of an environmental case involving over 1000 villagers in Pingnan County (*Pingnanxian qianyu cunmin huanbao song'an shimo*). February 12.

Caijing. 2012. China's mass incidents rise 29 percent annually (*Wo guo huanjing qunti shijian nianjun dizeng 29%*). October 27. http://tinyurl.com/dycoh82.

Caixin. 2012. September 3rd society: A proposal to quickly establish a system for environmental public interest litigation (*Jiusan xueshe: Guanyu jinkuai jianli huanjing gongyi susong zhidu de ti'an*). March 12. http://tinyurl.com/7mz2dtv

Central Committee of the Chinese Communist Party. 1979. Central Committee of the Chinese Communist Party instructions on guaranteeing the practical implementation of the criminal law and criminal litigation (*Zhonggong zhongyang guanyu jianjue baozheng xingfa, xingshi susongfa qieshi shishi de zhishi*), September 9. http://tinyurl.com/7dpdwfy

Chen, Aijiang, and Pengli Cheng. 2011. How do villagers mitigate environmental health risks? (*Cunmin shi ruhe huajie huanjing jiankang fengxian de?*). *Journal of Nanjing Agricultural University* (Nanjing Nongye Daxue Xuebao) 11(2): 27–32.

Chen, Yingfeng. 2006. The power of action and limits to the system: The middle class in urban activism (*Xingdongli yu zhidu xianzhi: Dushi yundong zhong de zhongchan jieceng*). *Sociological Studies* (Shehuixue Yanjiu) 21(4): 1–20.

Chen, Yueqin. 2006a. A successful Chinese environmental lawsuit (*Zhongguo yige chenggong de huanjing gongyi susong anli*). *China Commercial Law Web* (Zhongguo Min Shang Falü Wang), May 26.

China environment yearbook 2001 (*2001 Zhongguo huanjing nianjian*). Beijing: China Environment Press.

China environment yearbook 2002 (*2002 Zhongguo huanjing nianjian*). Beijing: China Environment Press.

China environment yearbook 2010 (*2010 Zhongguo huanjing nianjian*). Beijing: China Environment Press.

China law yearbook 2011 (*2011 Zhongguo falü nianjian*). Beijing: Law Press.

China statistical yearbook on environment 2001 (*2001 Zhongguo huanjing tongji nianjian*). Beijing: China Statistics Press.

China statistical yearbook on environment 2009 (*2009 Zhongguo huanjing tongji nianjian*). Beijing: China Statistics Press.

China statistical yearbook 2010 (*2010 Zhongguo tongji nianjian*). Accessed through chinadataonline.org

Chu, Wanzhong. 2010. An investigation of the environmental courts by the Yunnan high court uncovers embarrassing problems (*Yunnan sheng gaoyuan diaoyan huanbao fating faxian ganga shi*). *Legal Daily* (Fazhi Ribao), October 18. http://tinyurl.com/4hkyt2f

Deng, Xinjian. 2009. The Guangzhou city procuratorate issues guidelines on civil public interest litigation which explain how to solve four tough problems in upholding environmental and rights protection (*Guangzhoushi jianchayuan chutai minshi gongyi susong zhidao yijian pojie huanjing baohu weiquan sidao nanti*). *Legal Daily* (Fazhi Ribao), August 27. http://tinyurl.com/yjvveaz

Dr. Water (*Shui Bo*). "How public interest litigation can act as a shield for malicious accusations" (*Gongyi susong qineng dangzuo eyi wugao de hushenfu*). http://tinyurl.com/yljhye3

Duan, Hongqing. 2005. Background: Who will pay the bill for Songhua river pollution? (*Beijing: Shei wei Songhuajiang wuran maidan?*) *Caijing*, December 12.

Gao, Wei. 2010. Serious environmental pollution constitutes a crime (*Yanzhong wuran huanjing ji goucheng fanzui*). *China Environmental News*, August 27. http://tinyurl.com/6tyewyy

Guo, Guoting. 2004. Being a human rights lawyer (*Zuo yiming renquan lüshi*). In *Concerning justice: A sweeping conversation with Chinese lawyers* (Yu zhengyi you guan), ed. Guojun Zhao, 98–123. Guangzhou: Huacheng Publishing Company.

He, Ning Hai. 2004. One mountain village's difficult road towards environmental protection (*Yige xiao shancun de huanbao jianxin lu*), *Southern Weekend* (Nanfang Zhoumo), September 16. http://tinyurl.com/yb9vwv9

He, Weifang. 1999. Realizing social justice through the judicial system: A perspective on Chinese judges' situation (*Tongguo sifa shixian shehui zhengyi: dui Zhongguo faguan xianzhuang de yige toushi*). In *Toward an age of rights* (Zou xiang quanli de shidai), ed. Yong Xia, 179–250. Beijing: China Univ. of Political Science and Law Press.

He, Weifang. 2005. Preface. In *Concerning justice: A sweeping conversation with Chinese lawyers* (Yu zhengyi you guan), ed. Guojun Zhao, 1–2. Guangzhou: Huacheng Publishing Company.

Huang, Jinrong. 2006. A rising legal movement (*Yi chang fangxing weiai de falü yundong*). In *Public interest litigation*, ed. Jinrong Huang, 131–58. Beijing: Zhongguo Jiancha Publishing Company.

Jiang, Li. 2006a. Citizen suits in American environmental law and their inspiration for China (*Meiguo huanjing fa zhong gongmin susong zhidu jiqi dui woguo de qishi*). *Industrial Safety and Environmental Protection* (Gongye Anquan Yu Huanjing) 32(1): 1–3.

Jiang, Mingzhuo. 2006b. Baotou breaks through the difficulties associated with water pollution litigation (*Baotou shoupo shui wuran susong kunjing*). *The 21st Centrury Economic Herald* (21 Shijie Jingji Baodao), January 9.

Jiang, Ping. 2005. Only bow your head to truth (*Zhi xiang zhenli ditou*). In *Concerning justice: A sweeping conversation with Chinese lawyers* (Yu zhengyi you guan), ed. Guojun Zhao, 16–28. Guangzhou: Huacheng Publishing Company.

Jiang, Yajuan. 2006c. *Environmental law: A case course book* (Huanjing faxue: anli jiaocheng). Xiamen: Xiamen Univ. Press.

Jinhong community. 2007. Our living environment is getting worse by the day, we want to be further from the maglev! (*Juzhu huanjing riyi ehua, women yao yuanli cixuanfu!*). Copy on file with the author.

Kuang, Xiaoming, and Huijian Xu. 2010. Award winning essay from a conference on using law to boost the development of the Lake Poyang ecological economic zone, October 25. http://tinyurl.com/3t3sgfc

Kunming Daily. 2010. The environmental court at the Kunming Intermediate Court: An umbrella protecting Kunming's natural beauty (*Chengqi Kunming qingshan lüshui de baohusan – Ji Kunming Zhongji Fayuan huanbao fating*). July 6. http://tinyurl.com/25esss2

Lai, Yun. 2006. 1721 plaintiffs (*1721 yuangao*). *NGO Report* (Minjian Baogao): 28–31.

Lan, Hua, ed. 2004. *Environmental law cases* (Huanjing falü anli). Shanxi: Shanxi Educational Press.

Lan, Rongjie. 2008. Empirical research on the localization of litigation rules (*Susong guize difanghua shizheng yanjiu*). *Law and Social Development* (Zhengzhi yu Shehui Fazhan) 14(2): 13–22.

Laoting Tourism Bureau. 2011. Brief introduction to the Laoting county Luan river eco-tourism area development project (*Laotingxian luanhekou shengtai lüyouqu zonghe kaifa xiangmu jianjie*), April 2.

Laoting County Government. 2012. Laoting county Luan river eco-tourism area development project (*Laotingxian luanhekou shengtai lüyouqu zonghe kaifa xiangmu*), February 7. http://tinyurl.com/72jz2cm

Lei, Qing. 2010. Kunming plans to establish an "environmental public interest litigation relief fund" to help with the litigation cost problem (*Kunming nijian "huanjing gongyi susong jiuji jijin" pojie susong chengben nanti*). *Kunming Daily* (Kunming Ribao), April 5. http://tinyurl.com/4u53xht

Li, Shenrong, ed. 1999. *Pingnan county gazetteer* (Pingnan xian zhi). Beijing: Fangzhi publishing company.

Li, Yanfang, ed. 2003. *Typical cases in environmental protection law* (Huanjing baohufa dianxing anli). Beijing: Renmin Univ. Press.

Li, Yongshe. 2004a. Hu Jintao's instruction: Construct an army of lawyers to protect justice and prevent corruption (*Hu Jintao zhishi: Jianshe lüshi duiwu, weihu gongzheng fangzhi fubai*). Xinhua News Agency, March 24. http://tinyurl.com/ykj7y57

Liang, Congjie. 2005. Proposal by CPPCC delegate Liang Congjie on quickly establishing a stronger environmental protection public interest law *(Quanguo zhengxie weiyuan Liang Congjie guanyu jinkuai jianli jianquan huanbao gongyi susong fa de ti'an)*. In *Public interest environmental litigation* (Huanjing gongyi susong), ed. Tao Bie, 455–457. Beijing: Law Press

Lin, Hong, and Yapeng Ding. 2009. Environmental lawsuits make people unwilling to sue (*Huanjing guansi rang ren bu gan da*). *Xinhua Daily* (Xinhua Ribao), February 23. http://tinyurl.com/yzmwulw

Lin, Shiyu. 2003. One village's fate (*Yige cunzhuang de mingyun*). *Procuratorate Daily* (Jiancha Ribao), April 25. http://tinyurl.com/yaaf7hx

Liu, Sida. 2008. How to study the Chinese legal profession? *(Ruhe yanjiu zhongguo lüshi ye?)*. Chinese Lawyer (*Zhongguo Lüshi*), 8: 98–100.

Liu, Sida. 2008a. *The lost polis: Transformation of the legal profession in contemporary China* (Shiluo de chengbang: Dangdai Zhonguo falü zhiye bianqian). Beijing: Peking Univ. Press.

Liu, Sida. 2011. The logic of fragmentation: An ecological analysis of the Chinese legal services market *(Geju de luoji: Zhongguo falü fuwu shichang de shengtai fenxi)*. Shanghai: Shanghai Joint Publishing Company.

Liu, Wuzhang. 2007. Pan Yue: Special interest groups are the principal culprits of environmental destruction (*Pan Yue: Teshu liyi tuanti zheng chengwei pohuai huanjing shou'e*). *Southern Weekend* (Nanfang Zhoumo), January 18. http://tinyurl.com/yflpmeq

Luo, Aihua. 2009. A tannery's illegal pollution in Panyu, Guangdong: The procuratorate prosecutes (*Guangdong Panyu yi pigechang weigui paiwu: Jianchayuan zuo yuangao xi*). *People's Daily* (Renmin Ribao), August 10. http://tinyurl.com/6xcb33t

Luo, Yajuan. 2010. Environmental disputes over rural industrial pollution: A case study of Dongjing village (*Xiangcun gongye wuran zhong de huanjing kangzheng: Dongjingcun ge'an yanjiu*). *Journal of Xuehai* (2): 91–97.

Lü, Zhongmei, and Yong Wu. 2007. The practice of environmental public interest litigation in the current litigation system (*Huanjing susong shixian zhi susong zhidu gouxiang*). In *Public interest environmental litigation* (Huanjing gongyi susong), ed. Tao Bie, 20–40. Beijing: China Law Press.

Lü, Zhongmei, and Alex Wang. 2009. *Environmental public interest litigation: A China-US comparison* (Huanjing gongyi susong: Zhongmei zhi bijiao). Beijing: Law Press.

Lü, Zhongmei, Zhongmin Zhang, and Xiaoqing Xiong. 2011. An investigation into the status of environmental justice in China (*Zhongguo huanjing sifa xianzhuang diaocha*). *Faxue* (Legal Studies) 4: 82–93.

Meng, Dengke. 2009. Public interest lawyers: Heroes or troublemakers? (*Gongyi lüshi: Yingxiong haishi diaomin?*). *Southern Weekend* (Nanfang Zhoumo), May 31. http://tinyurl.com/y9qwt3o

Meng, Dengke. 2010. Environmental court head: Environmental public interest litigation urgently accumulates practical experience (*Huanbao fating tingzhang: Huanjing gongyi susong jidai jilei sifa shijian*). *Southern Weekend* (Nanfang Zhoumo), October 12.

Ministry of Justice. 2008. 2008–2012 Work plan on establishing and strengthening a system to prevent and punish corruption (*Jianli jianquan chengzhi he yufang fubai tixi 2008–2012 nian gongzuo guihua*). http://tinyurl.com/yhlcrnn

Ministry of Justice. 2008a. 2008 Green legal aid initiative launched (*Falü yuanzhu lüse xingdong qidong*). http://tinyurl.com/37jldcx

National Development and Reform Commission and the Ministry of Justice. 2006. 2006 Notice of the National Development and Reform Commission and the Ministry of Justice on printing and distributing the measures for the administration of lawyers' fees (*Guojia Fazhan Gaigewei, Sifa Bu guanyu yinfa "lüshi fuwu shoufei guanli banfa" de tongzhi*), effective December 1.

National People's Congress. 1999. Administrative review law of the People's Republic of China (*Zhonghua Renmin Gongheguo xingzheng fuyifa*), effective October 1, 1999.

News Probe (*Xinwen Diaocha*). 2003. The chemical plant next to Xiping village (*Xipingcun pang de huagongchang*). Broadcast April 12. http://tinyurl.com/yecgebo

Pan, Yue. 2004. Environmental protection and public participation (*Huanjing baohu yu gongzhong canyu*). *People's Daily* (Renmin Ribao), July 15.

Pan, Yue. 2006. An environmentally friendly society under the goal of harmonious society (*Hexie shehui mubiao xia de huanjing youhaoxing shehui*). *Twenty First Century Economic Herald* (21 Shiji Jingji Daobao), July 15. http://tinyurl.com/8yote33

People's Daily (*Renmin Ribao*). 2008. Xie Zhenhua: Energy efficiency and pollution reduction targets become part of provincial government evaluations (*Xie Zhenhua: Jieneng jianpai chengwei shengji zhengfu zhengji kaohe neirong*). March 11. http://tinyurl.com/37qppsj

People's Daily (*Renmin Ribao*). 2010. Environmental supervision orders are a scrap of paper, local government becomes a protection umbrella (*Huanbao 'dubanling' chengwei yi zhi kong wen, dangdi guanfang cheng baohusan*), October 26. http://tinyurl.com/2acgsyw

Pingnan County Statistical Bureau (*Pingnan xian tongji ju*). 2006. 2005 National economy and social development statistical report (*2005 nian guomin jingji he shehui fazhan tongji gongbao*), March 28.

Qian, Bai. 2007. The Shanghai-Hangzhou maglev: Why is it 22.5 meters? (*Huhang cixuanfu: Weishenme shi 22.5 mi?*). *Oriental Outlook* (Dongfang), March 22, 64–66.

Qie, Jianrong. 2002. An especially big fishery pollution case in Laoting reaches a first decision (*Laoting teda yuye wuran an yishen panjue*). *Legal Daily* (Fazhi Ribao), April 29. http://tinyurl.com/ybho689

Qie, Jianrong. 2007. The fine for Songhua River pollution is a year late (*Songhuajiang wuran fakuan chilai yinian*). *Legal Daily* (Fazhi Ribao), January 25. http://tinyurl.com/6mk8jtq

Qie, Jianrong. 2008. When in danger, why does the environmental court take orders? (*Huanbao fating weihe zongshi shouming yu weinan zhi shi?*). *Legal Daily* (Fazhi Ribao), October 6. http://tinyurl.com/73p3osg

Qie, Jianrong. 2009. Pollution victim Li Yujun prevails in compensation case over cancer death (*Wuran shouhaizhe Li Yujun aizheng siwang suopei'an shengsu*), *Legal Daily* (Fazhi Ribao), July 8. http://tinyurl.com/85njgkf

Qiu, Xuyu. 2006. *Poor lawyer, rich lawyer* (Qiong lüshi, fu lüshi). Beijing: Law Press China.

Sha, Lin. 2003. A timely rain: Wang Canfa (*Jishiyu: Wang Canfa*). *China Youth Daily* (Zhongguo Qingnian Bao), September 10. http://tinyurl.com/6admakb

Shandong Province. 1994. Shandong provincial regulations on handling environmental disputes (*Shandongsheng huanjing wuran jiufen chuli banfa*), effective July 1.

Shanghai Maglev Dispute. 2007. Anti-maglev BBS board (1,327 posts). Accessed May 27, 2007 (subsequently deleted). Copy on file with the author.

Shanghai Maglev Dispute. 2007. Petition to Wen Jiabao. Accessed April 1, 2007 (subsequently deleted). Copy on file with the author.

Shanghai Maglev Dispute. 2007. Shenchengyuan community peititon to the National People's Congress. Accessed April, 1, 2007 (subsequently deleted). Copy on file with the author.

Shen, Qiaohong. 2012. Public interest litigation now includes 'organizations' (*Gongyi susong jiaru 'zuzhi'*). *Southern Weekend* (Nanfang Zhoumo), September 15. http://tinyurl.com/9e8lwzv

Shi, Yucheng. 2003. An exploration of some of the problems with a system for environmental public interest litigation (*Huanjing gongyi susong zhidu goujian ruogan wenti tansuo*). *Contemporary Legal Studies* (Xiandai Faxue) 26(3): 156–60.

Shu, Taifeng. 2008. Could an environmental protection court possibly hold ground? *(Huanbao fating nengfou shouzhu yipian heshan?)*, Oriental Outlook (*Dongfang Zhoukan*), August 25. http://tinyurl.com/bjcj745.

Song, Qian. 2006. A short discussion of violations of rights in environmental lawsuits (*Qianyi huanjing qinquan susong moshi*). *People's Court Daily* (Renmin Fayuan Bao). http://tinyurl.com/ya99f5b

Standing Committee of the National People's Congress. 2001. Judges law of the People's Republic of China, 2001 amendment (*Zhonghua Renmin Gongheguo faguan fa, 2001 xiuding*), effective June 30, 2001.

Standing Committee of the National People's Congress. 2007. Lawyers law of the People's Republic of China, 2007 revision (*Zhonghua Renmin Gongheguo lüshifa, 2007 xiuding*), effective June 1, 2008.

Standing Committee of the National People's Congress. 2009. Tort law of the People's Republic of China (*Zhonghua Renmin Gongheguo qinquan zeren fa*), effective July 1, 2010.

Standing Committee of the National People's Congress. 2012. Civil Procedure Law of the People's Republic of China, 2012 amendment (*Zhonghua Renmin Gongheguo minshi susong fa, 2012 xiuding*), effective January 1, 2013.

State Council. 2005. Decision on carrying out the scientific development outlook and strengthening environmental protection (*Guowuyuan guanyu luoshi kexue fazhanguan jiaqiang huanjing baohu de jueding*), effective December 3, 2005. http://tinyurl.com/6ohkc5m

State Council. 2005a. Regulations governing the registration of appraisers (*Sifa jiandingren dengji guanli banfa*), effective September 30, 2005. http://tinyurl.com/84hu92c

State Council. 2006. The State Council's written reply on the water pollution prevention plan for the Songhua river basin (2006–2010) (*Guowuyuan guanyu Songhuajiang liuyu shuiwuran fangzhi guihua 2006–2010 nian de pifu*). August 23. http://tinyurl.com/7mpvf6o

State Council. 2007. Measures for the payment of litigation costs (*Susong feiyong jiaona banfa*), effective April 1, 2007. http://tinyurl.com/ybnqz85

State Council. 2011. Energy conservation and emissions reduction comprehensive work plan for the 12th five year plan (2011–2015) period (*Guowuyuan guanyu yinfa "shi er wu" jieneng jianpai zonghexing gongzuo fangan de tongzhi*). http://tinyurl.com/6zhh6x7

State Council. 2011a. State Council work report on environmental protection (*Guowuyuan guanyu huanbao gongzuo qingkuang de baogao*), October 25.

State Environmental Protection Agency. 2006. SEPA convenes a press conference to discuss good work on water pollution prevention along the Songhua River (*Huanbao zongju zhaokai Songhua Jiang shui wuran fangkong xianjinshiji baogaohui*). May 16. http://tinyurl.com/78xabp5

Supreme People's Court. 1992. Notice on "opinion on applying the Civil Procedure Law to several issues" (*Zui Gao Renmin Fayuan yinfa guanyu shiyong Zhonghua Renmin Gongheguo Minshi Susongfa ruogan wenti de yijian*), July 14. http://tinyurl.com/cwe7efc

Supreme People's Court. 2001. Interpretation on problems regarding the ascertainment compensation liability for emotional damages in civil torts (*Zui Gao Renmin Fayuan guanyu minshi qinquan jingshen sunhai peichang zeren ruogan wenti de jieshi*), effective March 10, 2001.

Supreme People's Court. 2001a. Supreme People's Court's various regulations regarding evidence for civil suits (*Zui Gao Renmin Fayuan guanyu minshi susong zhengju de ruogan guiding*), effective April 1, 2002. http://tinyurl.com/yk2v3av

Supreme People's Court. 2005. Notice of the Supreme People's Court on accepting joint action cases by the people's courts (*Zui Gao Renmin Fayuan guanyu renmin fayuan shouli gongtong susongan wenti de tongzhi*), effective January 1, 2006.

Supreme People's Court. 2006. The interpretation of the Supreme People's Court on some issues concerning the specific application of law in the trial of criminal cases involving environmental pollution (*Zui Gao Renmin Fayuan guanyu shenli huanjing wuran xingshi anjian juti xingyong falü ruogan wenti de jieshi*), effective July 28, 2006.

Supreme People's Court. 2010a. Annual work report (*Zui Gao Renmin Fayuan gongzuo baogao*). http://tinyurl.com/6qzwcoc

Supreme People's Court. 2010b. Various regulations regarding the provision of judicial guarantees and services to accelerate transformation of the mode of economic development (*Guanyu wei jiakuai jingji fazhan fangshi zhuanbian tigong sifa baozhang he fuwu de ruogan yijian*), effective June 29, 2010.

Supreme People's Court. 2011. Annual work report (*Zui Gao Renmin Fayuan gongzuo baogao*). http://tinyurl.com/7qgfp9c

Supreme People's Court. 2012. Annual work report (*Zui Gao Renmin Fayuan gongzuo baogao*). http://tinyurl.com/8z7hkvw

Supreme People's Court. 2012a. Introduction to the people's courts (*Renmin fayuan jianjie*). http://tinyurl.com/cchj5ru

Supreme People's Court Gazette. 2005. Liu Yaodong sues Yongda company (*Liu Yaodong su Yongda gongsi*). *Supreme People's Court Gazette* (Zhongguo Renmin Gonghego Zui Gao Renmin Fayuan Gongbao) 5: 40–42

Supreme People's Procuratorate. 2012. Supreme People's Procuratorate 2012 work report (*Zui Gao Renmin Jianchayuan gongzuo baogao*). http://tinyurl.com/7jwaqa2

Sun, Ruizhuo. 2010. How to solve the "no cases to try" embarrassment of environmental courts? (*Huanbao fating "wu'an keshen" ganga ruhe pojie?*) *Shenzhen Evening News* (Shenzhen Wanbao), October 19. http://tinyurl.com/6bpujsy

Tang, Zhengxu. 2007. The correct view of judicial authority is the proper meaning of rule of law (*Zhengque de sifa quanweiguan shi fazhi de yingyou zhiyi*). *China Court Web*, October 18. http://tinyurl.com/yhuymun

Tianjin Television Station. 2004. Who will pay for the fishermen's losses? (*Yumin de sunshi shei lai pei?*) October 14. http://tinyurl.com/y8ptqul

The World (*Huanqiu*). 2007. Investigation: America's fake thinktanks (*Meiguo wei zhiku diaocha*). December 16: 38–42.

Wang, Canfa, ed. 2005. *Cases in environmental and natural resource protection law* (Huangjing yu ziyuan baohufa anli). Beijing: Renmin Univ. Press.

Wang, Jin. 2006. *Environmental justice: For whom the bell tolls, a collection of classic environmental cases from US federal courts* (Huanjing zhengyi: Sanzhong wei shei er ming). Beijing: Peking Univ. Press.

Wang, Lili. 2005a. *Green media* (Lü meitei). Beijing: Tsinghua Univ. Press.

Wang, Yichao, Hongqing Duan and Feng Wang. 2005. The pain of the Songhua river (Songhuajiang zhi tong). *Caijing*, November 28.

Wang, Zhiqiu. 2008. The Guiyang environmental court looks forward to breaking through a bottleneck (*Guiyang huanbao fating qidai dapo pingjing*). *People's Daily* (Renmin Ribao), September 18.

Wei, Hongqian. 2007. "Strict enforcement" toward a grassroots environmentalist (*Dui yige minjian huanbao renshi de "yange zhifa"*). *Fangyuan*, November: 21–22.

Wen, Jiabao. 2007. Government work report (*Zhengfu gongzuo baogao*), March 5. http://tinyurl.com/7k54bxn

Wen, Jiabao. 2008. 2008 State Council government work report (2008 *Nian guowuyuan zhengfu gongzuo baogao*). http://tinyurl.com/ygwfzbv

Worker's Daily (Gongren Ribao). 2002. Fishermen invest millions without return (*Yumin touzi baiwan quan wu*). July 20. http://tinyurl.com/ye8wdox

Wu, Ge. 2006. Lawyers, who do you serve? (*Lüshi, ni wei shei fuwu?*). Blog post on file with the author.

Wuxi Intermediate Court. 2011. Wuxi City Intermediate Court work report (*Wuxishi Zhongji Renmin Fayuan gongzuo baogao*), January 19. http://tinyurl.com/4mzvwqn

Xing, Hong. 2004. Thoughts on environmental protection public interest litigation in China (*Guanyu woguo huanjing baohu gongyi susong de sikao*). *Journal of South China Normal University* 2: 137–138.

Xinhua News Agency. 2008. Representative Zhongmei Lü suggests establishing an environmental bench (*Lü Zhongmei daibiao: Jianyi sheli huanjing shenpanting*). March 8. http://tinyurl.com/ya5u749.

Xinhua News Agency. 2009. 44,502 female judges in Chinese courts, 23.48% of the total (*Quanguo fayuan gongyou nü faguan 44052 ren, zhan faguan zongshu 23.48%*). January 28. http://tinyurl.com/d67emsg

Xiong, Zhiqiang. 2010. Three counties in Jiujiang establish an environmental protection bench (*Jiujiang sanxian chengli huanbao heyiting*). *China Environmental News* (Zhongguo Huanjing Bao), September 9. http://tinyurl.com/3xj7w26

Xu, Hui. 2005. Why public interest lawsuits? Market society, distributive justice and public interest litigation (*Weishenme gongyi susong?*

Shichang shehui, fenpei zhengyi yu gongyi susong). World Environment 5: 25–27.

Xu, Linling. 2009. The king of litigation: Yan Yiming (*Susong zhi wang: Yan Yiming*). *Southern People Weekly* (Nanfang Renwu Zhoukan), May 9. http://tinyurl.com/bq75bex

Yang, Jianmin. 2002. Still our charming nature (*Hai women qingshan lüshui*). *Fangyuan*, March: 40–42.

Yang, Kai. 2010. 'Plant beans and get melons' and the start of environmental public interest litigation (*Zhong dou de gua de jieguo yu huanbao gongyi susuong de kaiduan). Environmental Law and Resources Law Review* (Huanjing Ziyuanfa Luncong) 8: 301–314.

Yang, Yifan, Hanfeng Chen, and Qun Zhang. et al. 2010a. *The legal history of the People's Republic of China* (Zhonghua Renming Gongheguo fazhi shi). Beijing: Shehui Kexue Wenxian Publishing Company.

Ye, Wentian. 2006. Seize GDP: Yancheng cancer village chemical pollution investigation (*Duoming GDP: Yancheng aizhengcun huagong wuran diaocha). China Business Journal* (Zhonguo Jingying Bao), April 24. http://tinyurl.com/42edqam

Yuan, Dingbo. 2009. Water pollution targets weak law enforcement, environmental courts hold up an umbrella protecting natural beauty (*Shui wuran jizhong zhifa ruanlei, huanbao fating chengqi qingshan lühui baohusan). Legal Daily* (Fazhi Ribao), March 3. http://tinyurl.com/ykqyds9

Zhang, Hubiao. 2010. Problems of legitimacy (and surpassing them) in protecting environmental rights: The case of Xiamen PX (*Huanjing weiquan de hefaxing kunjing jiqi chaoyue: Yi Xiamen PX anweili). Lanzhou Xuekan* 9(204): 115–118.

Zhang, Lijun. 2006. A discussion of personal environmental rights (*Lun geren huanjing quan). Environmental and Resources Law Review* (Huanjing Ziyuanfa Luncong) 6: 61–80.

Zhang, Shijun. 2006a. Infringing environmental rights in the Fujian pollution case with over 1000 farmers (*Fujian qianyu nongmin huanjing wuran qinquan an). In Impact litigation in China 2005* (Zhongguo yingxiangxing susong 2005), ed. Ge Wu, 24–34. Beijing: Law Press.

Zhang, Xiaohong. 2006b. Using the law for a living (*Yi falü wei ye). Legal Daily* (Fazhi Ribao). http://tinyurl.com/y8sr7rq

Zhang, Zitai, ed. 2007. *Frontline research on handling environmental disputes: Chinese, Japanese and Korean scholars discuss* (Huanjing jiufen chuli qianyan wenti yanjiu: Zhong Ri Han xuezhe tan). Beijing: Tsinghua Univ. Press.

Zhao, Lei. 2008. China's busiest court (*Zhongguo zui mang de fayuan*). Southern Weekend (Nanfang Zhoumo), December 4. http://tinyurl.com/ygg3n4t

Zhang, Sha. 2012. Environmental incidents repeatedly recur, delegate suggests establishing environmental courts to strengthen supervision (*Huanjing wuran shijian pinfa, daibiao jianyi sheli huanbao fating qianghua jianguan*), Chongqing Daily, March 13. http://tinyurl.com/ct4tokg

Zhongnan University of Economics and Law. 2007. A system for public interest litigation: A summary (*Gongyi susong zhidu zongshu*). Working paper on file with the author.

Zhou, Litai. 2005. Who protects lawyers' rights? (*Shei lai weihu lüshi de quanyi?*). In *Concerning justice: A sweeping conversation with Chinese Lawyers* (Yu zhengyi you guan), ed. Guojun Zhao, 199–210. Beijing: Huacheng Publishing Company.

Zhu, Jingwen. 2007. *Report on China law development: Database and indicators* (Zhongguo falü fazhan baogao). Beijing: Renmin Univ. Press.

Index

Made in the USA
Middletown, DE
18 January 2015